R00004 30700
CHICAGO PUBLIC LIBRARY
HAROLD WASHINGTON LIBRARY
00430700

D0908631

SHAKESPEARE'S HIDDEN LIFE:

Shakespeare at the Law

1585–1595

SHAKESPEARE'S HIDDEN LIFE:

Shakespeare at the Law

1585-1595

W. NICHOLAS KNIGHT

MASON & LIPSCOMB, *Publishers*
NEW YORK

ISBN: 0-88405-003-3

Library of Congress Catalog Card Number: 73-84881

Printed in the United States of America

Designed by Andor Braun

To

SUSAN HARRISON KNIGHT

and our

PAULINE, NATHANIEL, JESSICA

and PORTIA

"A pattern to all princes living with her,
And all that shall succeed."
Henry VIII, Act V, scene ii.

Table of Contents

LIST OF ILLUSTRATIONS

The following will be found between pages 118 and 119

For who would bear the whips and scorns of time,
The oppressor's wrong, the proud man's contumely,
The pangs of despised love, *the law's delay,*
The insolence of office and the spurns
That patient merit of the unworthy takes,
When he himself might his quietus make . . .

Hamlet III. i. 70-75

. . . who, by a seal'd compact,
Well ratified by law and heraldry,
Did forfeit, with his life, all those his lands
Which he stood seized of, to the conqueror:
Against the which, a moiety competent
Was gaged by our king; which had return'd
To the inheritance of Fortinbras,
Had he been vanquisher; as, by the same covenant,
And carriage of the article design'd,
His fell to Hamlet.
. . . to recover of us, by strong hand
And terms compulsatory, those foresaid lands
So by his father lost:

I. i. 86-95, 102-104.

I

The Biographers and the Lost Years

> . . . the air; which, but for vacancy,
> Had gone . . .
> And made a gap in nature.
> *Antony and Cleopatra* II. ii. 221–223.

1. *The Problem in Shakespearean Biography*

READERS of Shakespearean biographies are apt to be struck by a strange phenomenon. This is the fact that, in these biographies, there seems to be an almost total separation or nonconjunction between Shakespeare's world-familiar plays and his little-known personal life. Repeatedly, both biographers and literary critics have pursued their separate lines of inquiry as though these were logically divisible entities with nothing to tell or teach each other. Even when Shakespeare's work and life are considered together, these are often partitioned into autonomous sections or, in extreme cases, into individual volumes.

There has thus grown up among scholars, and been transmitted to the interested public, the conviction that these two areas of scholarship and knowledge are unbridgeably divorced from each other through the nature of their content and through the methodologies employed in dealing with the poet's writings and his life. If, on occasion, an effort is made to build a critical bridge between these two areas of concern, this is too often done in a manner which only emphasizes the lack of substantial knowledge of the degree to which Shakespeare's personal life is inextricably interwoven with the work of his pen.

A favorite technique of those who wish to span the gap between life and work but feel unable to do so through the presentation of fact, is psychological analysis, in which the fiction of literature is employed to create another fiction, that of the internal fantasy-life of the author—be he Shakespeare or the biographer himself. Well done, this can make fascinating reading. But it has contributed little to our solid knowledge of Shakespeare.

The purpose of this book is neither to compartmentalize nor to fantasize. Its aim is to demonstrate how many of Shakespeare's preoccupations in his writings echo and harmonize with facts which can be legitimately drawn and deduced from existing documents on his life. From this we can proceed to reconstruct the type and variety of day-to-day associations which the playwright must have had in order to be able to develop the themes which thread through his plays. To do this requires the immediate acknowledgment that such an attempt to meld Shakespeare's life and work in intimate relationship runs counter to the widespread belief that, at this long remove, there can be little reasonable hope of finding anything new regarding the poet's personal life and activities, and that the pool of knowledge regarding his life has been filled, however inadequately.

But such pessimism has little justification. For even if no new documents or facts on Shakespeare come to light, we are far from having exhausted the possibilities of interpretation and deduction obtainable from already existing documents and records. Fresh insights, based upon new and more perceptive arrangements of already familiar facts, are not only possible but inevitable, in Shakespearean scholarship as in other areas of scholarly research. Nor need we believe that no new facts pertaining directly to Shakespeare's life will come to light. It is indeed one of the purposes of this book to present several such facts which open a much wider window upon the poet's life during what are so often termed his "hidden" or "lost" years.

Today's reader of Shakespearean biography often finds himself in one of several positions when it comes to knowledge about the dramatist's life. Those who think nothing is known will be surprised to learn how much information the christening and burial records at Stratford can tell us about Shakespeare's various family relationships: to his younger three brothers and sister, to his first daughter, conceived before marriage, to his twins, and particularly to his only son, Hamlet ("Hamnet"). Yet one also finds from the same data that the person's precise birth and death dates cannot always be determined from these records. Those who believe that only a little is known may be surprised to discover that on specific days we can reconstruct precisely what was going on in Shakespeare's life from testimony in several court trials, as revealing as any diary written in the first person. And yet even such testimony must be carefully winnowed and weighed. Many who feel, on the other hand, that much about the poet's life is known may be surprised that, as mentioned above, it is not positively known when he was born or died (despite the Stratford-upon-Avon parish record which reads: 1564, Apr. 26. C. [christened] Gulielmus Filius Johannes Shakspere). Nor is it known when or where he was married, how well he did in school or when he left it, when he departed from Stratford, or how he became an actor or with which company. However we are able to make fairly reasonable deductions and conclusions regarding most of these incidents.

Perhaps the single greatest surprise to those who assume that Shakespeare's life is fairly well recorded comes when they are told, as some scholars assert, that anywhere from seven to ten years of the poet's life—in fact, those very years, from twenty-one to thirty-one years of age, when he was going through what was undoubtedly his major formative period—are a complete blank. But such conclusions are no longer justified. Much new factual information is becoming available as the result of recent scientific and technological advances, and from new methodologies, particularly those involving sophisticated critical and interdisciplinary techniques. Furthermore, the new material generally tends to confirm and strengthen the overall picture already formed of the man and his work. The new findings result in a more authentic reconstruction of the poet's life. They relate this life more closely to our contemporary perception of what reality, existence, living, and humanhood are to ourselves, were to the past, and will, for the most part, remain for the future. Our present age, with its diversity, contradictions, tolerance, techniques and increases in knowledge can, or ought to be able to, render past periods in their own terms more than was formerly possible. It is this possibility, combined with the perennial interest in Shakespeare that will result in a greater and greater knowledge of Shakespeare's hidden life, during what have become known as the "lost years," from approximately 1584–1585 to 1592–1595.

2. *The Biographers*

FACED WITH the wide gaps in the biographical record between his leaving Stratford and his being heard of in London (about 1584 to 1595), biographers have tried many expedients in dealing with the lost years. The crucial time span is often either ignored, conjectured about, or simply fancifully embroidered. Primary evidence is sparse and often misleading. The earliest information, apparently referring to the period 1585 to 1595, comes from the then (1661–2) new vicar of Stratford, John Ward. It introduced a major biographical myth, that of Shakespeare as the natural poet. At this time Shakespeare's younger daughter, Judith Quincy, was in Stratford and his nephew, Thomas Hart, was alive. The vicar reports:

> I have heard y^{t} [i.e. that] M^{r}. Shakespeare was a natural wit, without any art at all; hee frequented y^{e} [the] plays all his younger time, but in his elder days lived at Stratford:

> and supplied ye stage with 2 plays every year, and for y^t^ had an allowance so large, y^t^ hee spent att ye Rate of a 1,000 £ a year, as I have heard.[1]

This smacks of town gossip, and the intimate details could be ascribed to the knowledge that Shakespeare was a wealthy playwright. Does "younger time" cover the time he left school, presumably upon his completion of the curriculum in 1577, to the time he was officially listed as an actor (1595); or from 1595 to 1610 when he was known as a playwright, which would mean that his "elder days" are from 1610 to 1616? Although the times are unclear, Ward has instigated the easy notion that Shakespeare simply had a natural interest in plays as a viewer (perhaps in Stratford, certainly in London), which developed into his being a playwright and that he finally retired to Stratford.

Thomas Fuller's *Worthies of England* was published in 1662, the same year as John Ward's comment, and may well have served as a stimulus to the vicar's observation. Fuller wrote:

> He [Shakespeare] was an eminent instance of the truth of that Rule, *Poeta not fit, sed nascitur*, one is not made, but *born* a Poet. Indeed his Learning was very little, . . .

Ben Jonson had already written for all to read and unfortunately to remember, in his eulogy in the 1623 Folio, that Shakespeare ". . . hadst small Latin and less Greek, . . ." Fuller continued:

> . . . so that as *Cornish diamonds* are not polished by any Lapidary, but are pointed and smoothed even as they are taken out of the Earth, so *nature* it self was all the *art* which was used upon him. (*p.* 126)[2]

So, from the very beginning, partially based upon a misunderstanding of Jonson's observation, coming from a man associated with both Oxford and Cambridge, the idea of Shakespeare as a man of nature, simply and easily following the dictates of his poetic craft, emerged.

Some twenty years later, John Aubrey jotted down literary data (*Brief Lives*), some about Shakespeare in preparation for a composite volume edited by Anthony Wood to come out in 1690. John Aubrey's information does not cover many pages but its density is rich with both probability and also misinformation, raising, for the first time, questions about the livelihood of Shakespeare's father, and about Shakespeare's youth. The text has to be carefully dissected in order to determine what it can solidly tell us about the young Shakespeare: his occupations; his acting; the opinions others held of him; and his early, continuing, and final relationship to his family in Stratford. Aubrey remarks in his notes: "I have been told heretofore by some of the neighbours, that when he [Shakespeare] was a boy he exercised his father's Trade [mistakenly presumed to be that of a Butcher, rather than a glover], but when he kill'd a Calfe, he would doe it in a *high style*, & make a Speech."[3] There is a possibility, which might also explain the legend of Shakespeare's poaching deer, that the "hunting of the deer" and "to kill a calf in high style" (or sometimes a fox or a cat) were occasional games or traditional rituals, for which the talented Will would have been good at providing extempore speeches or ballads. These recollections Aubrey has garnered may have been triggered by such passages as, in *Hamlet*:

Why, let the stricken deer go weep,
The hart ungalled play;
For some must watch, while some must sleep:
So runs the world away.

(III. ii. 282–285)[4]

This Hamlet sings when he has driven Claudius to distraction by the play within the play. A similar instance may have prompted the other phrases. When Polonius says that in his youth he played Julius Caesar slain in the Capitol, Hamlet responds with, "It was a brute part of him to kill so capital a calf there." (III. ii. 111.) Amongst the actors, working backwards from notorious lines from famous plays, legend may have created the Butcher story to account for Shakespeare's father's trade and the deer-poaching episode for why he left Stratford, further embellished by passages about deer from *Merry Wives of Windsor*, the only play Shakespeare wrote with a contemporaneous setting.

At any rate, John Aubrey is the first to introduce the idea that Shakespeare had a series of occupations beginning with helping his father at his trade, either while still at school or after leaving (1575–1577). Aubrey continues in tantalizingly questionable detail: "This Wm. being inclined naturally to Poetry and acting, came to London I guesse about 18." That would be in 1582, which was also the year other sources indicate he married the twenty-six-year-old Anne Hathaway. Aubrey also says, ". . . and was an Actor at one of the Play-houses and did act exceedingly well: . . ." From various sources we know Shakespeare was cast in older or father-figure roles. This is of interest since it appears from legal documents and his writings he is preoccupied with his father. A way of handling any fears of that figure is to become or replace the father. He was King Hamlet's Ghost in his own *Hamlet*, Old Adam in his *As You Like It*, and in Jonson's *Every Man in His Humour* he was probably Knowell, Senior.

Aubrey continues to follow Shakespeare's occupational progress: ". . . now B. Johnson [i.e. Ben Jonson] was never a good Actor, but an excellent Instructor. He [Shakespeare] began early to make essays [attempts] at Dramatique Poetry which at that time was very lowe; . . ." This is probably not in reference to the sonnets nor to the narrative poems but more likely to his very early inferior dramas, perhaps *Titus Andronicus*, or to inferior earlier drafts of his later plays. What is not clear is whether these were attempted in Stratford or later in London. It is an intriguing reference to Shakespeare's early works and their state or reception at one time. Its possibilities will be pursued in the next chapter.

Aubrey continues, ". . . and his Playes tooke well: . . . He was wont to goe to his native Country [i.e. the county of Warwickshire] once a yeare." At least we cannot take seriously the suggestion that Shakespeare stayed away from Anne from the time he left Stratford until his retirement. The ties to Stratford were strong, even during the lost years. Aubrey then charmingly chats to himself: "I thinke I have been told that he left 2 or 300 £ per annum there and thereabout: to a sister. . . ." Is that what Shakespeare told his fellow actors in London about his wife Anne, eight years his senior? Perhaps it does refer to his sister Joan Hart, but it is a considerable amount of money.

Aubrey introduces another possible career into Shakespeare's life: ". . . Though as Ben Johnson sayes of him, that he had but little Latine and lesse Greek, He understood Latine pretty well: for he had been in his younger yeares a Schoolmaster in the Countrey. [*In margin,* 'from M^r - Beeston.']"[5] William Beeston is a source not to be ignored in so far as his father, Christopher, was a fellow member of Shakespeare's company in 1598; Shakespeare and Beeston acted together in Ben Jonson's *Every Man in His Humour* at that time. As the ultimate source is an actor, so Shakespeare's involvement with plays as an actor is stressed for the first time. This aspect of his theatrical skills is not spoken of much in the Stratford sources. Aubrey's information has the appearance of specificity but it is tantalizingly elusive in its dates, sources, and confirmability. The irony is that the earliest data on Shakespeare, the closest to the original sources, appears to be fraught already with myths and legends, and is at points highly suspect.

Thus, by the end of the seventeenth century, some of the basic difficulties which plague Shakespearean biography already existed in early reportage. None of the reports is consciously disturbed by any break in biographical time. The continuum is preserved by believing, after the fact, that Shakespeare's inclination to poetry drew him from Stratford to London, in the case of Aubrey at a rather early age, with little means of financial support except the sale of his early plays written between 1582 and 1592. However, Aubrey also incidentally introduced the possibility that Shakespeare was a schoolmaster, which qualifies the reservations Jonson, Ward and Fuller held about Shakespeare's learning. This, like the other legends, could have its origins in some of the passages remembered from *Love's Labour's Lost* and *Merry Wives of Windsor* where Latin lessons are recollected; but it does suggest that some "learning" on the part of Shakespeare was recognizable by his fellow actors, although he was probably, if a teacher at all, merely a tutor or actor-instructor in a country home. This, among other suggestions, has been put forth recently by Frederick J. Pohl in *Like to the Lark: The Early Years of Shakespeare.* The number of years between the end of his schooling (1577–1580) and his unequivocal presence in London (1594) allow ample time for Shakespeare to possibly have pursued several occupations or endeavors in, around or at farther reaches from Stratford before coming to the London area around 1588. But, in either case with regard to Shakespeare's learning, Aubrey's information further suggests that Shakespeare must have completed and greatly benefited from his schooling. By the seventeenth century the composite biography results in a meager but relatively logical picture: The lad does well in school and helps out his father; upon finishing school, he takes up a post in the country from 1577 to 1582, with skills provided by his education; he understands Latin fairly well; he is drawn by his own talents to poetry, plays, acting, and the theatre. In 1582 or shortly thereafter, he goes down to London, and writes inferior products at first, but then achieves some success as a playwright.

The standard eighteenth-century biography of Shakespeare is Nicholas Rowe's *Life*, based on information from

Betterton's travels to Stratford, and prefixed to the 1709 edition of the plays. Possibly reasoning backward to find an explanation for Shakespeare's "little Latin," Rowe does disclose some financial constraint upon Shakespeare's prospects, although he is in error as to its origin:

> . . . He [Shakespeare] was the Son of M^{r}. *John Shakespear*, and was Born at *Stratford* upon Avon, in *Warwickshire*, in *April* 1564. His Family, as appears by the Register and Publick Writings relating to that Town, were of good Figure and Fashion there, and are mention'd as Gentlemen. His Father, who was a considerable Dealer in Wool, had so large a Family, ten Children in all [Shakespeare had only three brothers and one sister] that tho' he was his eldest Son, he could give him no better Education than his own Employment. He had bred him, 'tis true, for some time at a Free-School, where 'tis probable he acquir'd that little *Latin* he was Master of: But the narrowness of his Circumstances, and the want of his assistance at Home, forc'd his Father to withdraw him from thence, and unhappily prevented his further Proficiency in that Language. . . . Upon his leaving School, he seems to have given intirely into that way of Living which his Father propos'd to him; and in order to settle in the World after a Family manner, he thought fit to marry while he was yet very Young. His Wife was the Daughter of one *Hathaway*, said to have been a substantial Yeoman in the Neighbourhood of *Stratford*. In this kind of Settlement he continu'd for some time, 'till an Extravagance that he was guilty of, [supposedly caught poaching deer] forc'd him both out of his Country and that way of Living which he had taken up; and tho' it seem'd at first to be a Blemish upon his good Manners, and a Misfortune to him, yet it afterwards happily prov'd the occasion of exerting one of the greatest *Genius*'s that ever was known in Dramatick Poetry.[6]

Rowe launches into what is now regarded as a myth, unsupported by any evidence of a local deer park, or by the facts of judicial procedure of the time.[7] The deer poaching story may be based on mocking games that Shakespeare might have participated in, and could have led to harassment from local parties of civic or social prominence. Chiefly, however, the myth is designed to account for Shakespeare's unaccountable departure from Stratford, leaving his wife and three very young children living with his parents in presumably narrow circumstances with certainly as many as four, some said nine, of William's siblings. Surely, felt the Stratford sources and folklore, it was better to have a famous youth leave by force, as the result of an understandable boys-will-be-boys prank, or petty crime, than to entertain the possibility, recalled by London sources, that Will Shakespeare deserted his family to become an actor, running off in hard times, to take the uncertain post of a servant in a London playhouse. It is equally possible he may have left for a time to take a tutor's post in the country, or to pursue an unknown trade, perhaps already begun in Stratford, more befitting his acquired skills.

The damage in the biographical transmission had been done, however, and was continued by Alexander Pope. Rowe had returned to Jonson's seemingly derogatory remark about Shakespeare's feeble proficiency in Latin. In his 1725 edition of Rowe's *Life*, Pope dropped entirely the reference to Shakespeare having to know Latin in order to write his *Comedy of Errors*. This made it easy for the classicist Samuel Johnson to insist erroneously that all of Shakespeare's works, dependent upon Greek and Roman writers, were based upon English translations, and go on to remark upon Shakespeare's lack of taste, decorum and, of course, learning. The neoclassical period from Milton to Johnson looked upon Shakespeare merely as a natural genius, ignoring many of Ben Jonson's critical evaluations to the contrary, and produced the vision of Shakespeare as an untutored poet, unaware of the classics and classical tongues in which they prided themselves and by which they measured education. No wonder they felt free to alter Shakespeare's text and his plays' actions. Likewise, they were almost totally uninterested, until late in the century with Edmond Malone (to be discussed in Chapter III), in Shakespeare's biography. The man behind the dramas had been written off as an uneducated country boy, whose talent grew under the influence of Marlowe, Jonson, and the University Wits of the London stage. His education, his Latin, his teaching, his other skills, which his contemporaries had noted as evident in his calligraphy, dropped from view. During the Age of Enlightenment, neoclassicism cast a dark shade upon what had been known about Shakespeare in the seventeenth century, a shadow from which we still have not completely emerged. For, as Schoenbaum (perhaps the first modern scholar of Shakespeare's biography) points out:

> . . . through Malone's achievement the inadequacies of Rowe's essay were now recognized. There are not more than eleven biographical facts mentioned in it, according to Malone's analysis, and of these critical examination reveals eight to be mistaken and one doubtful; the remaining two, records of baptism and burial, were furnished by the Stratford parish register. Malone exaggerates, but not a great deal. (*p.* 236)

As Schoenbaum has recognized, Edmond Malone marks the beginning of critical Shakespearean biography.

After the midpoint of the eighteenth century, and as information accumulated, there came an awareness of the gaps in the biographical data. About this time William Oldys labored at the College of Arms on a life of Shakespeare, destined for a bookseller, and which, according to John Taylor (*Record of My Life*, London, 1832, I, 28.) would contain "ten years of the life of Shakespeare unknown to the biographers and commentators." We can only wonder what Oldys might have found about the lost ten years; perhaps his knowledge as an antiquarian and the fact that he was the son (illegitimate) of Dr. William Oldys, the Chancellor of Lincoln and Advocate of the Admiralty, might have helped him uncover, or interpret, materials of value. But upon his death there were only scraps of paper found on the project. What, if anything, was he on to?

In the early part of the nineteenth century the Romantics returned to the talk about Shakespeare, not as a man, or even a dramatist, but as the Genius: the Poetic Genius for Keats, and the Tragic Philosopher for Coleridge. Shakespeare, for this period, was a man with an intense awareness of the agonized wanderings of the tormented soul, the ability to be universal in his "negative capability," and his sublime gifts of the imagination. Hazlitt captured the Romantics' rapture in a lecture on January 27, 1818:

> He was nothing in himself; but he was all that others were, or that they could become. He not only had in himself the germs of every faculty and feeling, but he could follow them by anticipation, intuitively, into all their conceivable ramifications, through every change of fortune, or conflict of passion, or turn of thought. He had 'a mind reflecting ages past,' and present:—all the people that ever lived are there . . . He had only to think of anything in order to become that thing, with all the circumstances belonging to it.[8]

Bardolatory was rampant; Shakespeare was the Universal Man; he did not need to read the Classics—he embodied them. So much for his learning, so much for his reading, so much for his sources, so much for this thought. Shakespeare the man, ignored by the eighteenth century, was swallowed up as the Oversoul of the nineteenth. There were some dissenters, but they were, and have remained, overshadowed. Even these, for the most part, indulged in blatant subjectivism, projecting their own lives upon the unknown; and then they criticized Shakespeare's inaccuracy when they were able to correct him through their research. The result was, on the one hand, to increase the airy nothing of conjecture and, on the other, to further denigrate what practical and scholastic knowledge Shakespeare had. From this universal blank or mystery man, and the concomitant unwarranted assumption of his ignorance, Schoenbaum has accurately suggested that the belief arose that someone *else* was the playwright: someone erudite, learned, perhaps with advanced (even legal) training must have been the writer of the plays; not Shakespeare, but rather, say, Sir Francis Bacon; or Bacon, Southampton, Elizabeth, James, Marlowe and others working together, or seriatim! The evidence of legal knowledge may have been correct but the conclusions drawn were absurd. Victorian critics and editors also played into the hands of the Baconists and others by holding that major portions of Shakespeare's canon and parts of individual texts could not have been written by him because these pieces were too vulgar to be penned by what they anachronistically assumed were Shakespeare's Romantic genius and Victorian morality.

Fortunately, several nineteenth-century scholars provided more scholarly scrutiny by studying the documents and by applying critical tools of reason and logic. Halliwell-Phillipps' *The Life of William Shakespeare* (London, 1848) after intense and thorough study and reproduction of the many documents pertaining to Shakespeare's and his family's life, concludes that taking the narrow circumstances of the poet's home into consideration ". . . reason will be found quite sufficient for Shakespeare's important step of joining the metropolitan players." (p. 134). He does not suggest what Shakespeare was doing at the time he left Stratford, and goes on to admit that the position with the players would have been of "very mean rank." That many theatrical companies passed through Stratford each year, and that once Shakespeare left his house he could easily return to visit his family are facts employed by Halliwell-Phillipps to ease nineteenth-century moral discomfort over the questions of why he would leave, and why he would stay away from, his wife and three children. He then goes on to cite as genuine a Collier forgery that places Shakespeare with Burbage at Blackfriars Theatre in 1589. So, Halliwell-Phillipps presumed Shakespeare went from school to marriage to London with no discernible occupation or craft other than his rise from a servant boy holding horses to one of the chief players by 1589. He supports this with documentary evidence now known to be forged.

F. Fleay, in his *The Life and Work of Shakespeare* (1886), expanded upon what seems to be a more logical assumption: that Shakespeare left *with* one of the traveling company of players (Leicester's Men), so that when he arrived in London he was at least credited with having been a strolling player, though a minor one and still poor. However, this leaves us with two problems: what professional company would welcome him so easily, and would Shakespeare have run off with a group of players affording him so little surety? Nevertheless, this has more or less remained the current assumption furnished with a specific company (Leicester's or the Queen's), a specific year (1587) and made plausible by Shakespeare's obvious talent, evidenced subsequently, and by the company's good prospects and high reputation.

The twentieth century has offered a number of possible occupations for Shakespeare. As one of a few, J. W. Gray in 1905 reconsiders in his *Shakespeare's Marriage and Departure from Stratford* the supposition that Shakespeare was a teacher for a while. The idea by now has a number of virtues to recommend it: It places Shakespeare in a situation upon leaving school; it might involve an initial period of separation from his family; it could easily develop prospects for going to London. Furthermore, evidence from the scholastic atmosphere of his early plays and references in these and others to schoolboy Latin seem to support the claim—but, of course, these might just as well have arisen from the bench side as the desk side of the schoolroom. The conjectures at the beginning of this present century rapidly become legion with the expanded awareness of the breadth of Shakespeare's knowledge.

By 1913, Dr. F. J. Furnivall and Mr. John Munro, editors of *Cassell's Illustrated Shakespeare*, allow the reader a gallimaufry of possibilities. They indicate that upon leaving school at the age of fourteen to sixteen, Shakespeare may have held one or several of the following positions before he turned to the theatre. He could have been a schoolmaster in the country, an abecedarius (tutor), an apprentice to a butcher, an apprentice to his father (a glover, and possibly a dealer in wool), a doctor, a guardian of the insane, anticipator of trends in science, biology, astrology, etc. Munro continues: "If we are to give credence to the voluminous literature which has dealt with his intellectual attainments, he must have followed almost every trade and profession—and all almost simultaneously!" (p. xiii). What did he live on, Munro wonders? The conclusion is that we just don't know. Was his marriage a happy one? It is seriously doubted. It is therefore obvious he would seek his fortunes elsewhere. Ergo, he needed to win money and fame, so he left in 1586 to become an actor and author; and on and on go the number of possibilities and the fabrications to support them. The most respected resolution has now become the familiar one: "'The Queen's Players—not known to be the company with which Shakespeare is always connected—came for the first time to Stratford, in 1587. And this was probably the turning-point in Shakespeare's life. At any rate, sooner or later, he left his birth-town for London, and took the way to fame and fortune." (p. xvi). That is how Munro handles the problem of why, and for and with what Shakespeare left Stratford.

Arthur Acheson in 1920 attacks the subject head on in *Shakespeare's Lost Years in London*: 1586–1592. He rejects the suggestion that Shakespeare left Stratford with the Earl of Leicester's men. He has as his purpose to prove that Shakespeare came to London as a bonded servant of James Burbage's for a term of a few years; thus Acheson manages to make an early connection with the group of players that would become the Lord Chamberlain's Men. It is this company of which Shakespeare ultimately became a member. The book is clearly designed to answer the latest question which had emerged: How does the biographer transfer Shakespeare from Stratford to the right acting company? A straight line is the shortest way between two points.

Joseph Quincy Adams, who served as Director of the

Folger Shakespeare Library in Washington, D.C., published his *Life of William Shakespeare* in 1923, the tercentenary of the printing of the First Folio of Shakespeare's plays. Schoenbaum's observations on Adams are quoted at length so that Schoenbaum, as the most recent biographer (1970), may himself be observed.

> The Lost Years provide a test of mettle. Adams is the first biographer of note to build upon Aubrey's remark, derived from the actor Beeston, that Shakespeare 'had been in his younger years a schoolmaster in the country.' Acceptance of this possibility frees one from the painful necessity of separating a young husband from his wife and small children. Moreover, *The Comedy of Errors* is based upon Plautus, who had a place in the grammar-school curriculum; both this play and *Love's Labour's Lost* include pedants in their *dramatis personae*, both contain echoes of the classroom and tags from school textbooks. But Adams clearly best relishes his final, triumphant argument: 'Lastly, not to exhaust the reasons that might be cited, a career as school-teacher would splendidly equip the non-university trained Shakespeare for his subsequent career as a man of letters.' Why such should be the case is not self-evident, at least to this writer, and one suspects that the soul of the pedagogue in Adams has surfaced.
>
> (*p.* 699).

Schoenbaum, with glee equal to what he would ascribe to Adams, is thus able to relegate still another writer to the subjectivist school in his theory of projection in Shakespearean biography.

What remains the most reasoned and most widely accepted scholarly response to the data pertaining to the departure from Stratford is that expressed by E. K. Chambers in his *William Shakespeare* (Oxford, 1930) I, pp. 21–24. There he says: [1] that no precise data for the Hegira between 1584 and 1592 can be ascertained; [2] that he went directly to London cannot be insisted upon; and [3] that although much could have gone on in those eight years we remain ignorant of what happened. He does favor, along with Adams, Aubrey's statement of Shakespeare's being a schoolmaster, or more probably an "abecedarius." He rejects as conjecture any attempts to make Shakespeare an apothecary, a student of medicine, a soldier, a printer, but Chambers will grant ". . . a roving and apperceptive mind, conversant in some way with many men and manners, and gifted with that felicity in the selection and application of varied knowledge, which is one of the secrets of genius." (p. 24). After sifting the evidence to date, Chambers concludes:

> The main fact in his earlier career is still that unexplored hiatus, and who shall say what adventures, material and spiritual, six or eight crowded Elizabethan years may have brought him. It is no use guessing. As in so many other historical investigations, after all the careful scrutiny of clues and all the patient balancing of possibilities, the last word for a self-respecting scholarship can only be that of nescience.
>
> 'Ah, what a dusty answer gets the soul,
> When hot for certainties in this our life!'
>
> (*p.* 26).

The conjectures were not to be silenced by Chambers' conclusions. His colleague in the British government's Education Department in London, John Dover Wilson, who wrote *The Essential Shakespeare* (1932), provided still another hypothesis: Shakespeare was educated in the role of a singing-boy in the household of some great Catholic nobleman, then was an actor-playwright for Lord Strange's Men, entered Southampton's entourage perhaps as a tutor, and possibly toured Italy with Florio. An impressive background, indeed. The respected Edgar I. Fripp in volume I of *Shakespeare: Man and Artist*, (1938) returned to the possibility of Shakespeare's following the Earl of Leicester's players, with Burbage among them, when they passed through Stratford.

But the remaining biographical attempts, written between 1949 and 1968, explaining what happened during the "lost years" have had the most popular reception and had the farthest reaching, current impact. Marchette Chute, in *Shakespeare of London* (1949), plays up the

Puritanism in the Hathaway family. She presumes Anne Hathaway's Puritanism kept her from accompanying her actor husband to London, and in fact may have driven him off; and that he stayed away from her for the nearly twenty years he lived in London in hired lodgings. He left Anne within three or four years of his marriage, and he went because Stratford was too small for him, she says. And, although the actual date of his arrival is unknown, 1588 would have been a propitious time to arrive, on account of the Elizabethan exuberance surrounding that mystically double numbered year, which saw the defeat of the Spanish Armada.

Hardin Craig, read by innumerable college students as editor of a one-volume *Complete Works of Shakespeare*, exceeds E. K. Chambers' skepticism about the lost years, wiping the slate clean and giving the gap a complete blank.

> THE SEVEN DARK YEARS
>
> With this entry of the baptism of his children, the connection with the records of Stratford and vicinity for William Shakespeare in the period of his youth and obscurity comes to an end. We are then faced with a great blank of seven or nine years which history has failed to fill and which conjecture has filled entirely too full.[9]

The brevity of his handling of this span in Shakespeare's lifetime helped to create generations of college students who seldom recall the passage and are often not even aware of the gap in Shakespeare's biography. While those who have obtained their Shakespeare from the public performance of plays are susceptible to the conclusion that we know nothing about Shakespeare's life, college graduates are apt to fall into the pit of believing that not only do we know a lot about Shakespeare, but we know everything there is to know or can be discovered about him. Misinformation is replaced with total misconfidence.

With the approach of the quatrecentenary (1964) of Shakespeare's birth (1564), biographies abounded but they shed no additional clarity on the lost years. The possibility of acting troupes to run off with is increased by sheer quantity: "In 1587 Leicester's and the Queen's were both in Stratford, as well as three other companies [Stafford's Men, Essex's players and another company]."[10] F. E. Halliday continues, "There has been much ado about Shakespeare's 'lost years,' either the seventeen years between the collapse of his father's fortunes and the first definite mention of his name in London, or more narrowly, the seven years between the christening of Hamnet and Judith and Robert Greene's attack on 'Shakescene' in 1592. . . . We can weave any romance we fancy about these early years of Shakespeare." (pp. 50–51). Halliday, like Chambers, favors the case for the schoolmastership, however. His reason is not clear, but he says that ". . . we must assume that he [Shakespeare] was in Stratford until at least 1587." (p. 53). It does keep him there to see the actors and allows him to make it to London for the Armada victory in 1588. As did Marchette Chute, he presumes Will is no longer in love with Anne. He conjectures the crisis was a quarrel with Anne, ". . . precipitated perhaps by her puritanical, churchwarden brother Bartholomew, who cannot have approved of his writing." (p. 53).

> He was going, . . . because the great literary revival was in the air, because, although he was not conscious of it, London had need of him; in short, because he must.
>
> (*p*. 54)

First-rate scholarship on these matters continued to emerge in the 1960s. We find a contemporary scholar's response to the data in James G. McManaway's excellent booklet (done up partly to silence the Baconians) for The Folger Shakespeare Library, "The Authorship of Shakespeare" (1962). Here a voice, in the tone of E. K. Chambers, reminds us that "The author of the plays was not a formally trained lawyer—or doctor, or soldier, or sailor—however vividly and appropriately technical terms are often used" (p. 34) and "The year of Shakespeare's arrival in London is unknown, as are the circumstances that brought him." (p. 15). Mark Eccles' *Shakespeare in Warwickshire* (Madison, Wisconsin, 1963) reveals that one of the players of the Queen's company died June 13, 1587, and therefore they were one actor shy when they came to Stratford. Thus, if one were to choose to which company Shakespeare might have become attached, in 1587, the Queen's may now appear to have the edge. The hidden questions still remain: would they have selected Will as a replacement? and would he have upped and gone, leaving his wife, two-year-old twins and a daughter? It has, however, been taken up as the most reasonable conjecture and simplest explanation. But if this is his primary occupation why does he not appear in any actor or author list until 1595?

The anniversary of his birth in 1964 brought out many publications. A pamphlet printed in England for the Public Record Office (*Shakespeare in the Public Records*) states, "In 1589, . . . he [Shakespeare] was twenty-five years old and was probably in London and a member of one or other of the Companies of Players operating under the patronage of various prominent figures in Elizabethan society." (p. 5). A. L. Rowse in his *William Shakespeare* (1964) solidifies the current theory: Shakespeare helped in his father's shop, and with the business; and one cannot reject the possibility of his being a schoolmaster, or an usher in the country.

> Still, there was no future in being an usher, with his ambitions and responsibilities. By nature he was a poet, and one fine day in the later 1580's—the opportunities were specially inviting in the year 1587, with five companies visiting Stratford, including Leicester's and the Queen's, the former below strength and the latter wanting a man—he took the road to London. (*p.* 61).

Biography and detailed narrative techniques intermingle in Rowse.

In the 1970s the novelist of the earlier Shakespearean (*Nothing Like the Sun*) in Anthony Burgess succeeds in making the moment come very much alive in his new biography of the Bard:

> In that last Stratford summer of his youth [1587] Will would see a brilliant clown [Will Kemp of the Queen's Men] with sad eyes and a decaying body. It may have been to him that he made a stammering or confident application to be considered as a member of the company. Thou art too old, laddie, to be a prentice in the craft. Canst mend plays? Will might then show what he had done: an act in draft of *The Comedy of Errors*, a stanza or so of his Venus and Adonis poem. Thou hast a fair hand. Canst copy fast? And he is well enough set up, is he not? Let us see how he makes an entrance.
>
> Something like that. Back from the inn where the players lodged to Henley Street, to bundle up his few clothes, beg a little money from his father, be sprayed by tearful farewells. And then to cease to be Will of Stratford. The role of Sweet Master Shakespeare awaited him in a bigger town—filthy, gorgeous, mean, murderous, but the only place where a member of his new breed, without land, without craft, could hope to make money and a name.

There scholarly data is carried into fictionalized biography, but with an intelligence, logic and delight of its own, worthy of the subject matter.

S. Schoenbaum in his monumental *Shakespeare's Lives* (1970) in which for 838 pages he submits all previous biographies and biographers to an acid test and reduces the known facts to the bare minimum, almost produces through his acute scholarly skill a nonbiography. Unhappily, when it comes to his own reportage, he himself does little better (but no worse) than Rowse or Burgess. Yet one is delighted when the critical mind that has been turned so devastatingly on others experiences an original moment in life. Schoenbaum pleasantly reveals what brought him the energy to embark upon such an undertaking as his *Shakespeare's Lives*. His readers are told that it was on that late afternoon in Stratford-upon-Avon on the first of September, 1964 (four hundred years after

Shakespeare's birth) as ". . . outside the late summer sun still shone brilliantly, [that Schoenbaum] could barely make out the monument and bust in the shadows of the north chancel." and there "pondered the inconceivable mystery of creation." (p. vii). Schoenbaum's own conclusion from all the evidence about Shakespeare's departure from his native town is as follows:

> . . . eventually, whatever the circumstances, he [Shakespeare] left Stratford. 'Such wind as scatters young men through the world,'
>
> To seek their fortunes further than at home,
> Where small experience grows,
>
> carried him from his drowsy childhood town to a world of larger experience, in much the same way as the happy gale blows Petruchio to Padua from old Verona. (*p.* 116).

Unlike Petruchio, who is looking to marry wealthily in Padua, Shakespeare already had the financial burden of a wife and three little ones in Stratford. And so, for the biographers of the past, the "lost years" have retained their enchanting mystery. With all these attempts and failures to explain why Shakespeare left Stratford and what happened to him for ten years, it is no wonder the general reader believes that there are mysteries surrounding Shakespeare's life and that little is known and nothing more can be discovered about him. This book's purpose is to tell what must have happened during the so-called "lost years," based on more solid information and reasonable conclusions than biographies have hitherto provided. Many critics and scholars differ in their interpretation of the man who was the author of the plays and in their evaluation of his personal life. Some are led to disagree to such an extent, or as a result of witnessing this nonagreement (even contradictory interpretations) by scholars, they say that the author of the plays was not Shakespeare. Agreeing that the Shakespeare who wrote the plays was the

Shakespeare of Stratford, there are those who argue over his education and learning. Still others say nothing can be known about his intellectual background and reading, except through his works. Yet, upon analyzing his writings for personal opinions, the evidence falls on both sides of many questions. The resulting answers are ambiguous. (Does he support or reject the dethronement of Richard II or the killing of Caesar?) He abides, or withdraws from answering specific problems. He dramatizes the issues, not the answers; he shows us the consequence of the dialectic process, we are told. Despite the number of schools of thought about Shakespeare's ideas, background and purposes, it is astonishing that upon review a wide variety of scholars, often even those at odds on other matters, agree directly, implicitly, or sometimes inadvertently that Shakespeare must have had a career which operated as a considerable influence upon his thought—a career other than that of an actor or dramatist. What has, up until recently, largely been a conjecture held by scholars of diverse and often conflicting persuasions, is now supported by new evidence. In turn this new fact about Shakespeare's private life allows various pieces of previously known data to fall into a more complete picture of Shakespeare's personal interests, concerns, and preoccupations. In spite of current Shakespearean scholarship's incredulity, the voices who suggested that Shakespeare had a knowledge of the technicalities of jurisprudence, an interest in legal theory, and an involvement in the legal institutions of his day, and was not just an observer, litigant, or commentator, but one with a career in the law were indeed very close to being correct.

Those who did not believe that Shakespeare was the author and favored Bacon, or others, did so chiefly on the basis of the plays' evidencing a "profound command of legal intricacies."[12] For centuries many writers with a legal background have been convinced that Shakespeare was a lawyer: "Another tradition says that he was an attorney's clerk; and that he was so at one time of his life, I, as a lawyer, have no doubt."[13] Many scholars rejecting any claim that Shakespeare had a legal background, have inadvertently produced evidence to the contrary: ". . . had Shakespeare been a lawyer accustomed to write with legal abbreviations, we might reasonably accept this interpretation."[14] These comments might elicit Hippolyta's response from *A Midsummer-Night's Dream*:

> . . . all their minds transfigured so together,
> More witnesseth than fancy's images
> And grows to something of great constancy;
>
> (v. i. 24–26).

What follows, then, is a re-creation, and not a fantasy, using for the first time individual facts which, having been rejected or ignored in the past, have not been woven into whole cloth. The purpose of the ensuing narrative is to account for what Shakespeare was doing before and after the time he was last heard of in Stratford (1585) and his uncontested presence in London (1595); to provide the most complete array of evidence for the case of Shakespeare's legal career, or background in the law; and to indicate how this background influenced the legal elements in the plays, and in turn how he used the plays to promulgate ideas about the legal institutions, and to effect changes in the juristic theories and practices of his day. Since what follows does not seek to be a complete biography, we shall pursue only a few themes, particularly those pertaining to his views on equity, justice and the law, in order to disclose how an harmonic concern on Shakespeare's part for these topics can be deduced from his art and from his personal documents; uncovering for the first time his surprising legal, social and political attitudes and preoccupations and how forcefully these were held and applied.

II

The Hidden Life From 1585 to 1595

When to the sessions of sweet silent thought
I summon up remembrance of things past,
I sigh the lack of many a thing I sought,
And with old woes new wail my dear time's waste;
Then can I drown an eye, unused to flow,
For precious friends hid in death's dateless night,
And weep afresh love's long since cancell'd woe,
And moan the expense of many a vanish'd sight:
Then can I grieve at grievances foregone,
And heavily from woe to woe tell o'er
The sad account of fore-bemoaned moan,
Which I new pay as if not paid before.
    But if the while I think on thee, dear friend,
    All losses are restored and sorrows end.

(Sonnet xxx)

1. *Shakespeare's Father's Success and Failures*

SHAKESPEARE sighed the lack of one thing he sought; all losses were not to be restored. His thirteenth year was an unfortunate one, and in retrospect may even have initiated him into adolescence with a crisis. Possibly it aggravated the childish fantasy with which Launcelot Gobbo taunts Jessica in *The Merchant of Venice*: "Marry, you may partly hope that your father got you not, . . ." (III. v. 11–12). Shakespeare's father, John Shakespeare, like feather'd Mercury, had vaulted with such ease into his position of Mayor or High Bailiff of Stratford and then something dreadful began to happen:

and indeed it takes
From our achievements, though perform'd at height,

The pith and marrow of our attribute.
So, oft it chances in particular men,
That for some vicious mole of nature in them,
As, in their birth—wherein they are not guilty,
Since nature cannot choose his origin—
By the o'ergrowth of some complexion,
Oft breaking down the pales and forts of reason,
Or by some habit that too much o'er-leavens
The form of plausive manners, that these men,
Carrying, I say, the stamp of one defect,
Being nature's livery, or fortune's star,—
Their virtues else—be they as pure as grace,
As infinite as man may undergo—
Shall in the general censure take corruption
From that particular fault: . . .

(*Hamlet* I. iv. 20–26)

Look here upon the former father:

See, what a grace was seated on this brow;
Hyperion's curls; the front of Jove himself;
An eye like Mars, to threaten and command;
A station like the herald Mercury
New-lighted on a heaven-kissing hill;
A combination and a form indeed,
Where every god did seem to set his seal,
To give the world assurance of a man:

(*Hamlet* III. iv. 55–62)

Whatever it was for John Shakespeare, it puzzled his will and his native hue of resolution sicklied o'er and enterprises of great pitch and moment with this regard their currents turned awry and lost the name of action. But Will would perform in measure, time and place and in some way restore his mother's losses and sorrows end, "Yes, truly; for look you, the sins of the father are to be laid upon the children," as Launcelot Gobbo says also in his taunting. Key to this biographical study is the event of his mother, Mary Shakespeare, perhaps reluctantly, becoming party to a transaction, which resulted in a significant loss to William's inheritance. The passage in *The*

Merchant might continue to apply to Will's feelings: ". . . so the sins of my mother should be visited upon me."

> Truly then I fear you are damned both by father and mother: thus when I shun Scylla, your father, I fall into Charybdis, your mother: well, you are gone both ways.
>
> (III. iv. 17–20)

This may appear to be a very romantic use of text, or misuse of words from fictional characters, products of the imagination. Several types of characters in different plays voicing identical, or similar sentiments can constitute a preoccupation on the part of the author; and if allied concerns cluster in the same play, or in plays written close together, they may serve as clues—the closest evidence we can get—to what touched Shakespeare's thought. The foregoing montage, despite its seemingly melodramatic application, does suggest how a young boy upon whom nothing was lost might be affected by his father's surprising and ultimately public decline.

John Shakespeare had risen through his trade and his popularity to become what would now be called the mayor of Stratford-upon-Avon, then a prosperous and not insignificant community in Warwickshire. John was a glover ["A great round beard, like a glover's paring knife" (*Merry Wives of Windsor* I. iv. 21)]; he dressed leather ["As proper men as ever trod upon neat's leather have gone upon my handiwork" (*Julius Caesar* I. i. 29); ". . . his hide is so tanned with his trade, that he will keep out water a great while; . . ." (*Hamlet* V. i. 186–187)]; and dealt in wool and farm produce ["Fifteen hundred shorn, what comes the wool to?" (*Winter's Tale* IV. iii. 35)]. He was to leave no will to his son, Will, who would eventually receive the house, [". . . give me the poor allottery my father left me by testament; . . ." (*As You Like It* I. i. 76–77.]. But John's father Richard left his son, on February 10, 1561, an estate valued at £38. 17s. From 1561 to 1563, John was one of the two chamberlains of Stratford; and in 1565, he was elected one of the fourteen aldermen whose public costume was a black gown, and subsequently he was allowed to prefix his name with "Master." In 1568 (the year of the publication of a book that will play an important part in the narrative), John Shakespeare received his town's highest honor, when he was selected High Bailiff. As the town's chief officer, he was also a justice of the peace presiding at the monthly sessions of the Court of Record. When his term expired in 1571, he was selected High Alderman and deputy to the new Bailiff, who was his close friend, Adrian Quiney. Shakespeare's father had been selected first citizen of Stratford and had with the aid of the town steward presided over numerous legal and business transactions such as cases of debt, and violations of town ordinances; he had distributed warrents of restraint, for arrest, and to keep the peace; he had sealed leases, looked after town lands and investments. The very young Will Shakespeare from 1568 to 1571, when he was between four and seven years of age, was brought up in the womb of prosperity and public acclaim.

Adrian Quiney was John Shakespeare's close associate in the town's business matters. Quiney, older than John by a generation and a sort of mentor to him, was a mercer and in his lifetime had been selected three times as Stratford's Bailiff. The year that John became Bailiff (1568), he and Adrian went up to London on borough business, drawing their expenses from the Stratford Council. This was the very path William was to follow in the 1580's; who knows what contacts his father had in the London area as the result of his town's legal and financial dealings. This was not the only time John and Adrian went to the city together; legal details from their second trip document their activity more precisely.

In September of 1571, when Adrian Quiney once more became Bailiff, John Shakespeare, as Chief Alderman, was his assistant. Following their establishment in their new offices, the two men again went in January 1572, during Hilary term, to the London area to represent Stratford in the law courts situated in the City of Westminster.

For future reference it will be helpful to explain briefly the term times of the English court calendar. They are: Hilary, Easter, Trinity, and Michaelmas, in that order. Hilary Term, lasting a month, refers to St. Hilary, bishop of Poitiers (d. 367) whose feast falls on January 13. Easter Term goes from eighteen days after Easter to the Monday following Ascension Day (forty days after Easter). Trinity Term is the period from the Wednesday after Trinity Sunday until the Wednesday two weeks later (a fortnight as the English would say). Trinity Sunday follows Pentecost (or Whitsunday) which is the seventh Sunday after Easter and fifty days from the second day of Passover. Michaelmas Term is associated with Michaelmas Day, the feast celebrated on September 29 in honor of the archangel Michael. This feast day is an ominous date for Shakespeare's father and Shakespeare's inheritance. Adjusting these dates to 1972, the Terms would work out as follows: Hilary—January 23 to February 21; Easter—April 20 to May 15; Trinity—May 31 to June 14; and Michaelmass—October 9 to November 28. During these periods the law courts would be in session.

Commissioned by Stratford, Adrian and John went down to Westminster on matters of conflict between the town and the lord of the manor, the Earl of Warwick. While there John Shakespeare completed some personal business of recovering a debt of £50 from a Banbury glover at the Court of Common Pleas in Westminster Hall. On the other hand, in the same court he was being sued for a £30 debt by a former steward of Stratford. John was acquiring but not giving; he did not pay what he owed. This was to return to plague him at a more critical time.

But now he was at his height—". . . leasing meadows from the former Clopton estate, and in October 1575 he bought two more houses, with gardens and orchards, in the town for £40;" and before that he "had stood surety for an acquaintance at Shottery, Richard Hathaway, for two debts which were paid when harvest came in."[1] John's confidence was such that in 1575/1576 he started to apply to the Herald's College for a grant of a coat of arms. John would be styled a gentleman. William Shakespeare would have been the son of a gentleman, might have gone to the University, or more likely could have become an Inns of Court man and gone on to be a barrister, perhaps a judge or justice. However, John's reach exceeded his grasp and things began to fall apart. It would be left to William twenty years later to finally attain for his father what he had desired to pass on to him.

From the age of thirteen to his thirty-seventh year, the time of his father's death in 1601, when it is thought the last version of *Hamlet* is written, Shakespeare witnessed in his father a decline which had a considerable effect upon William's prospects, plans and conduct of his life, even what he wrote about. A paragraph from Marchette Chute, narrates one aspect of this well:

> It was at this point in John Shakespeare's career, when everything seemed to be going so well for him, that something suddenly went very wrong. He attended the meeting of the Stratford Council in the normal way on September 5, 1576, as he had been doing for the past thirteen years. Since his election to the Council he had been absent on only a single occasion, and in the past eleven years he had never been absent at all. But at the meeting of the Council in the following January [1577], John Shakespeare was absent. He was absent at the next meeting, and the one after that, and in fact he never returned again as a regular member. For the rest of his life he only attended one meeting of the Council, and for five years he broke completely with the official governing body of Stratford after more than a decade of devoted, loyal attendance.[2]

It was in the winter of 1576 that the "vicious mole of nature" began to work upon John, which only ceased when he was buried twenty-five years later outside the church edifice in the yard, even though he had held high office. It was his son who was placed beneath the floor of the chancel next to the north wall.

A chronology of Shakespeare's father's decline can be

constructed from the documentary evidence. Even the earliest biographer, Nicholas Rowe, was aware of these declining circumstances, but he attributed them to what turned out to be an exaggeration in the number of Shakespeare's siblings.

> . . . that tho' he was his [father's] eldest Son, he could give him no better Education than his own Employment. He had bred him, 'tis true, for some time at a Free school, where 'tis probable he aquir'd that little Latin he was Master of: But the narrowness of his Circumstances, and the want of his assistance at Home, forc'd his Father to withdraw him from thence, and unhappily prevented his further Proficiency in that Language.

Although this may be an attempt on Rowe's part to account for Jonson's remark concerning Shakespeare's little Latin and Greek (despite the fact that Shakespeare would have received a substantial education at the Stratford Free School) there is a presence, behind its purpose, of a financially constrained childhood and increasing domestic wants needing to be supplied. The first sign of this trouble, serious only in retrospect, was John's absence from the January Council meeting in 1577. The first indication that the problem might have financial ramifications is in 1578 when John is called upon to give to the levy for the supply of additional soldiers. The aldermen must have been aware of some difficulty since they assessed him only 3s. 4d, half the amount they assessed themselves. John did not even pay the reduced fee and finally was excused completely. Likewise, he was relieved of his duty to pay a weekly poor tax of 4d, which indicates that his financial state was a cause for serious concern. They forgave him his fine for nonattendance at Election Day in September of that year at the same time they invoked heavy fines upon two other absentee members. This forgiveness on the part of the town fathers is not matched by the former steward of Stratford's again opening his suit for £30 in this same year in the Court of Common Pleas in Westminster, where only seven years before money was being awarded to John. In 1578, when William Shakespeare was fourteen, his father was being forgiven his poor tax by the Council and being sued for debt in Westminster Hall. Stratford was extending mercy but London was calling for justice.

And then, Will's future was tampered with. To pay off these mounting debts and those of a number and amount unrecorded, John Shakespeare's consumption in 1578/79 was to touch Shakespeare's mother. Mary's endowment was taken by John and the act ultimately cut off what was to be from her to her son. At this time John disposed of Shakespeare's mother's estate. Records show that Mary's interest in a large amount of land in Snitterfield was sold to her nephew Robert Webbe for only £4, but this is probably an error in the record. Since Webbe sells it later for £40, that is likely what the Shakespeares received, the price being also closer to what was needed. It was nevertheless a desperate measure since outright possession, rather than merely an interest in the title, was nearly forthcoming upon the death of a mortally ill relative. The eighty-six acres of Asbies were let. Furthermore, the additional Wilmecote estate, consisting of fifty-six acres and a dwelling house, was mortgaged.[3] According to the legal agreements, the Shakespeares apparently kept title to at least the last two properties. Outright ownership and conveyance was a complicated business to determine by sixteenth-century English law from such documents. The Shakespeares had entered on slippery, legal ground where assurances were never really certain. This was the beginning of the end; the valuable properties had been lost; they had been given away to feed some defect, some flaw, watching "this canker of our nature come/In further evil" (*Hamlet* v. ii. 69–70).

In April 1579, Shakespeare's fifteenth birthday warned that his last year of formal schooling was approaching. It also turned out to be a cruel month, for his eight-year-old-sister Anne died, to be restored only in a wife of the same name three years later. That summer John Shakespeare was not furnished with a pattern of familial action which would give solace to his condition. A relative of the same name, a John Shakespeare of Balsall, a Warwickshire town north of Stratford, succumbed to despair and hanged himself in his house on 23 July 1579.[4] John, William's father, at least decided 'tis nobler to take action against a sea of troubles and to try to end them.

1580 was the year of judgment when all the debts came due. A particular transaction in this year will be analyzed which bears more immediately upon the narrative, after some evidence of the continuing decline is provided. John's mortgage of £40 on his wife's property had fallen due so he sells property in Snitterfield outright to cover it, but cannot meet the total debt. This specifically is what has the long-range effect upon William. It looked as if all were going to have balanced. Chaos would not come again, except for an extraordinary problem involving once more a call for justice from Westminster, but this time from a higher court, close to the Crown itself—the Court of Queen's Bench.

What trouble had come upon the already perplexed and aggravated John Shakespeare? In 1580, the same year as the sale of Snitterfield, John, in attempting to meet the mortgage for £40, lost precisely that considerable sum for losing his temper. He and a Nottingham hat-maker, John Audley, are bound over to the Court of Queen's Bench to give security against a breach of the peace. This, ironically, is the kind of case he would have presided over as a justice of the peace. William Shakespeare would be cited to keep the peace in the very same court sixteen years later, and act in Jonson's *Every Man in His Humour* where a number of characters are involved in a similar case before a Justice Clement. Queen's Bench is in the same Hall of Westminster as the Court of Common Pleas, where John had gone in 1572 to recover a debt. It is all the more astonishing, then, that he does not make the journey to appear and stand surety by giving oath in person to keep the peace. Was it because of not being of the mind, or will to do it, or would there have been something physically wrong with John making it an impossibility? Whatever it was it cost him dearly. He did not appear, and no one could act as attorney in such matters, only *in personam* presence was recognized. John Audley did not appear either, hence Shakespeare's father was fined £20 for his own absence and £20 for not bringing Audley into the court. £40 *was the amount he owed on the mortgaged estate*! He had sold outright other lands to meet the sum and now these incomes were consumed by this sequence of indiscretions. When William Shakespeare was cited to keep the peace by the same court in 1596, but was not served upon or fined, although he avoided loss, it was, nevertheless, a painful reminder of what his father had had so ruinously laid upon him. The actions of his father in 1580 were to plague Shakespeare by their consequent loss, additional cost, and time in years spent in the very court which at his father's height could give him £50, and when he had fallen low demand £40.

In 1582 Shakespeare marries the eldest daughter of the well-to-do farmer Richard Hathaway of Hewland Farm. To her marriage, Anne Hathaway brought eight years of seniority, £6, 13s. 4d from her father's will, and two to three months' pregnancy by Will's sexual will. Shakespeare's father had formerly stood surety for her father who had died the year before the marriage. Fortunately, John Shakespeare, while relinquishing land, rights and estates outside Stratford, had his home on Henley Street and room there for Will and Anne. In addition at this time it appears that John's conflicts break out in local enmity. The narrative is picked up by F. E. Halliday:

> Shakespeare's courtship and hasty marriage coincided with an episode that must have added to the disturbance of that already sufficiently disturbed year, for at this time his father was threatened with some sort of violence at the hands of four of his fellow townsmen. Anyone thus threatened could go to a justice of the peace and make oath that

> he stood in fear of his life or some bodily hurt, whereupon a judge would order the sheriff of the county to attach the alleged offender and make him enter a bond to keep the peace. In the summer of 1582, therefore, John Shakespeare craved 'sureties of the peace against Ralph Cawdrey, William Russell, Thomas Logginge and Robert Young, for fear of death and mutilation of his limbs.' Little is known about Russell and nothing about Logginge, but Robert Young was a well-known dyer, and Ralph Cawdrey a substantial butcher, tenant of the Angel Inn, and at this time bailiff of Stratford. What happened further we do not know, but it may be significant that in September Alderman Shakespeare attended his first Council meeting since 1576 in order to register his vote for his old friend John Sadler as bailiff. It cannot have made life any easier for the Shakespeares to have been at enmity with Ralph Cawdrey.[5]

It sounds as if the disturbance was partly a political matter, possibly a financial one. William, along with his father, showed his affinity for the Sadlers by having John Sadler's son and daughter-in-law as godparents for his twins in 1585 and he gave his children their names—Judith and Hamnet (i.e. Hamlet). The date 1585 and his expanding family are the time and the circumstances which find the dramatist leaving Stratford; however, in order to understand why he does, the sequence of John's problems has to be completed to provide the full testimony of how serious he thought his condition to be, and of what directly impinged upon Will Shakespeare's preoccupation and occupation.

In 1586 John Shakespeare had to stand surety for his brother Henry who was often fined for fighting and was also in debt. These litigations have been enumerated by F. E. Halliday: Henry Shakespeare

> . . . owed £5 to Christopher Smith of Stratford and another £22 to Nicholas Lane, a farmer and money-lender of Bridgetown on the other side of the [Avon] river. Although his brother John had just lost £10 by standing surety for a local coppersmith who had failed to appear in court, he guaranteed £10 of Henry's debt, or so it was al-

leged by Lane, who sued him for that sum. John, however, denied the responsibility, contested the suit through all its stages, and when judgment was given against him appealed to a higher court. At the same time he embarked on another lawsuit.

Apparently, one of John's flaws was his tendency to help persons who could not be relied upon, and to hope in turn that others would treat him as mercifully. In the same year, after ten years of nonattendance, John Shakespeare is finally removed as Alderman. A new alderman is appointed to replace him ". . . for that Mr. Shaxspere dothe not come to the halles when they be warned nor hathe not done of longe tyme."[6] It is believed that his enemy at law Ralph Cawdrey probably proposed the motion. Most commentators suppose that in this or the following year (1586 or 1587) of court actions against his father, legal attempts on his parents' part to repossess properties lost, and John's ouster from the local government structure, when William had reached his maturity, William Shakespeare left Stratford for London. The theory goes on to suggest that he may have followed the Queen's Men who had given theatrical performances in the town, as had the less prominent Leicester's Men and three other companies. The year is convenient because of the presence of the acting companies (but there were almost always one or two any year), but it presumes that since he became a dramatist, actor, and part owner of a theatre a number of years later, the histrionic craft must have been his sole interest.

But there were, beyond conjecture, reasons closer to his own and his father's circumstances prompting his departure for the London area around this time. Of course, neither his narrow circumstances nor the attraction of the players rules out the influence of either factor upon his actions, in fact his reasons for leaving may have been several. It is doubtful, however, that the husband of a well-to-do woman, father of three children, and son of parents in financial difficulties and public decline would run off to follow a theatrical group passing through town with little promise of security or monetary support. But that he would leave at this point for more occupational advantage and possible real family gain in his father's need and fall from civic influence is quite apparent. He may have made initial contacts with some of the players which would serve beneficial purposes later, after he pursued more pressing matters. Schoenbaum (p. 246) presumes Shakespeare stepped immediately into one of the major roles in an acting company, but it seems very unlikely that he could or did step directly into anything like the position of a major role as an actor, or as a writer.

The situation with John Shakespeare remained unabated. He is not recorded as being of any trade after holding civic office. The problems will become graphically clear when we trace the most important legal case surrounding just one transaction from 1577 to 1599. His circumstances were publicly and officially recorded in 1592 and are given an interesting interpretation by one commentator:

> His absenteeism extended to church, and in September 1592 he was listed for failure to attend church—a legal fault in an age when church attendance was required by statute. It has sometimes been claimed that the elder Shakespeare stayed away from Church of England services because he was a Roman Catholic, or because he was a Puritan, but the evidence is against such claims. The official records state that John Shakespeare was absent 'for fear of prosecution for debt.' We cannot know definitely the root cause of his difficulties, but the story reminds us of the classic decline of the alcoholic.[7]

John Shakespeare dies in 1601 and is buried without particular distinction as to place and without a monument. This is around the time it is thought the final version of *Hamlet* was completed and performed:

QUEEN: Do not for ever with thy vailed lids
Seek for thy noble father in the dust:

Thou know'st 'tis common; all that lives must die,
Passing through nature to eternity.
HAMLET: Ay, madam, it is common.
QUEEN: If it be,
Why seems it so particular with thee?
HAMLET: Seems, madam! nay, it is; I know not 'seems.'
'Tis not alone my inky cloak, good mother,
Nor customary suits of solemn black,
Nor windy suspiration of forced breath,
No, nor the fruitful river in the eye,
Nor the dejected 'haviour of the visage,
Together with all forms, moods, shapes of grief,
That can denote me truly: these indeed seem,
For they are actions that a man might play:
But I have that within which passeth show;
These but the trappings and suits of woe.
KING: 'Tis sweet and commendable in your nature, Hamlet,
To give these mourning duties to your father:
But, you must know, your father lost a father;
That father lost, lost his, and the survivor found
In filial obligation for some term
To do obsequious sorrow: but to persever
In obstinate condolement is a course
Of impious stubbornness; 'tis unmanly grief;
It shows a will most incorrect to heaven,
A heart unfortified, a mind impatient,
An understanding simple and unschool'd:
For what we know must be and is as common
As any the most vulgar thing to sense,
Why should we in our peevish opposition
Take it to heart? Fie! 'tis a fault to heaven,
A fault against the dead, a fault to nature,
To reason most absurd; whose common theme
Is death of father, and who still hath cried,
From the first corse till he that died to-day,
'This must be so.' We pray you, throw to earth
This unprevailing woe, and think of us
As of a father: (I. ii. 70–108)

Although replacing his father in responsibility, unlike Hamlet he receives no inheritance, nor election; but, of course, by this time Shakespeare in himself has recouped his father's losses, although not the one which has so specifically rankled, and his mother does automatically receive the partial life interest in the house on Henley Street. His father left no will; it is not known if he left debts, or whether William had met them by that time, or accepted responsibility for them.

The unfinished, poorly constructed, or problematic, *Timon of Athens* was written by Shakespeare sometime from 1601 to 1606, say many, and some suggest even an earlier date as they feel it is not in the later style. Its condition may have resulted from Shakespeare's having looked back too closely, too autobiographically upon his father's life. Its content certainly shows that Shakespeare was aware of the nature of his father's experiences; perhaps the play itself suffers from William's inability to sufficiently distance himself for once in his art (as he does in *Hamlet*) from what struck him so directly in his life. As this section of our narrative opened with a montage of Shakespeare's possible reaction to his father's civic and financial affairs, it will serve more than mere symmetry to close it with direct statements by Shakespeare about a civic figure at his height, falling into debt and bankruptcy, scorned by his fellow citizens save for one colleague, (Adrian Quiney?) driven from public office, falling into a malevolent condition and ending in an ignominious grave in *Timon of Athens*.

LUCULLUS: And how does that honourable, complete,
free-hearted gentleman of Athens, thy very
bountiful good lord and master?

(III. i. 9–11)

SECOND LORD: In like manner was I in debt to my
importunate business, but he would not hear
my excuse.

(III. vi. 15–16)

FLAVIUS; I did endure
Not seldom, nor no slight checks, when I have
Prompted you in the ebb of your estate
And your great flow of debts. My loved lord,

Though you hear now, too late—yet now's a time—
To pay your present debts.
TIMON: Let all my land be sold.
FLAVIUS: 'Tis all engaged, some forfeited and gone;
And what remains will hardly stop the mouth
Of present dues: the future comes apace:
What shall defend the interim? and at length
How goes our reckoning?
TIMON: To Lacedaemon did my land extend.
FLAVIUS: O my good lord, the world is but a word:
Were it all yours to give it in a breath,
How quickly were it gone!

(II. ii. 148–163)

FLAVIUS: Why then preferr'd you not your sums and bills,
When your false masters eat of my lord's meat?
Then they could smile and fawn upon his debts
And take down the interest into their gluttonous maws.

(III. iv. 49–52)

TIMON: Who dares, who dares,
In purity of manhood stand upright,
And say 'This man's a flatterer'? if one be,
So are they all; for every grise [*i.e. step*] of fortune
Is smooth'd by that below: the learned pate
Ducks to the golden fool: all's obliquy;
There's nothing level in our cursed natures,
But direct villany. Therefore, be abhorr'd
All feasts, societies, and throngs of men!
His semblable, yea, himself, Timon disdains:

(IV. iii. 13–22)

FIRST BANDITTI: Where should he have this gold? It is some poor fragment, some slender ort [*i.e. fragment*] of his remainder: the mere want of gold, and the falling-from of his friends, drove him into this melancholy.

(IV. iii. 400–403)

TIMON: I do proclaim
One honest man—mistake me not—but one;
No more, I pray, — and he's a steward.
How fain would I have hated all mankind!
And thou redeem'st thyself: but all, save thee,

I fell with curses.
Methinks thou art more honest now than wise;
For, by oppressing and betraying me,
Thou mightst have sooner got another service:
For many so arrive at second masters,
Upon their first lord's neck.

(IV. iii. 503–513)

TIMON: I have a tree, which grows here in my close,
That mine own use invites me to cut down,
And shortly must I fell it: tell my friends,
Tell Athens, in the sequence of degree
From high to low throughout, that whoso please
To stop affliction, let him take his haste,
Come hither, ere my tree hath felt the axe,
And hang himself. I pray you, do my greeting.
FLAVIUS: Trouble him no further; thus you still shall find him.
TIMON: Come not to me again: but say to Athens,
Timon hath made his everlasting mansion
Upon the beached verge of the salt flood;
Who once a day with his embossed froth
The turbulent surge shall cover: thither come,
And let my grave-stone be your oracle.
Lips, let sour words go by and language end:
What is amiss plague and infection mend!
Graves only be men's works and death their gain!
Sun, hide thy beams! Timon hath done his reign.
[*Retires to his cave.*]
SENATOR: His discontents are unremoveably
Coupled to nature. (V. i. 208–228)

2. *Shakespeare's Schooling and His Law Hand*

THE FINANCIAL problems of the father of the young lad of thirteen, Will Shakespeare, may or may not have been critical enough to force his withdrawal from school, as some have thought to be the fact. He may have had to leave to supplement the income, but he certainly would not have had to leave to save money, since his father's civic position allowed him to attend the Stratford Grammar School free. It is true that Will, as eldest son, would be expected to have to earn money as an apprentice to his father, a glover, or perhaps to a butcher, or one of the tradesmen of his father's acquaintance. If he did particularly well in school, he could teach in the country, or for one of the local gentry, where he might have translated and produced the earliest version of *Comedy of Errors* for his pupils. These are all possibilities not excluded by what will be suggested he might have done whenever it was that he finished his schooling, and, as shall be demonstrated, could write well and have, from the excellent education of the Stratford school, a considerable amount of Latin.

Early weekday mornings Will would leave his home on Henley Street and walk toward the River Avon but have to turn right at the Market Cross onto High Street, which in a block became Chapel Street. This point was near the imposing New Place, now in disrepair. Eventually, it was to be his own house and to become such a symbol of his accomplishment in Stratford. Then Chapel became Church Street where the Grammar School adjoined the Guild Chapel on the corner at which Chapel Street and Chapel Lane intersected with Church Street and Scholars (Tinkers) Lane. From his plays it is learned that Shakespeare retained, at later dates, recollections of his Latin lessons in verses of Mantuan appearing in *Love's Labour's Lost*, and of Horace in *Titus Andronicus*, probably from his grammar book. The grammar school's ". . . master was paid £20 a year and provided with a house. This equaled the salary of the master of Eton and enabled the borough to employ first-class men. Thomas Jenkins, for example, who was master from 1575 to 1579, the years when young William should have been in the upper school, was fellow or scholar of St. John's College, Oxford, B.A. April 6, 1566, M.A. April 8, 1570. A high-school principal of equivalent education would be a Ph.D. of Harvard."[8]

Shakespeare would have learned his Latin from Lily's *A Short Introduction of Grammar* as he cites a passage from it in *Titus Andronicus* (IV. ii. 20–23). His curriculum had him reading plays by Plautus and Terence; his first play, *Comedy of Errors*, is heavily dependent upon his knowledge of Plautus in the original Latin. James G. McManaway presents an excellent list of works studied at the school in English, Latin and Greek (pp. 13–14). Shakespeare recalls with humor a pedantic teacher of Latin in Holofernes (*Love's Labour's Lost*); and Latin lessons in *The Taming of the Shrew* (III. i) and *Merry Wives of Windsor* (IV. i). Edmond Malone, the late eighteenth century barrister, having analyzed Shakespeare's free school, judged the proficiency Shakespeare attained in Latin to consist of a knowledge of the language which if not profound, was at least competent. Despite the notorious accusation by Ben Jonson, who was associated with both Oxford and Cambridge after going to Westminster School, it is now assumed that although not a scholar of Latin, Shakespeare had a good background in the language, and knew some Greek, evidenced by his translations of Plautus and Ovid (*The Rape of Lucrece*).

The grammar schools provided competence in few things, and of these above all they concentrated on language (Latin) and penmanship. Before entering the school at seven in 1572, Shakespeare would have had to have learned to write and read. Possibly his mother taught him, but there is no evidence that Mary or John could write. There is ample data in fact suggesting that they could not write; instead of affixing their signatures to those documents we possess, they made their marks. This does not necessarily mean they could not also write, but whenever "Jhon Shacksper" appears on an official or legal document a copyist, clerk or recorder has written the name.[9] Perhaps Will had to learn from "Sir Willy," as William Gilbert was called, who was, amongst other things, the local scrivener. As scrivener Gilbert had to know a number of writing hands: secretary hand, Italianate, Chancery, and legal hand. Soon after young Shakespeare learned to work well with his horn book (*Love's Labour's Lost* v. i. 48, and *Richard* III, I, i. 34–57) and his Absey book (*King John* I. i. 196 and *Two Gentlemen of Verona* II. i. 22), little Will may have been exposed to alternate ways of making his letters very early in his life. The Grammar School would give him strenuous training in an excellent Secretary hand. And so, whether it came when he was thirteen in 1577, as a direct result of his father's financial problems, or in the ordinary course of events in 1580 at the age of sixteen, Shakespeare was out upon the world of Stratford-upon-Avon with the aid of an imaginative mind, some good Latin, and a Secretary hand to do him service. There was no getting around it, he had to earn money by the sweat of his brow, or by pushing a pen, if he had a nimble hand.

> I know the hand: in faith, 'tis a fair hand;
> And whiter than the paper it writ on
> Is the fair hand that writ.
>
> (*Merchant of Venice* II. iv. 12–14)

Perhaps he returned to William Gilbert to acquire another hand or applied to any of a number of acquaintances who had the skill: the deputy steward, or town clerk; a former teacher; one of his father's lawyers; or one of their clerks.

Besides being able to turn to a number of others, Shakespeare could teach himself penmanship and various hands from a copy book. The first and finest handwriting manual of the Chancery hand to be had was Ludovico degli Arrighi's *Operina*. Rome, 1522. He could thus learn the legal script, or Chancery hand necessary for a clerk, such as is referred to in Charles Dickens' *Bleak House*:

> 'Who copied that? . . .'
> 'Is it what you people call law-hand? . . .'
> 'Not quite. Probably'—Mr. Tulkinghorn examines it as he speaks—' the legal character which it has was acquired after the original hand was formed.'
>
> (Chapter II)

Working at it over a period of time, particularly if he did much writing or translating on his own by candlelight, Shakespeare as a copyist, could have produced a good hand fast, quite like that of which Hamlet boasts:

> I sat me down,
> Devis'd a new commission, wrote it fair:
> I once did hold it, as our statists do,
> A baseness to write fair, and labour'd much
> How to forget that learning; but sir now
> It did me yeoman's service . . .
> Folded the writ up in form of the other,
> Subscribed it, gave't the impression, . . .
> (V. ii. 31–36, 51–52)

Shakespeare knows enough about legal forms to have Hamlet not only produce fair copy in a hand he had learned in the past, but to have the writ in correct form and fold, and properly subscribed and sealed.

The leading Shakespearean handwriting expert, Sir Edward Maunde Thompson, speaks of evidence for such a legal hand on the part of Shakespeare as he examines the dramatist's signatures.

> The signature to the deposition [Belott-Mountjoy 1612] is WILLM SHAKP with a sweeping stroke dashed through the tail of the p. If we were to apply the rules of mediaeval abbreviation to the signature we might determine the final letter p with its added stroke to be read as *per*; and had Shakespeare been a lawyer accustomed to write with legal abbreviations, we might reasonably accept this interpretation. But the poet was not a lawyer, nor is there any reason for supposing that he had in his mind any thought of exact and methodical abbreviation according to rule, when he thus subscribed his name. We should prefer to regard the underwritten flourish in this instance as serving the same purpose as the over-written flourish in the Blackfriars deeds, that is as simply indicating that the name was shortened and nothing more.[10]

Just as Ben Jonson mixed Italianate and Secretary hand to

produce his personal style, what Sir Edward may be noting is Shakespeare's mix of Secretary and his legal hand. The under-written flourish to indicate abbreviation, rather than merely adornment, which Thompson identifies, did not come into use until the eighteenth century. The evidence informs us that, like Hamlet, Shakespeare had not forgotten his learning of legal hand when he signed on May 11th, 1612 the deposition signature with the abbreviation of *per* as was the practice of those involved in the Elizabethan legal professions.

Although not ever being able to be a formally trained lawyer, Shakespeare could have found a trade in Stratford as a solicitor's clerk, a lawyer's copyist, a scrivener's apprentice, a helper to the curate, or an aid to the town deputy (the office his father had held), where he would write out documents. There, to borrow a description from Dickens' *Bleak House*, he would deal

> . . . in all sorts of blank forms of legal process; in skins and rolls of parchment; in paper—foolscap, brief, draft, brown, white, whitey-brown, and blotting; in stamps; in office-quills, pens, ink, India-rubber, pounce, pins, pencils, sealing-wax, and wafers; in red tape and green ferret; in pocket-books, almanacks, diaries, and law lists; in string boxes, rulers, ink-stands—glass and leaden, penknives, scissors, bodkins, and other small office-cutlery; in short, in articles too numerous to mention; . . .
>
> (Chapter x)

William Gilbert, the scrivener, among others could have found him piecework, odd jobs, or instruction that might employ his skills perhaps as an abecedarius. When Will was only seven, in 1571, his schoolmaster, Walter Roche, left teaching to become a lawyer in Stratford, but he continued to live in Chapel Street, three doors from New Place. Shakespeare's father employed the services of several lawyers, the one in Stratford was named William Court who lived across the street from New Place and in London, John Harborne, J. Stovell, Edward Huberd, and Stephen Powle. The Shakespeares also employed lawyers and scribes residing in nearby Worcester. William Underhill, who at this time was the owner of New Place, was a lawyer and a member of the Inner Temple, one of the four Inns of Court, or major schools, where lawyers were trained in London. Shakespeare's father had been deputy to the town steward; as Bailiff, had had the steward under him; and had held judicial offices as Justice of the Peace and chief magistrate of the Court of Record. The town steward, or town clerk at this time, from 1575 to 1587, was Henry Rogers. Later a cousin of Shakespeare's, Thomas Greene, becomes town clerk. He names his children after William and Anne, rents rooms in Shakespeare's residence, is subsequently Treasurer of Middle Temple, and stands surety for membership into that august legal body for the dramatist John Marston. Any of these men could have directly provided, or obtained, a place for the young Shakespeare in a Stratford law office.[11] "Thou art clerkly, thou art clerkly, . . ." (*Merry Wives of Windsor* IV. v. 58). There he would have been exposed to his "'se offendendo'" (v. i. 9), "crowner's quest law" (l. 24), and "his action of battery" (l. 120) which appear in *Hamlet*; but primarily learn how to put quill to "parchment made of sheep-skins" (l. 123), to draw deeds of gift, to make warrants and to become a proper fine penman, like the one in *Merchant of Venice*:

> This justice's novice! . . . a youth,
> A kind of boy, a little scrubbed boy,
> No higher than thyself, the judge's clerk,
> A prating boy . . .
> the boy, his clerk.
> That took some pains in writing.[12]

3. *Court of Queen's Bench:* Shakespeare *v.* Lambert

IN 1578, when Will Shakespeare could write fair copy, knew Latin, and could work in a law office, his father, as the result of his financial decline, entered into a legal transaction which profoundly affected Shakespeare's life. Some have said it caused him to leave school. It might have influenced his initial trade and intellectual development; may have been the major factor which brought him from his family and Stratford to London; and its study leads to discovering where he was hidden from scholarly sight during the number of silent years including the most crucial period of his development. The property central to this matter was not originally his father's, but rather his mother's. As part of the dowry portion to her marriage in 1557, Mary Shakespeare had brought an estate. Like father, like son; John Shakespeare, like William, married the year after his bride's father died, making her a beneficiary. Mary Arden was the youngest daughter of John Shakespeare's father's landlord, Robert Arden. Robert left Mary ten marks and the freehold estate of Asbies: "all my land in Willmcote cawlide [i.e. called] Asbyes and the crop apone the grounde sowne and tyllide as hitt is." Later records disclose that this included a dwelling house and forty-four acres of land: "one virgate of ground and four acres of arable land."[13] Some twenty years after the marriage in 1578 John Shakespeare finds that this property will serve to forestall his accelerating decline.

In 1578 there are several clear and specific evidences of the seriousness of John Shakespeare's financial state. Halliwell-Phillipps, the first person to look carefully at, and unscramble, the documents pertaining to John, describes what happened at this time:

> At a meeting of the Town Council held on 29 January there was a levy upon the inhabitants of the town for the purchase of military accoutrements, and the note of this taxation is preceded by the following resolution, — 'at this hall yt ys agreed that every alderman, except suche underwrytten excepted, shall paye towardes the furniture of the pikemen, ij billmen, and one archer, vj.*s.* viij.*d*, and every

> burgess, except suche under-wrytten excepted, shall pay iij. *s*. iiij.*d*,'

As was mentioned earlier, "Mr. Shaxpeare" is excepted and had to pay only iij.*s*. iiij.*d*, which was half the expected amount. Later that year on November 14th, John Shakespeare has to mortgage his wife's estate of Asbies. On that same day, "In a list of 'debtes which are owinge unto me, Roger Saddeler,' a baker of Stratford, appended to his will of 14 November, 1578, is the following entry, — 'item, of Edmonde Lambarte and . . . Cornishe, for the debte of Mr. John Shaksper, v. li[i.e. £5]."[14] This indicates that Edmund Lambert, Mary Shakespeare's brother-in-law, along with someone else had had to stand surety for a debt of John's to Roger Sadler. It was to Edmund that John and Mary had mortgaged Asbies for £40 for the two years until 1580, with no intent to sell, thus increasing their debt to him.

Edmund received no interest on the advance, for he enjoyed the rents and profits from the farm while he held it in security for the bond. The clever John had already leased the property for twenty-one years after the due date of the mortgage to George Gibbes for the annual payment of "'the moiety of one quarter of wheat and the moiety of one quarter of barley.'" This is found in the complicated Wilmecote Fine filed in Hilary Term 1579 at Westminster Hall (*cf.* 202). John Shakespeare was looking for cash, and attempting to set up a future income. In the same law term, the note of a fine levied when the estate at Aston-Cantlowe (Asbies) was mortgaged to Edmund Lambert is recorded "before the Queenes Majesties justices of the comon plees att Westminster" (p. 15, *cf.* also p. 11). "Wilmecote" and "Aston-Cantlowe" estates are the general geographical indications used interchangeably for what will henceforth be referred to as the estate of "Asbies," to avoid confusion. The Shakespeares, from later testimony, clearly felt that the recovery of the estate would result from the simple repayment of the borrowed sum. William Shakespeare is fully aware of this kind of transaction as he puns on the method of conveyance in his *Comedy of Errors*:

> DROMIO: There's no time for a man to recover his hair that grows bald by nature.
> ANTIPHOLUS: May he not do it by fine and recovery?
> DROMIO: Yes, to pay a fine for a periwig and recover the lost hair of another man.
>
> (II. ii. 73–75)

Not a week after the mortgage arrangement had passed before the Town Council announced on 19 November "item, yt ys ordered that every alderman shall paye wekely towardes the releif of the poore iiij.*d*, savinge Mr. John Shaxpeare and Mr. Robert Bratt, who shall not be taxed to pay anythinge." (p. 235). The Corporation was being lenient and then kind in the face of John's difficulties, particularly since he had not attended any of their monthly meetings for the past year.

A while later, in 1578, John and Mary Shakespeare state, in official documents (to be analyzed in Chapter IV) what by that time William then understood to be the case, and what his parents clearly understood the arrangement to be, at the time they entered into the mortgage on November 14, 1578. When the transfer of the estate to Edmund Lambert took place, John and Mary were in lawful possession of the Asbie property through Mary's direct inheritance, consisting of forty-four acres and a house in Wilmecote, Warwickshire. Upon receipt of £40 from Edmund living in Barton-on-the-Heath they were satisfied that he should have and enjoy the premises until such time as they repaid him the £40. Thereby Edmund took possession of the property and received its produce and profits (*cf.* p. 14). John Shakespeare had formulated an indenture bearing the date upon, or about the fourteenth day of November, in the twentieth year of the reign of our Sovereign Lady the Queen's Majesty that now is. As the Lambert testimony goes on to say, in which indenture there is a conditional provision contained that, if John did pay unto him the sum of forty pounds upon the feast day of St. Michael the Archangel in the year of our Lord one thousand five hundred and eighty, at his dwelling house in Barton-on-the-Heath, Warwickshire, that then the bargain and agreements would cease and become void (*cf.* p. 15). John would be able to obtain his wife's dowry to settle upon William if in two years he paid the said £40 on September 29, 1580 to Edmund Lambert at his home in the Cotswolds.

To prevent the loss of Asbies, John Shakespeare turns once again to manipulating his wife's inheritance. In 1579 he disposes

> . . . of his wife's reversionary interests at Snitterfield for the exact amount that he had borrowed from the Lamberts in 1578, a transfer that he had perhaps arranged with a view to the redemption of the matrimonial estate at Wilmecote.
>
> (I, 59)

Shakespeare's earliest play deals with such matters:

> DROMIO: Will you send him, mistress, redemption,
> the money in his desk?
>
> ADRIANA: Go fetch it, sister. This I wonder at,
> That he, unknown to me, should be in debt.
>
> (*Comedy of Errors* IV. ii. 46–48)

Halliwell-Phillipps continues to explain the Elizabethan practice concerning mortgages:

> It must be borne in mind that it was at that time the practice in mortgages to name a special day for the repayment of a loan, the security falling into the indefeasible ownership of the mortgagee when the terms of the contract were not rigidly observed. There was not then the general equity of redemption which, at a later period, guarded the legitimate interests of the borrower.

Without a "grace period" on mortgages, loans, or bonds, such transactions after the due date became outright sales, transference of property, or loss of collateral. Again Halliwell-Phillipps:

> The reversion that was parted with in the year 1579 consisted of a share in a considerable landed estate [1/7 of two dwelling houses and 100 acres] that had belonged to the poet's maternal grandfather, a share to which John and Mary Shakespeare would have become [ironically] absolutely entitled upon the death of Agnes Arden [the Ardens are recalled by Arden Wood in *As You Like It*], who was described as 'aged and impotent' in the July [5th] of the following year, 1580, and who died a few months afterwards [just after the due date of the Asbies mortgage], her burial at Aston Cantlowe having taken place on the 29th of December [*cf. M.N.D.* I. i. 3–6.].
>
> (I, 59, 61)

1580, the year of the mortgage due date, arrives, with John having, obtained through an unwise transaction at least the £40 for the payment, over and above other transactions and business. It is also the year of the birth of their last child, a boy on May 3rd; they christened him Edmund to flatter or insure goodwill from their helpful relatives, Edmund Lambert and his wife Joan (Arden), (Mary's sister, for whom the Shakespeares had named their first daughter and then another who survived). Critics have wondered why Shakespeare gave his brother's name to the archvillain of *King Lear*; it was undoubtedly not that close a relative named Edmund of whom he was thinking.

Poor John, in attempting to avoid debt, only dug himself in deeper. He "... was fined £20 in Queen's Bench [of course if a male is on the throne it is known as the Court of King's Bench] for not appearing to find surety for keeping the peace, and another £20 as a pledge for a Nottingham hatmaker; two others were fined £20 as pledges on Shakespeare's behalf."[15] Anthony Burgess suggests,[16] that in staying away from Church to avoid being seized for debt, John (and one hundred and forty other men from various communities in the Midlands) was cited for not keeping the King's peace. First, he had stopped attending Church; then, he was absent from Council meetings; and now, in addition, he did not show up at Westminister Hall before Queen's Bench, for which he was fined a total of £40, (what he had obtained from selling off the rights of his wife's estate and what he needed to fulfill the payment of the mortgage on Asbies). Furthermore, two others had lost the total of £40 for having stood surety for him. Lambert and Cornishe had just before stood surety for him on a loan from Sadler. The fact that there were two in each case indicates an attempt to make assurance doubly sure. Perhaps by September 29th, 1580, Edmund Lambert had had enough of supporting John Shakespeare's fines, sureties, debts, and mortgages. There must have been quite a scene at Edmund's place in Barton-on-the-Heath that day.

William was to immortalize Edmund in *King Lear* as one who illegitimately stole the paternity of a brother. Although the testimony was given seventeen years later (and the text will appear in Chapter IV) in a case William undoubtedly pursued in his father's name, one can hear John's voice in the Shakespeare family's concern to set the record straight against the Lamberts. John and Mary say that the response of Lambert is a lie and therefore does not require an answer by law. They ask that the judgment be given in their favor immediately and for all time, because, according to the condition or provision mentioned in the identure of bargain and sale of Asbies, *John did go to the dwelling house of Edmund Lambert in Barton-on-the-Heath on September* 29, 1580. *There John offered to pay Edmund the* £40 *he owed in order to redeem Asbies. This sum, which John had brought to give him, Edmund refused to receive.* He said John owed him other money and unless he paid him all the debts he owed him, as well as the £40, he would not receive the payment for Asbies. Perhaps Edmund became more mellow than the Shakespeares would later officially admit, and placated John by assuring him that he could have the estate when and if he made such total payment. Some understanding was reached because John was not sued for the King's peace upon Edmund on the Feast of St. Michael the Archangel, and the Shakespeares did not go to law to get the land back, both activities John was prone to engage in about this time. After all, it was a close relative who had been extremely kind in the past and, although appearing harsh, it was a clever way of clearing up all the debts owed him.

However, the loss of income must have continued to rankle. As time went on, it was not only a loss of income for John, but for his eldest son as he came of age; perhaps it even meant the loss of a separate residence. Early in his writings Shakespeare introduces Christopher Sly from Barton-on-the-Heath into *The Taming of the Shrew* and he has him owing money to the alewife of Wincote (*cf.* Induction. ii. 18–25). Despite the fact that the subsequent legal action is carried on in his parents' names as parties concerned, Will, as eldest son, certainly had expectations in the estate of Asbies, particularly upon his marriage in 1582 when he had no house of his own; when his parents with four children were in the throes of experiencing loss, debt and finally rejection; and when Anne Hathaway's newly widowed mother had an even larger family. By February 2, 1585, to his surprise, with the birth of twins, William had the responsibility of five mouths to feed, let alone the need for more room. With what must have seemed for the Shakespeares a considerable amount of inequity, Edmund Lambert continued to refuse acknowledging the agreement for recovery of the estate on into 1587, long after the due date of the mortgage of 1580 had passed.

In *Hamlet*, Shakespeare meditates upon the emptiness of such compacts as that his father and Old Lambert had entered into and particularly if the party should die:

> This fellow might be in's time a great buyer of land, with his statutes, his recognizances, his fines, his double vouchers, his recoveries: is this the fine of his fines, and the recovery of his recoveries, to have his fine pate, full of fine

> dirt? will his vouchers vouch him no more of his purchases, and double ones too, than the length and breadth of a pair of indentures? The very conveyances of his lands will hardly lie in this box; and must the inheritor himself have no more, ha?
>
> HORATIO: Not a jot more, my lord?
>
> HAMLET: Is not parchment made of sheep-skins?
>
> HORATIO: Ay, my lord, and of calf-skins too.
>
> HAMLET: They are sheep and calves which seek out assurances in that.
>
> (V. i. 111–125)

Old Lambert dies in the latter part of April in 1587, and with him any verbal agreement about the return of the Asbies property in Wilmecote upon payment. He has a son. "Am not I Christopher Sly, old Sly's son of Burton-Heath, by birth a pedlar . . . Ask Marian Hacket, the fat alewife of Wincot, . . ." John Lambert inherits Edmund's estate and along with it the Shakespeare instruments pertaining to the indenture upon Asbies in Wilmecote. This is at the height of John Shakespeare's public embarrassment from having been replaced as Alderman within the year, suing and being sued to keep the peace with parties fearing life and limb. John Shakespeare now faces his antagonist in John Lambert. The report of this encounter furnishes the first evidence of William Shakespeare's involvement—the only recorded data indicating even his mere existence between 1585 and 1592.

Sometime between April and September of 1587, John Shakespeare decided to go to John Lambert to see if he would accept just the mortgage payment upon which his father had put additional verbal provisions. The testimony continues to report that after the death of Edmund, and after John's legal inheritance of Asbies as son and heir, the Shakespeares approached the new possessor, offered the £40 payment, and asked him if he would allow them to have Asbies according to their right and title, and the promise his father had made to them. John Lambert denied them in all things declaring that he recognized no such rights, that they had no evidence of such title, and that he disavowed any such promise. He successfully prevented them from repossessing Asbies.

John Lambert obviously regarded the transaction between his father and Shakespeare's father as complete; signed, sealed and delivered; the business finished. Because, he said, his father paid John Shakespeare £40, and for such consideration, John Shakespeare did give, grant, bargain and *sell* Asbies to Edmund Lambert and his heirs (i.e. himself), to have forever. Furthermore, the younger Lambert goes on to say, John Shakespeare did *not* pay the £40 to his father on Michaelmas Day (September 29), 1580 according to the explicit provision stated in the indenture. Therefore at the time of his death, Edmund Lambert had lawful and absolute possession of the estate of Asbies. After his father's death the property descended rightfully to John Lambert. Therefore he, by both law and equity, now possessed it according to his rights and proper title. In the face of John Lambert's adamant response, John Shakespeare saw that it would be hopelessly expensive and legally torturous to obtain action on behalf of his provision for redemption, which had been extended by verbal agreement, and settled for the opportunity to get, if not the estate, some remuneration in recognition of the financial equity still residing in his claim.

John Lambert had Asbies; John Shakespeare wanted it returned upon payment of £40, but the annual income on the property now could exceed the payment of the loan. No wonder the one John could afford to repossess it, and the other, not want to give it up. So, finally, on September 26, 1587, threatened with litigation by the Shakespeares and seeing it as the cheapest way out, John Lambert agreed to recognize the mortgage and pay the Shakespeares £20 for the absolute title to the estate; the abolition of all claims whatsoever to the property. This, then, would involve William Shakespeare personally since he was of age (twenty-three), the eldest son and heir, and had to be willing to consign any rights to the property lying in him. John Shakespeare and Mary Shakespeare his wife, together with William Shakespeare their son (*Johannes Shackespere et Maria uxor ejus, simul cum Willielmo Shackespere filio suo*) told Lambert that they would be willing to confirm Asbies as in his absolute possession by delivering all deeds, titles, instruments of conveyance, writings and such evidence concerning the estate to him whenever they were asked to do so. John Lambert on that day (September 26, 1587) in Stratford faithfully promised John Shakespeare that he would faithfully pay him £20. Nevertheless John Lambert disregarded his promise, and according to the Shakespeares schemed with fraudulent intent to deceive them and deprive them of their payment, never giving them the £20 he had promised.[17] John Shakespeare was faced once again with a verbal agreement he could not depend upon from the Lamberts. What the Lambert family was doing was protected under strict interpretation of the common law. However they may have been taking unfair advantage of John Shakespeare's unfortunate circumstances, a fact that is recognizable warranting the moderation of the law by an equitable judge. The due date of the mortgage coincided with a heavy forfeit laid upon John Shakespeare by Queen's Bench. Perhaps hardship could be argued; perhaps a higher court might exercise some mercy; perhaps the verbal agreements could be enforced; perhaps—?

John, Mary and William waited a year before deciding to take the matter to the courts in Westminster. After attempting on June 20, July 3, and July 17 in the Stratford Court of Record to regain other funds from a John Thompson, who owed him money, John Shakespeare went to John Lambert at Barton-on-the-Heath on the first of September, 1588 to see if he would act upon the proposed arrangement to give the Shakespeares £20 to relinquish their claims on Asbies. John Lambert refused to do so; and, hence, ten years after making the original alienation to Edmund Lambert, John Shakespeare had a Bill of Complaint containing a claim for £30 in rights and damages sent to attorney John Harborne to file at Michaelmas Term (October 9–November 28) 1588, in the Court of Queen's Bench in Westminster.

Perhaps it is on this occasion that William Shakespeare first crossed the stone Clopton Bridge to take the road to London from Stratford, and the complaint to his father's lawyer in London, John Harborne. Biographers, such as Charles Knight (*cf.* Schoenbaum, p. 390), are only partially accurate when they describe Shakespeare's journey to the London area. It is said that the budding young dramatist must have traversed the hills between the counties of Warwickshire and Oxfordshire, through the bare downs and the great park of Woodstock, passing through Oxford and then from town to town and village to village, finally to the outskirts of London. At this point the road divided passing through fields and hedgerows leading to the hills of Hampstead and Highgate giving a commanding view of the City from the north. The presumption is that he proceeded toward Highgate. It now seems likely he may have taken the southern fork in the road and headed directly for the City of Westminster, rather than London. Surely his father would not go for £30 when he did not go to the same court only eight years before and consequently lost a £20 fine, a £20 surety and sureties from others who had put up pledges for him.

Perhaps Shakespeare went over to Westminster Hall to check on the progress of the suit upon Harborne's filing of the Complaint which opens with:

> Warr.—*Memorandum quod alias, scilicet, termino Sancti Michaelis ultimo preterito, coram domina regina apud Westmonasterium venit Johannes Shackspere, per Johannem Harborne, attornatum suum, et protulit hic in curiam dicte domine regine tunc ibidem quandam billam suam versus Johannem Lambert, filium et heredem Edmundi Lamberte nuper de Barton Henmershe in comitatu predicto yoman, in custodia marescalli & c., de placito transgressionis super casum; et sunt plegii de prosequendo,*

> *scilicet, Johannes Doo et Ricardus Roo, que quidem billa sequitus in hic verba, . . .*[18]

Of course Shakespeare would be interested in the document and eager to know of the outcome, particularly since the case refers to him twice with the phrase "*simulcum Willielmo Shackespere filio suo.*"

William Shakespeare's attention was diverted in the direction of Westminster Hall from time to time for a long period. The case presented by John Harborne for the Shakespeares, and John Boldero for the Lamberts, remained in Westminster's Court of Queen's Bench for three years in which, upon receipt of the additional £30,

> . . . the said John Shakespeare and Mary his wife, together with William Shakespeare their son, have always been ready both to confirm John Lambert's possession of the aforesaid premises [Asbies] and to deliver to the same John Lambert all writings and evidences concerning the said premises.[19]

The Bill of Complaint does not appear in the Court Records until Michaelmas Term 1589, a year following the filing. In that year John is still attempting to obtain money from William Green, John Thompson and Richard Sultun in the Stratford Court of Record.[20] Finally, the Westminster court case is set for hearing during Hilary Term (January) 1590. There are no further records of it in Queen's Bench, but it is reopened in the higher court of Chancery eight years later. In 1590 there may have been an out-of-court settlement, or the case dropped; but the appearance in another court later clearly indicates that the Shakespeares had all too obviously not received satisfaction, and that William was not to have his inheritance when he needed it.

4. *William Shakespeare of Westminster*

THE STRATFORD Parish Register records the last official reference to Shakespeare's presence in Stratford before the next official indication, ten years later, that he was then in London. There are several other accepted evidences, by interpretation and interpolation, but the span separating the unequivocal references is that of the ten years, from February 2, 1585 in Stratford, to March 15, 1595 when his name appears in the Declared Accounts of the Treasurer of the Royal Chamber. Shakespeare's first child, Susanna, was baptized on May 26, 1583 after his marriage that took place in late November, or early December, of 1582; the marriage license being dated November 27, 1582. Two years later, on February 2, 1585, Anne and William's twins were baptized. If one wants to be overbearingly precise, this means, of course, that Shakespeare could have left Stratford for any considerable length of stay in the London area after May, or June, 1584. The twins were named Judith and, rather significantly, Hamlet ("Hamnet"; *l* and *n* being interchangeable as in "chimbley" for "chimney" when following an *m*). Judith and Hamnet Sadler were friends and neighbors, and they in turn would give William's name to one of their children in 1598. Shakespeare in all probability left Stratford sometime after February 2, 1585 and before October 1588. He may have easily returned on occasion between term times when the courts were not in session, when the theatre season was not on, or when there was plague in London, particularly during the summer. He might have consulted with his parents on the legal action against John Lambert between April and September 1587. Some feel he left Stratford in the wake of the companies of players passing through in 1586 and 1587. If he had, he probably would have been noted in some players' list and the likelihood of his running away for such employment leaving three young children, his wife and all else upon his parents with their difficulties can only be proposed with difficulty. At precisely this time, in 1586, a distress was issued, or a write of distraint (*distringas*) upon failure to pay a debt, for the seizure of John Shakespeare's goods. The sergeants reported it could not be acted upon since extreme poverty made its execution impossible ('quod predictus Johannes Shackspere nihil habet unde distringi potest').[21] As a lawyer's clerk in Stratford, Shakespeare could continue his trade even more lucratively in Westminster, being set up, or advised by, his father's London attorney, John Harborne, while keeping his eyes on the case for his parents that would bring considerable money to them in their need. Perhaps even a loophole might develop through which he could obtain a return (which is attempted later) of the dwelling and farm to use as a separate residence, or to have as an income.

Perhaps, on the one hand, William Shakespeare was already in London following the theatre seasons, or pursuing during term time greater legal opportunities as a copyist or solicitor's clerk than Stratford could provide. By 1587, if he had been formally apprenticed at any trade his time would be up. Perhaps, on the other hand, it was not until the court case was initiated that he first arrived with some play manuscripts under his arm to attend the forthcoming suit because his father could not. At any rate, William Shakespeare's knowledge of conveyances, recoveries, and indentures evidenced in his early plays makes it logical that he would, or did, pursue what was his family's, and certainly now his case when it came to the Court of Queen's Bench in Westminster Hall. The texts indicate that Shakespeare must have acquired the complex knowledge of English real property law from somewhere.

Westminster Great Hall is an imposing structure which towers over its surrounding courts, chambers and chapels. It is the oldest and largest hall in England, built by William the Conqueror's son, William Rufus. It is a staggering 250 feet long and 70 feet wide, with a ceiling so high that it gives the impression of being outside. Formerly, the Hall was used by the kings of England for their feasts, parliaments and tennis matches. Since the thirteenth century, Westminster Hall has been used as a place for the various law courts in the one room, meeting regularly during term time. As one enters the arched entrance door, the Court of Common Pleas, where John Shakespeare recovered a debt earlier, is on the right. This is where the civil suits are held. At the far end of the Hall is where the *Shakespeare* v. *Lambert* case was pending from 1588 to 1590, in the Court of Queen's Bench presided over by the Attorney General. Across the Hall in the southeast corner is the Court of Chancery where Shakespeare is to have several petitions to the Lord Chancellor later in his life. The Keeper of the King's Conscience is accompanied by his Masters of Chancery for consultation, particularly his Master of Rolls who has access to previous cases. Anyone was free to enter and observe the goings on. In term time the Hall would be filled with judges such as Coke, Ellesmere, and Yelverton; Masters of the court such as George Carew and William Lambarde; Clerks of Chancery such as Powle and Hubard; attorneys such as John Harborne, J. Stovell, John Boldero, Nicholas Overbury; town recorders, clerks, deputies, justices of the peace, such as Shakespeare's father, Adrian Quiney, James Dyer, Thomas Greene, and Henry Rogers; jailers, prisoners, barristers, solicitors, clients, clerks, noverints, scriveners and copyists. All were looking for and pursuing their business at the law, consuming vast quantities of books, paper, parchment, ink, wax, ribbon, cloth, and also fees from litigants.

His case would take time. Shakespeare would have to have some means of continuing support. Perhaps Harborne could use him as, or knew someone who needed, a fellow who had served as a scrivener's apprentice, or an attorney's clerk, or an abecedarius, or a copyist doing odd jobs in Stratford. Or on his own, Will may have simply advertised his craft to obtain piecework. Places to advertise his skill might also be where he could pick up inexpensive law books such as discarded copies of Plowden's *Reports*, Christopher Saint Germain's *Doctor of Divinity and a Student of Lawes*, or William Lambarde's *Archaionomia*.

There is little conjecture, however, concerning William Shakespeare's skill in calligraphy. He had a fair and fast copyist hand. This is known from another resident of the City of Westminster, Ben Jonson, and from John Heminge and Henry Condell who edited the First Folio and acted with Will in Ben's *Every Man in his Humour.* All three testify to William's legibility and speed:

> I [Ben Jonson] remember, the players have often mentioned it as an honor to Shakespeare that in his writing, whatsoever he penned, he never blotted out a line. . . . he flowed with that facility that sometime it was necessary he should be stopped. . . .
>
> "De Shakespeare nostrat[e]," *Timber, or Discoveries*, 1641.

> His [Shakespeare's] mind and hand went together, and what he thought he uttered with that easiness that we [John Heminge and Henry Condell] have scarce received from him a blot in his papers.
>
> (Epistle to Readers, First Folio)

What his contemporaries are attesting to is Shakespeare's ability to produce fair copy. Since some of his plays were thought to have had to have been written in a few weeks' time, Shakespeare revised from earlier first drafts, in many cases producing fair copy in his own hand. This is an important clue to Shakespeare's writing method: he wrote plays at first in his spare time and at leisure; then, when called for to produce, would revise them into fair copy for the occasion. Unfortunately none of Shakespeare's manuscripts are left, unless it is his hand in the *Thomas More* play, or that he wrote *Edmund Ironside*, both remaining in manuscript and unascribed because they were never produced nor published in his lifetime, perhaps from having been censored. The manuscript copy of *Edmund Ironside* is in a legal hand, and thought by at least one scholar to be that of the hand that many claim, following Sir Edward Maunde Thompson, is Shakespeare's in the *Thomas More* play.[22]

When coming to London from Stratford, or coming to

attend the case at Westminster, Shakespeare had to have had a place to stay. He could have found one himself or through his father's old contacts, or by friends from Stratford already in London such as Richard Field, Bartholomew Quiney or John Harborne. Richard Field, who had dealings with John Shakespeare, travelled to London to become a printer and later, on April 18, 1593, indicates in the Stationers' Register that he will publish Shakespeare's first poems, *Rape of Lucrece* and *Venus and Adonis*, dedicated to the poet's patron the Earl of Southampton. Perhaps aid was forthcoming from Bartholomew Quiney, brother of Shakespeare's schoolmate Richard and son of Shakespeare's father's closest civic friend, Adrian Quiney. These are the usual suggestions but now it appears most likely that John Shakespeare's attorney would be the one in London who would have found a place and possible work for Shakespeare near the law courts.

If an address could be found for Shakespeare around this time, it would go a long way to suggest what he was doing in these silent years. One of the blanks preventing scholars from determining where Shakespeare was from 1585 to 1592 is the lack of evidence in the City of London of a residence for him during this time. After he moves to Southwark to be near the Swan Theatre in Paris Garden in 1596, he is assessed for prior taxes as a resident of St. Helen's Parish, Bishopsgate, which is on the road running north in London to the Theatre and the Curtain in Shoreditch. The assumption is that upon leaving Stratford he must have been living near the theatres in London. The Shakespeare family complaint against John Lambert is filed outside the City of London in the Court of Queen's Bench during Michaelmas Term (October 9th to November 28th) 1588 in Westminster Hall which is located in another city entirely, that of Westminster. The City of Westminster is a mile's journey from London to the west. Charing Cross and its little town is a halfway point at which one turns south, passing Whitehall on the right and

Scotland Yard on the left. Continuing down the street, Westminster Abbey can be first seen. The tower of the parish church of St. Margaret's then comes to view. The City, by some standards more of a town, is made up of a clutter of roofs, towers, castellated walls, gables, shops, dwellings and boarding houses, and taverns clustering about winding streets radiating from the antique edifice of Westminster Palace. To the west, St. James' Park sprawls with its occasional arcade of trees. The Great Hall is part of the Palace which surrounds it with officialdom. The huge complex stands like an overgrown medieval crown upon the shore of the Thames looking eastward across the water to London's walls, temples, Inns of Court, spires, cathedral, tower and bridge.

There is an address in a book at the Folger Shakespeare Memorial Library in Washington, D.C. which can be regarded as evidence for the interpretation thus far given to Shakespeare's hidden years. Until recently the Folger Library's autograph signature of William Shakespeare (W$\overline{m}$ SHAKSPERE) in William Lambarde's *Archaionomia* was not thought to be genuine. The book is a Latin translation of Anglo-Saxon law, printed in 1568. The presence of the signature, to be discussed in detail in the following chapter, seems to indicate that either Shakespeare knew the author, a famous jurist and one of the Masters of Chancery, or that Shakespeare had a more scholarly interest in the subject matter of legal history than has been thought. Since the signature was suspect, an address in the book was not taken seriously; in fact the address was used in the argument to increase the possibility of a forgery, as it was the kind of superfluous interference characteristic of a William Henry Ireland. Since the signature has never been regarded by the Folger as an Ireland forgery, and ink tests place it before any of John Payne Collier's work; since characteristics uncovered by me in March of 1971 strengthen its authenticity; and since numerous previously unknown connections between the volume's author and Shakespeare have subsequently come to light and will be mentioned later, the new Shakespeare address in the volume must at least be considered for its significance.

On the inside of the vellum cover of Lambarde's book, in an eighteenth century hand one can easily read:

Mr. Wm SHAKSPEARE
Lived at No. 1 Little Crown St.
Westminster
N.B. near Dorset steps
St. James's Park

Of course this could simply be misinformation, quite irrelevant to the genuineness of the signature. Or this could legitimately refer to anyone living before 1800 with the same name as the dramatist, without the signature being that of the unknown figure of the same name as the dramatist. However, let us presume that the eighteenth century owner of the volume could have genuine information pertaining to William Shakespeare the dramatist. Assuming even that, previous investigators were stymied by regarding it as a falsification because there was no such address, the place being unlocatable on any map. While Director of the Folger, Joseph Quincy Adams, presuming the signature to be genuine concluded in 1943 that "Little Crown Street seems to have disappeared in the first half of the eighteenth century, for it is not recorded in Rocque's minutely detailed plan of 1761." Responding to Adams' disclosure in the *Rylands Memorial Library Bulletin*, Ambrose Heal of Beaconsfield in the British *Notes and Queries* says that as opposed to Adams' despairing assertion:

> Rocque, however, shows Crown Court, and I suggest that it is identical with the Crown Street which appears in Horwood's Survey of 1799, and which is called Rose & Crown Court in the Plan of the Parish of St. Margaret's, Westminster, given in Strype's edition of Stow's Survey published in 1755. At the West end of this passage where it leads up to St. James' Park, there appears in Strype's

plan, to be an indication of a few steps which may well be the Dorset Steps mentioned on the document.

If this reading of the plan is correct. it would go to show that Dorset Steps were in existence in the middle of the eighteenth century and that 'Little Crown Street' was identical with the narrow end of Crown Court where it ran into Duke Street. It seems probable that this thoroughfare was not done away with until clearance was made for the erection of Sir Gilbert Scott's India Office and Foreign Office buildings in 1860.

(October 23, 1943, p. 263)

Fortunately several maps of the London area drawn in the Elizabethan period are extant and show Westminster in some realistic detail. One is in the Guildhall Library in London and is attributed to Georg Höfnagel, in *Civitates Orbis Terrarum*, 1572. It shows Westminster to the far left with the Great Hall, accompanying town, several by-streets and a corner of St. James' Park. Of still greater interest as the result of its angle of vision, date of drawing, and minute detail is Norden's Map of Westminster done in 1593, only three years after the *Shakespeare* v. *Lambert* case is in Queen's Bench, Westminster (reproduced in the picture section). Looking westward across the Thames one sees in detail the Hall, the Abbey, down "Tootehill Street" running beside St. James' Park, and across rows of houses on the streets, several of which end in crescents with houses backing up to "S. Jeames parke." Superimposing upon the Elizabethan maps the eighteenth century location of "Little Crown St." indicated by Ambrose Heal, we have Shakespeare's earliest known, probably first residence or lodgings outside Stratford, before he moved into the City of London and then Southwark (Bankside in Surrey).

This new location was south of the Cockpit Theatre at Court (Whitehall Palace), on the southeast edge of St. James' Park, northwest of Westminster Abbey, and slightly northwest of Westminster Hall, only a few streets. In that area there was a web of alleyways connecting to the wide and straight King's Street or main artery running north and south through Westminster. The location would also have been south of present Downing Street, where in the eighteenth century James Boswell had rooms. It was to this area that litigants would come in Westminster in droves from all over the country in term time to pursue their cases and suits. It was here in the numerous small houses that they fought for satisfactory hired lodgings.

There is now reason to believe Shakespeare was one of them from no later than the beginning of Michaelmas Term, 1588 to at least the end of Hilary Term, 1590. Ben Jonson, one of whose plays Shakespeare acted in, and is supposed to have been recommended to his Company by Shakespeare, or so a story says, lived in Westminster in Hartshorn Lane on the southeastern side of Charing Cross toward the Thames.

A great admirer of Shakespeare's plays was the esteemed headmaster of Westminster School at this time, William Camden,[23] who as head of the College of Arms received the Shakespeares' application for a coat of arms to become a gentleman. A writer named Thomas Watson, a friend of the dramatists Marlowe, Kyd, Greene, and Peele, was living in Westminster in 1579 and moved to St. Helen's, Bishopsgate, by 1587.[24] Shakespeare may have followed precisely the same pattern, since he is taxed as residing in St. Helen's, Bishopsgate sometime before 1596 as his first known London address. All this makes the address of Little Crown (Rose/Crown) Street near St. James' Park, Westminster found in the Folger copy of Lambarde's *Archaionomia* a feasible one for Shakespeare during the period from 1585 to 1593, and most probably during 1588–1590.

While in Westminster, Shakespeare bore the whips and scorns of time, the oppressor's wrong, the proud man's contumely (evidenced in his sonnets, the pangs of despised love), and above all the law's delay, the insolence of office and the spurns that patient merit of the unworthy takes; he watched the lawyers' "quiddities, his quillets, his cases, his tenures, and his tricks" (*Hamlet* v. i. 108–109) from the time leading up to the filing of the complaint by his father's attorney John Harborne in Michaelmas Term 1588, through its placement in the Court Records in Michaelmas 1589, and its being set for hearing in the following Hilary Term 1590. Legal terms in *Hamlet*, which may have been written in early draft closer to this time than has been thought, or his associations in its final form with his father, pertain to this case.

> . . . who, by a seal'd compact,
> Well ratified by law and heraldry,
> Did forfeit . . . all those his lands
> Which he stood seized of, to the conqueror:
> Against the which, a moiety competent
> Was gaged by our king; which had return'd
> To the inheritance of Fortinbras,
> Had he been vanquisher; as by the same covenant,
> And carriage of the article design'd,
> His fell to Hamlet. Now, Sir, young Fortinbras,
> . . . to recover of us, by strong hand
> And terms compulsatory, those aforesaid lands
> So by his father lost:
>
> (I. i. 86–95, 102–104)

No such seal'd compact nor articled covenant had been made nor could be produced by the father upon the Asbies estate to the inheritance of young Shakespeare; nothing was recognizable by common law and the claim was not actionable before Queen's Bench:

> Have I not seen dwellers on form and favour
> Lose all, and more, . . .
>
> (Sonnet CXXV).

Shakespeare, like his Hamlet, saw a son (Young Fortinbras) inherit what was his; and saw his father's brother (-in-law) steal the inheritance from his father in the first place, taking land of which John Shakespeare, in later testimony, said he was "lawfully *seised* in their demesne as of fee, as in the right of the saide Mary, . . ."

The book that the Folger Shakespeare signature is in was written by William Lambarde. The volume was perhaps given, or loaned, to the dramatist by the author as suggested by J. Q. Adams. At this point in 1590 when the case finds no solution in court Shakespeare as one of the plaintiffs, and John Harborne the attorney might have sought consultation. When the suit reappears. John and Mary are appropriately characterized in legal phraseology as ". . . your saide oratours [who] are of small wealthe and verey fewe friends and alyance in the saide countrie. . . ." On this basis they could turn to the Office of Alienations insofar as their suit fell under its jurisdiction. The Office of Alienations could advise John, Mary, and William Shakespeare about the current technicalities involved in their having alienated their Asbies estate to Edmund Lambert. It was this office's operations which determined the fines for alienation indicating whether a mortgage, sale, or other type of conveyance had taken place. The fine for alienation (or the conveyance fee to the Crown) for the Asbies property was set in Easter Term 1579, and in 1597 John Lambert was to cite it as evidence for a sale rather than a mortgage. The head of the Office of Alienations appointed by Lord Burleigh in 1589 was none other than William Lambarde. In the preceding year, Lambarde had rooms at Lincoln's Inn, one of the Inns of Court, or London law schools, and in 1563, in his student days there, he had been in charge of selecting the revels, or entertainments, for All Saints' Day. At precisely the time of the Shakespeare case in Queen's Bench Lambarde was engaged in writing a treatise, as he usually did for each office he held, for the Office of Alienations on making clearer distinctions between conveyances that were mortgages and those that were sales by differentiating and regularizing the fines more than had been done in the past.[25]

William Lambarde had written in 1581 a famous book called *Eirenarcha* on the duties of the Justices of the

Peace while he was one for the county of Kent. This would have been of interest to John Shakespeare, and some scholars believe that it was a source for Shakespeare's lower judicial types in his *Henry IV*, just as they believe that Lambarde's earlier *A Perambulation of Kent* was a source for the Dover passages and local setting in *King Lear*. On October 22, 1591, Lambarde was completing a manuscript, of which there are many copies, several of them in Lincoln's Inn, called *Archeion*, a study of all the major Elizabethan courts. It was a popular document, and many read it for its discussion on Chancery: "For remedy in which cases of Uses [conveyances of property], chiefly the Chancery Court was fled into, as the onely Altar of helpe and refuge." What Shakespeare's father, and now William, had found themselves in was a case for Chancery and the rulings of equity pertaining to uses and land law. William and his father were basing their claim on an informal agreement, and William would have to become acquainted with a Court of Conscience and a jurisdiction pertaining to equity; something familiar to Ben Jonson:

> Lies there no writ out of the Chancery
> Against this Vulcan? No injunction,
> No order, no decree? Though we be gone
> At Common Law, methinks in his despite
> A Court of Equity should do us right.
>
> *An Execration Upon Vulcan*

Chancery was a higher court of equity which offered to mitigate the harshness of the law. In Lincoln's Inn, where were some of John Donne's sonnets (which Shakespeare read) in manuscript, William Lambarde was writing in his manuscript on the high Courts:

> The final determination of any case was in the will of the sovereign, manifested ultimately in the High Courts of Star Chamber, Requests, and the Chancery. He [Lambarde] suggested that a man might sue his rights in the base court at home before proceeding outside the county. But if he did not recover his rights in this beginning, he

> then was able to seek justice in the King's High Court, where not only 'right and law' but also 'equity and good conscience prevailed.' On Chancery he emphasized 'the help of God which speaketh in that Oracle of Equity.' He endeavored then to show how the mercy of the sovereign extended through the Chancellor's office to bestow help directly to deserving persons whose causes had become confused in the courts of common law.
>
> (Dunkel, p. 131)

So, whether this information about mercy, equity and Chancery were sought or obtained around this time of 1590–1591 or later around 1594–1597, William Shakespeare decided to try his family suit in Chancery when he had the finances, connections, knowledge, and desire to do so, and at a time which coincided with the period when William Lambarde was Master of Chancery, from 1592 to 1601, where one of his main responsibilities remained the overseeing of cases involving the Office of Alienations. At least William Shakespeare knew of William Lambarde and his historical researches as evidenced by the dramatist's signature in *Archaionomia* (evidence of its authenticity will be discussed in chapter three). The likelihood that he knew of the other books by Lambarde bearing even closer connections to his lawsuits and his plays is very high indeed. The signature is bold enough to come from this period of Shakespeare's early life, from 1587 to 1597.

5. *Shakespeare's Sonnets and the Language of Law.*

DURING this initial contact with the high courts of law, how might Shakespeare have spent his time? Days may have found Shakespeare working in Westminster as a solicitor's clerk, researching and copying deeds and records, or earning money perhaps as a copyist, scrivener or noverint, one who does wills and testaments, compacts, covenants and the like; seeing plays along with the students at the Inns of Court; perhaps picking up, outside term time, odd jobs or bit parts in the theatres and at night by candlelight working on his own play manuscripts. Many Shakespeareans, particularly the followers of *Mr. W. H.* by Leslie Hotson, believe that the Sonnets, or many of them, come from this period of 1587/1588 and are addressed to either William Hatcliff or the Earl of Southampton, both members of Gray's Inn. Either of these figures Shakespeare might have met through his legal or theatrical connections from his acquaintances at taverns, the theatres, or Inns of Court. John Harborne or William Lambarde, who was on a commission with Bacon of Gray's Inn in 1588, may have gotten Shakespeare, as a lawyer's clerk, into some of the revels at Gray's Inn to see William Hatcliff as the Prince of Purpoole during the Christmas festivities of 1587/88. Lord Burghley, who had appointed Lambarde to his office in 1589, secured for the Earl of Southampton, who would subsequently be the patron of Shakespeare's early poetry, admission into Gray's Inn on February 29th, 1588. The Earl's father had been a member of Gray's Inn and had been Lord Chancellor of England and head of Chancery under Henry VIII. "The young Earl of Southampton, patron of poets, aged only sixteen, came down from Cambridge in 1589 to enter Gray's Inn, from the same college as the brilliant 'young Juvenal', Thomas Nashe, and his friend Robert Greene." [26] Nashe and Greene were to be jealous of this upstart Shakespeare whose poetry, acting, and, subsequently, his plays would so please their illustrious colleague.

The language of Shakespeare's Sonnets alone undeniably evidences his considerable learning in the law. This point survives all controversy over whom they are addressed to, or whether they were written in 1587/88, 1594 or later. Although the tantalizing "Mr. W. H." will remain enigmatic, that he was a member of Gray's Inn is virtually assured as the three leading candidates for the honor of addressee (William Hatcliffe, or the Earls of

Southampton or Pembroke) were all members of that Inn. It is not beyond Shakespeare's capacity to merely get the legal vocabulary up for the occasion; either the technical terms or, as several have thought, even the story the sonnets reveal might have been fabricated; but both devices are highly unlikely. The vocabulary is most fitting for their subject, a member of Gray's Inn (perhaps a patron); and a wider audience, select friends in the legal profession. No matter to whom, or when, and independent of other biographical data whose derivation from the Sonnets has been attempted, evidence of Shakespeare's early familiarity with many aspects of England's complex law, perhaps even evidence in this body of his writing alone for a clerkship, comes in abundance from the vocabulary of the Sonnets. It is in this legal language that he addresses his indebtedness to W. H., a close friend of higher station, or possible benefactor:

> Accuse me thus: that I have scanted all
> Wherein I should your great deserts repay,
> Forgot upon your dearest love to call,
> Whereto all bonds do tie me day by day;
> That I have frequent been with unknown minds
> And given to time your own dear-purchased right; . . .
> Book both my wilfulness and errors down
> And on just proof surmise accumulate;
> Bring me within the level of your frown,
> But shoot not at me in your waken'd hate;
> Since my appeal says I did strive to prove
> The constancy and virtue of your love.
>
> (CXVII)

The metaphor of the sonnet recapitulates a case involving the squandering of a loan upon a bond, not being able to repay it, having it recorded and recognized by law, being brought to trial for it, and at the last moment receiving a merciful appeal from the execution on the grounds that the intent of the illegal actions was honorable rather than malicious. In Sonnet XXXV, Shakespeare chides himself for being so forgiving of W. H.'s effrontery in stealing his mistress, and depicts a trial scene for an analogy.

All men make faults, and even I in this,
Authorizing thy trespass with compare, . . .
Thy adverse party is thy advocate—
And 'gainst myself a lawful plea commence; . . .
That I an accessory needs must be. . . .

Shakespeare by a similar comparison in Sonnet XLIX goes so far as to say he would prevent any unjust action from being brought against him, even by himself.

Against that time, if ever that time come,
When I shall see thee frown on my defects,
When as thy love hath cast his utmost sum,
Call'd to that audit by advised respects; . . .
Against that time do I ensconce me here
Within the knowledge of mine own desert,
And this my hand against myself uprear,
To guard the lawful reasons on they part:
To leave poor me thou hast the strength of laws,
Since why to love I can allege no cause.

The Sonnets are not simply salted with legal terminology. Shakespeare exquisitely incorporates the legal world as a framework with reference to the judicial quarter sessions when the itinerant judges appear in county courts in his famous "When to the sessions of sweet silent thought/I summon up remembrance of things past, . . ." (XXX, which begins the chapter).[27] Using a commission's examination (or Court of Assizes) and the setting up of a jury, he constructs the allegory of Sonnet XLVI (*cf. Hamlet* I. i. 86–104, particularly 11. 89–90):

Mine eye and heart are at a mortal war
How to divide the conquest of thy sight;
Mine eye my heart thy picture's sight would bar,
My heart mine eye the freedom of that right.
My heart doth plead that thou in him dost lie,—
A closet never pierced with crystal eyes—
But the defendent doth that plea deny

And says in him thy fair appearance lies.
To 'cide this title is impanneled
A quest of thoughts, all tenants to the heart,
And by their verdict is determined
The clear eye's moiety and dear heart's part:
As thus; mine eye's due is thy outward part,
And my heart's right thy inward love of heart.

There is scarcely a sonnet which fails to contain a legal reference. Entire sequences of legal action, and sets of law terms appear over and over in these poems—"warrantise" (CL); "most heinous crime" (XIX); "shall beauty hold a plea,/Whose action is no stronger than a flower?" (LXV); "Hence, thou suborn'd informer! a true soul/When most impeach'd stands least in thy control" (CXXV); "why of two oaths' breach do I accuse thee,/When I break twenty? I am perjured most" (CLII and *cf.* CXXIX; "Prison my heart in thy steel bosom's ward,/But then my friend's heart let my poor heart bail;/whoe'er keeps me, let my heart be his guard;/Thou canst not then use rigour in my gaol [jail]:" (CXXXIII); and in his proclamation to his mistress the Dark Lady (supposed by some scholars to be the Lucy Negro who ran a bordello in Clerkenwall mentioned in Gray's Inn's *Gesta Grayorum* in 1594[28]):

. . . not from those lips of thine
That have profaned their scarlet ornaments
And seal'd false bonds of love as oft as mine,
Robb'd others' beds revenues of their rents.
Be it lawful I love thee, as thou lovest those
Whom thine eyes woo as mine importune thee:
(CXLII)

Even more specifically, as is expected from a writer, there are references to pen and quill (LXXI, LXXXIII), ink (CVIII), and puns on "writ" (LXXI, CXVI, XXIII). The hand that did writs, warrants, deeds, documents, charters, conveyances, compacts, testaments, and wills has been forgotten and the error upon Shakespeare proved concludes, as he ironically said, "I never writ," perhaps one can "learn to read what silent love hath writ." A noverint or solicitor's clerk above all would have been familiar with the legacies, contracts and heirs apparent in the pleas of the first seventeen sonnets to Mr. W. H. to provide inheritors (*cf.* also XCIV and CXLVI), and the forms or means of conveyance in the numerous references to lease and use (IV, V, VI, XIII, XVIII, CXXXIV and CVII):

> Look, whom she best endow'd she gave the more;
> Which bounteous gift thou shouldst in bounty cherish:
> She carved thee for her seal, and meant thereby
> Thou shouldst print more, not let that copy die.
>
> (IX)

Shakespeare comes closest to mentioning his possible trade, when he is confronted with rivalry for the patronage of W. H. from other poets, such as Nashe, Chapman, or Greene.

> Who is it that says most? which can say more
> Than this rich praise, that you alone are you?
> In whose confine immured is the store
> Which should example where your equal grew.
> Lean penury within that pen doth dwell
> That to his subject lends not some small glory;
> But he that writes of you, if he can tell
> That you are you, so dignifies his story
> *Let him but copy what in you is writ,*
> Not making worse what nature made so clear,
> And such a counterpart shall fame his wit,
> Making his style admired every where.
>
> (LXXXIV)

Some of the quibble on legal terms used in address to his mistress are puns on the tertiary, beyond the secondary level of sexual desire and the primary level of the punning on his name: "Thus far for love my love-suit, sweet, fulfil./'Will' will fulfil the treasure of thy love/Ay, fill it full with wills. . . ." (CXXXVI); "So thou, being rich in 'Will,' add to thy 'Will'/One will of mine, to make thy large 'Will' more." (CXXXV); and in CXXXIV where Shakespeare comes closest to commenting upon his family's case against the Lamberts:

So, now I have confess'd that he is thine,
And I myself am mortgaged to thy will,
Myself I'll forfeit, so that other mine
Thou wilt restore, to be my comfort still:
But thou wilt not, nor he will not be free,
For thou art covetous and he is kind;
He learn'd but surety-like to write for me
Under that bond that him as fast doth bind.
The statute of thy beauty thou wilt take,
Thou usurer, that put'st forth all to use,
And sue a friend came debtor for my sake;
So him I lose through my unkind abuse.
Him have I lost; thou hast both him and me:
He pays the whole, and yet am I not free.

The sonnets indicate that before Shakespeare had become an established playwright, and before he owned any property, he had acquired a knowledge of the varied legal terminology pertaining to inheritance laws, arrest and court procedure, but most obviously to the accouterments accompanying legal documents, such as bonds, mortgages, writs, wills, compacts, articles, Chancery forms, covenants, and fair copies of the same embossed with seals, printed in fair style and proper hand. They also indicate his preoccupation with inheritance, wills, usury, increase, fear of loss, suits, court cases, penury, poverty etc. Often, in attempting to find to whom they are addressed and looking for the identification of particular characters mentioned, the obvious biographical evidence is ignored that Shakespeare had a natural use of legal terms and processes, not totally explicable from just picking them up on the street or by being a mere hanger-on at the law courts. He was at least deeply involved in his own family's litigation:

For how do I hold thee but by they granting?
And for that riches where is my deserving?

The cause of this fair gift in me is wanting,
And so my patent back again is swerving.
(LXXXVII)

Since he cannot offer any consideration he loses exclusive rights. Hopefully he might regain his rights:

Not mine own fears, nor the prophetic soul
Of the wide world dreaming on things to come,
Can yet the lease of my true love control,
Supposed as forfeit to a confined doom.
(CVII)

In his sonnets, as in the court case, Shakespeare wants to stand surety to prevent the forfeiture of a mortgage and says,

Let them say more that like of hearsay well;
I will not praise, that purpose not to sell.
(XXI)

6. *Shakespeare's Early Plays*

AT NIGHT, on occasion, Shakespeare would journey to the Inns of Court. Some of ". . . the young noblemen who were admitted to the Inns of Court used them more as gentlemen's clubs than as colleges for the study of law."

> The throng of young men who studied law either nominally or in dead earnest at the Inns of Court constituted the liveliest, brightest group to be found anywhere in Elizabethan London. They prided themselves on their manners, their breeding, their elegance of fashion and their wit. And they were the especial patrons of the theatre, deeming themselves *cognoscenti* of the stage. On high occasions they brought the actors to their own halls to put on plays specially commissioned by them. Thomas Hughes' *The Misfortunes of Arthur* was presented at Gray's Inn on the evening before Southampton became a member of that society.[29]

Shakespeare would have gone to the Inns of Court to talk over literature, translations, new styles of poetry, and plays, there borrowing books and manuscripts. On his own, a practice he may have initiated in Stratford, he was doing first drafts of his plays. He undoubtedly came to Westminster and London with a manuscript of *Comedy of Errors* already in hand. This first draft, perhaps performed in school or amongst friends or pupils, was revised for performance at the Inns of Court. It was selected for Gray's Inn's Christmas revels in 1594, a singular honor. However, if modern editors and critics are to be believed, who independently have accumulated a list of at least *eleven* major works by William Shakespeare produced within the year of his revision of the first draft of *Comedy of Errors* in 1594, the presumption must exist that he wrote the majority of these works in earlier years. His subsequent record, even at his height, shows he wrote on the average of two or three plays, or less, a year. It has been calculated that, in addition to the ten or eleven works produced or published, he must have been working on, or had in manuscript, three to five more by this time. Hence, by placing the works back in time according to his usual writing rate, and settling them in order of stylistic progress, a fascinating list of works, supplemented by some plays suggested by E. B. Everitt (*The Young Shakespeare*), emerges, that Shakespeare was turning out in some form or other during the lost years from 1585 to 1595.

Depending upon how much writing Shakespeare had accomplished in Stratford (from 1577 or 1580 to 1585 or 1587) when he came to Westminster, he would have manuscripts in first draft of several plays. Not only could he have done the earliest forms of *Comedy of Errors* and *Love's Labour's Lost* with their schoolboy associations and similar rhyming style, but also constructed as a single play the later trilogy of *Henry IV* Parts One and Two and *Henry V*. He may have attempted what resulted in a shapeless version of *King Lear*. At night in Westminster he may have worked on these while being a lawyer's clerk during the day. *Love's Labour's Lost* would be revised for performance for the Earl of Southampton in 1594 (Akrigg, pp. 207–215) in the same year as *Comedy of Errors*. *Famous Victories*, possibly a pirated copy of Shakespeare's first drafts of his second Henriad trilogy, was entered May 14, 1594 on the Stationers' Register (an Elizabethan copyright office), but it is known that Tarleton and Knell performed it at the Bull in Bishopsgate, and Tarleton died September 3, 1588. An early *King Lear* was entered on the same date. So by the year of his suit in Queen's Bench against Lambert, Shakespeare had, besides his initial interest in English history, two plays fit for private or academic entertainment: *Comedy of Errors* from the Roman playwright Plautus, and possibly Ariosto's *Suppositi*; and *Love's Labour's Lost*, erudite, and courtly, using language in a masquelike setting.

Comedy of Errors has a mercantile background complete with its particular kind of Roman law; and in it Shakespeare brought to the foreground complex arrest procedures and laws of debt. The play evidences the knowledge of such particularities as: earnest to bind, or downpayment (II. ii.); attachment, and breach of promise (IV. i.); arrest upon meane process, "One that before the judgment carries poor souls to hell", "he is 'rested on the case", subornation (IV. ii) and such exchanges as:

> OFFICER: He is my prisoner: if I let him go,
> The debt he owes will be requir'd of me.
> ANTIPHOLUS: Fear me not, man; I will not break away.
> I'll give thee, ere I leave thee, so much money,
> To warrant thee, as I am 'rested for.

Shakespeare's first play is about a father under bond looking for his lost twin sons in a foreign city with characters arresting and being arrested for debt. The content of the play clearly relates to what has been shown to be Shakespeare's and his father's experiences.

Love's Labour's Lost is resplendent with legal terminology.[30] The play uses juristic technicalities such as attainder, common-severalty, crime of perjury, acquittances, duties of apparitors, enfranchisement, treason, and quillets of the law. Of more particular interest are the references to inheritance, dowry, title, and especially mortgage debts:

KING: . . . Madam, your father here doth intimate,
The payment of a hundred thousand crowns;
Being but the one-half of an entire sum,
Disbursed by my father in his wars.
But say, that he, or we (or neither have)
Received that sum; yet there remains unpaid,
A hundred thousand more; in surety of the which,
One part of Aquittain is bound to us,
Although not valued to the money's worth.
PRINCESS: You do the king, my father, too much wrong,
And wrong the reputation of your name,
In so unseeming to confess receipt,
Of that which hath so faithfully been paid.

(II. i)

This denial of receipt is somewhat akin to the situation concerning Asbies estate in *Shakespeare* v. *Lambert*. Inheritance, dowry, and title are the principal subjects of *The True Chronicle History of King Leir and his three daughters, Gonorill, Regan, and Cordella.* This first draft of the later *King Lear* was written in the time following *Love's Labour's Lost*. The play was subsequently entered on the same day as *Famous Victories*, (May 14, 1594) after having been prepared for its production by Henslowe on April 6th and 8th, 1594. The concern of these plays for inheritances, debts, dowries, sums of money, sureties of land, titles, and above all not recognizing, or accepting payments cannot help but be echoes from Shakespeare's biographical preoccupation, particularly Edmund Lambert's having not honored the mortgage payment when tendered, until all other outstanding debts were paid by Shakespeare's father.

Unfortunately, the manuscripts have vanished. The drafts are no longer extant for a number of possible reasons: they may have been destroyed as they became available in print, used as actors' copy (play manuscripts became property of the theatres), copied into second and third drafts, subsequently burned, or lost. Sometimes, because a play was not performed, revised, or published, the manuscript is extant, as is the case of the *Thomas More* play manuscript written around 1591 or 1592, now thought by most to contain, along with four other hands, Shakespeare's own longhand in just one scene; the play had been censored and was never performed. *Edmund Ironside*, written around 1587 or 1588, was never performed and is the fifth of fifteen plays (#1994) in the Egerton manuscript collection housed by the British Museum. Edricus is an interesting figure in the play, dresses himself entirely in black and is self-styled a "crow." The play script is in a "late sixteenth century Secretary hand, especially as it was styled for legal documents," that which was "most generally employed for legal documents and forms because conventional and because it was considered 'rapid.'" "Though this manuscript was obviously written at high speed for stage use, and has only a few attempts at calligraphy, these few are sufficient to establish the competence of its professional scribe."[31] Everitt goes on to indicate that the hand is that of the author of the play, since additions to the text are made in the same hand, and the text contains no errors (ne'er a blotted line); furthermore he claims that the hand is the one believed to be that of Shakespeare's in the *Thomas More* play. It must be granted that the play itself is good enough to be like Shakespeare's other early pieces and particularly a number of early supposed "anonymous sources" of his later plays. The conclusion, then, is that *Edmund Ironside* is a very early play by William Shakespeare which was never revised or published; and furthermore that Shakespeare had the scribal skills of a noverint, a scrivener, or one who could write in eight styles of handwriting (evidenced by a single author in three different manuscripts): Text hand;

Roman hand; Engrossing Secretary; Mixed Secretary-Italic (preferred by Ben Jonson for his own hand); Italic, but the writer is most comfortable with older Secretary; late sixteenth Secretary; and Mixed Secretary (cultivated by the Stratford Free School, rather than the Italian and new Secretary influence of the London and Westminster schools). It makes considerably greater sense to believe that Shakespeare worked at more plays, beginning at an earlier time and composed from first or perhaps second drafts than that he went from *Comedy of Errors* (1594) to *Richard II* (1596) with only a year to improve his craft in between. And so, by the year of the filing of his case (1587) Shakespeare is possibly writing in his noverint hand a play named after his antagonist in court (Edmund); certainly two plays about debt and inheritance (three, counting *Lear*); and probably a first draft of the Henriad which in part is the story of a father worrying about his son's inheriting the throne, and of the son's managing to outdo the father and acquire more land for the kingdom.

Sir Edmund Chambers identifies *Titus and Vespasian* as an early version of Shakespeare's *Titus Andronicus*,[32] which is a bloody revenge play with many crudely similar features in story and structure to *Hamlet*,[33] particularly the original play, now lost, known as the *Ur-Hamlet*. Both earlier drafts of these plays were probably written in 1587 or 1588 around the time of Thomas Kyd's successful revenge play, *The Spanish Tragedy*. *Titus and Vespasian* was performed on April 15, 1592, preceded by *Harry the Sixth* on March 4th, by Lord Strange's Men, at the Rose. *Titus Andronicus* (revised from *Titus and Vespasian*) was performed as a new play on January 24, 1594 by the Earl of Sussex's Men, at the Rose. It was published that year "As it was Plaide by the Right Honourable the Earle of Darbie [i.e. Strange], Earle of Pembroke and Earle of Sussex their Servants."[34] *Titus* is the story of a father who has slain a son and who wreaks vengeance upon his superiors, whom he has served and who turn against him, until he destroys them and himself.

It is also at this Christmas season of 1587–1588, Hotson

believes, the majority of the sonnets were written, addressed to Hatcliff at Gray's Inn, of which Southampton was a member. In the next section, more substantial evidence will be analyzed to support the contention that Shakespeare's original *Hamlet* was written in first draft during the court case in 1588 or 1589, as many of its themes and phrases might suggest from association with the case, the sonnets, *Titus*, and *The Spanish Tragedy*. An extant, and regarded as a "bad quarto," version (*The Tragicall Historie of Hamlet Prince of Denmark, by William Shake-speare* (Quarto 1603), may have been translated into German (*Der bestrafte Brudermord oder: Prinz Hamlet aus Dannemark*, printed 1626) from a pirated printing of, or directly from a, first or revised draft of the *Ur-Hamlet*.[35] Henslowe reports a performance of *Hamlet* between February 19, and June, 1594 at the Rose. *The Spanish Tragedy*'s success in 1588 may have stimulated Shakespeare to turn to the revenge action of *Titus* and also to write an early *Hamlet*, with its concern about a father's losing land and a son's avenging him, and its many references to law, conveyances, lawyers and cases.

In 1589 the suit goes on to the Court Record in Westminster. This is when Shakespeare probably wrote *The Taming of A Shrew* (Quarto May 2, 1594) which contains considerable satire upon lawyers and is the first version of *The Taming of the Shrew* (Folio 1623), which drops that satire. This later adaptation was probably rewritten in 1593 (or earlier, from the first draft in 1589) for the performance reported by Henslowe between February 19th and June 1594. The later version manages to pillory John Lambert as Christopher Sly, Old Sly's (Edmund Lambert's) son of Barton-on-the-Heath, drunk, puffed up and owing money.

> HOSTESS: I know my remedy, I must go fetch the third borough [constable].
> SLY: Third, or fourth, or fifth borough, I'll answer him by law; I'll not budge an inch, boy: let him come, and kindly.
>
> (Induction i.)

The play in its second version mentions a manor court (I. ii), settlement by way of assurance and has a charming view of lawyers or litigants:

TRANIO: Please ye we may contrive this afternoon,
And do as adversaries do in law,—
Strive mightily, but eat and drink as friends.

Everitt believes in this year of 1589 Shakespeare also wrote a first draft, to await revision in 1595 as *King John* ("For this down-trodden equity, . . ." II, i. 241.), called *The Troublesome Reign of King John*, pirated and published in 1591. Amongst other things, John is accused of having given England as a fief to the Pope in return for being recognized as King. King John was buried in Worcester Cathedral, where Shakespeare obtained his marriage license. This play would mark the beginning of a sustained interest in English history plays which would at last win him recognition from his contemporaries, by allusion in 1592, and in print as author of *Richard III* on the title-page of the 1598 Quarto.

With the production of Christopher Marlowe's *Edward II*, interest turned to English chronicles once again and Shakespeare in 1590 and 1591 was, in some way not now altogether clear, working on a cycle of plays pertaining to the Wars of the Roses. What most probably explains the data furnished by the various texts and quartos is that his first drafts of the later trilogy were pirated and so *The Firste Parte of the Contention of the Two Famous Houses of York and Lancaster* (Quarto 1594) may be a first draft written in 1590 of what Shakespeare was to later revise (possibly in 1591) into *Henry VI, Part Two* (Folio 1623). As in *King John*, where equity is put down, so in *Henry VI, Part II* Shakespeare has Gloucester complain to the King:

Ah, gracious lord, these days are dangerous:
Virtue is choked with foul ambition
And charity chased hence by rancour's hand;
Foul subornation is predominant
And equity exiled your highness' land.

(III. i. 142–146.)

The True Tragedy of Richard Duke of York (Quarto 1595) by the same process relates to *Henry VI, Part Three.* These were followed by a first draft in 1591 of what was to become *Henry VI, Part One,* which in its earlier version was known as *Harry the Sixth. Harry the Sixth* results in the first acknowledged reference to Shakespeare's existence in London as a playwright, and is a play that Henslowe lists as being performed in 1594. It is probably at this time of 1590 or 1591 that Shakespeare helps Henry Chettle, Thomas Dekker, and, less certainly, Thomas Heywood with the *Sir Thomas More* play. Everitt believes *Edward III* (1591) to be Shakespeare's.

At any rate with *Henry VI*, Shakespeare was presumptuously making his bid for recognition, perhaps even to the men at the Inns of Court. He sets the important historical scene four (where the red and white roses are plucked) of Act Two of his *Henry VI, Part One* in Middle Temple Garden. Middle Temple had members from Stratford. One was William Combe who was admitted in 1571, a reader there in 1595, and counsel for Stratford in 1597; his nephew John "left a bequest of five pounds in 1613 'to Mr William Shackspere.'"[36] The scene goes on to mention Middle Temple Hall, where one of Shakespeare's plays would finally be put on some ten years later. His contemporaries, as the next section will explain, were incensed. William had loaded these plays with things that would fetch them at the Inns[37]: Jack Cade (*Henry VI, Part Two*) says the first thing his rebellion would do is kill all the lawyers; and they discuss amongst some fifty-odd legal technicalities (including those in the trial of the Duchess of Gloucester for witchcraft [*Henry VI, Part Two*]) those of title by confirmation, rigor of law, contract, distraining property, and disinheriting an heir!

1592 is the date most scholars presume Shakespeare's presence to be established upon the London scene as a dramatist, from the well-known reference by his rival Greene which will be examined shortly. By later allusions, plays that can be identified as undoubtedly his must have been written around this time. His *Richard III* and *Two*

Gentlemen of Verona were probably written that year. In the former, Shakespeare has Richard not allowing Buckingham to enter upon his promised title and land, the Earldom of Hereford, and it is a play about the corruption of justice on many levels; the latter has as its source Montemayor's *Diana* which was translated by Bartholomew Yonge who was a member of Middle Temple, and the play mentions unreversed decisions and appeal. In that year, the plague began to threaten the theatres' livelihood and Shakespeare embarked on other forms of poetic work such as the long narrative stanzaic poems dedicated to the Earl of Southampton. Thus Shakespeare for the next three years pursues a double role of producing plays for the public theatres and at least five works for performance before private or select audiences, while, undoubtedly, he added to his sonnet sequence.

On February 3, 1593 the plague broke out in London and the theatres remained closed virtually for the rest of the year, and much of the next. There were intermittent performances when the Earl of Sussex's Men returned to the Rose on December 26, 1593 and they did *Titus Andronicus* January 24, 1594: the Admiral's Men played at the Rose from May 14th to the 16th; and the Lord Chamberlain's Men (formerly Strange's) and Admiral's Men played from June 3rd to the 13th, 1594, at Newington Butts near Bishopsgate. During this time they performed *Titus Andronicus*, *Hamlet*, and *The Taming of a Shrew*.

With the reduced public performances, Shakespeare took this time to write *Venus and Adonis* which was published by Richard Field, formerly of Stratford, and entered by him on April 18, 1593. Likewise dedicated to the Earl of Southampton, *The Rape of Lucrece*, was entered May 9, 1594.

Venus and Adonis amongst other legal references mentions: lawgiver unable to enforce law (l. 251); client wrecked, when attorney mute (ll. 331–336); conveyance by seal manual:

'Pure lips, sweet seals in my soft lips imprinted,

What bargains may I make, still to be sealing?
To sell myself I can be well contented,
So thou wilt buy, and pay, and use good dealing;
  Which purchase, if thou make, for fear of slips,
  Set thy seal-manual on my wax-red lips.
(ll. 511–516)

He also mentions double penalty upon broken bond (ll. 517–522); and inheritance by next of blood ("Here was thy father's bed, here in my breast;/Thou art the next of blood, and 'tis thy right." (ll. 1183–1184) (*cf.* White, pp. 493–496). *The Rape of Lucrece* (*cf.* White, pp. 497–505) is replete with laws, duties, pleas, rights, notaries, justices, cases, as in such passages as:

My bloody judge forbade my tongue to speak;
No rightful plea might plead for justice there:
His scarlet lust came evidence to swear
That my poor beauty had purloin'd his eyes;
And when the judge is robb'd the prisoner dies.
(ll. 1648–1652)

Shakespeare, in the dedication of the second long poem feels more duty bound to his lordship perhaps from having not only welcomed the earlier piece but also having asked for plays on occasion which would account for the revision of *Love's Labour's Lost*, and possibly the new *A Midsummer-Night's Dream*. These successes undoubtedly supported the candidacy of *Comedy of Errors* before the private legal audience at the Earl's law Inn, which warranted the revision of that play for its particular hearers. Just before *Rape of Lucrece* was entered, so was *The Taming of a Shrew* on May 2, 1594. Shakespeare probably rewrote *Taming of the Shrew* and *Titus Andronicus*, both of which refer to the figure of Lucrece, during his off-time while escaping from the plague, and probably London, in 1593. At this time for popular consumption he had started *Romeo and Juliet* to end with its scene where the messenger Friar Laurence sends to Romeo is quarantined because of the plague. He then playfully parodies his public play in the private masquelike production of *A Midsummer-Night's Dream* in the "Pyramus and This-be" enactment, probably written in 1593 or 1594, and produced later (in 1594, 1595, or 1596) at any one of several major weddings among the nobility. *Love's Labour's Lost* is felt now by Akrigg to have been produced for the Earl of Southampton early in 1594 and that would mean some revising. At the end of the year the revised *Comedy of Errors* (possibly also known as *The Jealous Comedy*) is produced at Gray's Inn and as a Christmas entertainment for the Queen.

Shakespeare thus wrote two or three of these pieces a year from 1584 to 1594, and developed his technique and style over this period to attain the artistic level of that miraculous year, 1594. Scholars note that in 1594, besides the sonnets and the *Rape of Lucrece*, which alone would have established him in the literary community of his day, he produced *A Midsummer Night's Dream*, *Love's Labour's Lost*, and *Comedy of Errors* for the nobility and from February 19th to June of 1594 he produced for Henslowe at the Rose, *Henry the Sixth* (*Part One*, and two others), *Titus Andronicus*, *The Jealous Comedy* (possibly the early form of *Comedy of Errors*), *The Taming of the Shrew*, and *Hamlet*. This is at least *ten* major works comprising over 31,000 lines of poetry and prose, which at any rate was a phenomenal amount of literature by one author to appear and be heard, seen and read in one year, as it was in 1594. Shakespeare also may have had in manuscript by this time *Two Gentlemen of Verona*, *Richard III* and *Romeo and Juliet*; and have had performed his earlier versions of *Henry VI*, Part Two and Three and his early version of his other three Henry plays as a single play; and had published *Venus and Adonis*. His future was at last assured. He was recognized by the nobility, was a leading member of the Lord Chamberlain's Company, and was recognized by the Court.

There was, undoubtedly, a moment before this time that poor Will was not so fortunate of state, or so happy of mind. The period between the loss of the suit in Queen's Bench in 1590, coupled with his futureless trade of a copyist, and the time of the first performances and recognition of his plays in 1592 may have been filled with despair that patient merit of the unworthy takes, when he was scorned by time, pained by despised love from a disappointed affair, ignored by men of rank, experienced the law's delay, oppressed by those with money and lands, unjustly dealt with by those in office and made to feel as Titus does in *Andronicus*:

> And sith there is no justice in earth nor hell,
> We will solicit heaven; and move the gods,
> To send down justice for to wreak our wrongs.
> Come, Marcus, come;—kinsmen, this is the way.
> Sir boy, now let me see your archery;
> Look ye draw home enough, and 'tis there straight.—
> *Terras Astraea* [Goddess of Justice] *reliquit*;
> Be you remember'd, Marcus, she's gone, she's fled.
>
> (IV. iii.)

Shakespeare confided these feelings in one of his sonnets where he plumbs the depth of vanity around him and his own lack of purposeful or needful activity, approaching what he saw as his father's situation.

> Tired with all these, for restful death I cry,
> As, to behold desert a beggar born,
> And needy nothing trimm'd in jollity,
> And purest faith unhappily forsworn,
> And gilded honour shamefully misplaced,
> And maiden virtue rudely strumpeted,
> And right perfection wrongfully disgraced,
> And strength by limping sway disabled,
> And art made tongue-tied by authority,
> And folly doctor-like controlling skill,
> And simple truth miscall'd simplicity,
> And captive good attending captain ill:
> Tired with all these, from these would I be gone,
> Save that, to die, I leave my love alone.
>
> (LXVI)

He could have continued his "And . . ."s *ad infinitum* save for the necessity of the sonnet's couplet. However, thanks to the Earl's beneficent regard from 1593 to 1594 and the performances of his plays his outlook was altered:

When, in disgrace with fortune and men's eyes,
I all alone beweep my outcast state
And trouble deaf heaven with my bootless cries
And look upon myself and curse my fate,
Wishing me like to one more rich in hope,
Featured like him, like him with friends possess'd,
Desiring this man's art and that man's scope,
With what I most enjoy contented least;
Yet in these thoughts myself almost despising,
Haply I think on thee, and then my state,
Like to the lark at break of day arising
From sullen earth, sings hymns at heaven's gate;
For thy sweet love remember'd such wealth brings
That then I scorn to change my state with kings.

(XXIX)

As time swiftly passed in the busy theatrical season from 1594 to 1595 and he was about to revise *King John*, a play with a reference to equity by name, and to embark upon the literary accomplishments that were about to make his greatness visible in *Richard II* and the subsequent tragedies dealing with the states of kings, Shakespeare finally makes his undeniable appearance on official records. On the 26th and 28th of December (the 28th was the night of the *Comedy of Errors* at Gray's Inn) in 1594,[38] Shakespeare acted at Court as one of the Lord Chamberlain's Men, as is indicated by a payment to "Willm Kempe, Willm Shakespeare & Richard Burbage servants to the Lord Chamberleyne." This is entered into the Declared Accounts of the Treasurer of the Royal Chamber on March 15, 1595 for the performance of "two several comedies or interludes" before the Queen. And so we have spanned the silent and slow ten years between the official records of February 2, 1585 (Stratford Parish Register) and March 15, 1595 (Accounts of the Treasurer of the Royal Chamber), saving two references in the *Shakespeare* v. *Lambert* document in the Coram Rege

Roll for Queen's Bench 1588/89. We have deduced his life between his documented presence in Stratford when his twins were born, to his being at the law in Westminster, and his performance before the Queen in a comedy at her palace in Greenwich. What remains is to briefly examine two literary documents written in 1589 and 1592 which allude to Shakespeare as a copyist in Westminster and the author of *Hamlet* and *Henry VI.*

7. *Shakespeare as Noverint Turned Dramatist*

WE WILL NOW examine an intriguing passage which was printed in March of 1590, after having been entered on the Stationer's Register on August 23, 1589. In making sense of the passage, one must remember some facts pertaining to the date of the early *Hamlet.* Shakespeare, in all probability knew the story of Hamlet by 1585, since that is what he named his only son. Even if he named him after Hamnet Sadler, he probably would want to know the origin of the name, or he would be attracted to its literary associations with Amleth in a collection of novels by Francis de Belleforest printed in 1564. Painter's *Palace of Pleasure,* 1566, translated some of these novels and Shakespeare had read Painter by the time he wrote *Rape of Lucrece.* Shakespeare had written a number of plays by August 1589, one of them a revenge tragedy (*Titus Andronicus*) copying Thomas Kyd's *Spanish Tragedy,* and a number of early drafts of later plays (such as *Lear, Comedy of Errors,* portions of his various Henry plays). There is a bad quarto of Shakespeare's *Hamlet* which may, as T. S. Eliot thought, have come from an earlier draft. The anonymous *Hamlet* is recorded by Henslowe in a group of other plays by Shakespeare without credit to author as having been performed on June 9, 1594, and since it lacks his usual mark for a new play, this probably was not its maiden performance.[39]

The author of the passage, Thomas Nashe, had strong

feelings against noverints, scriveners, and copyists, as are witnessed by his later remarks in *Pierce Penniless* entered August 8, 1592:

> Looke to it you Booksellers & Stationers, and let not your shops bee infected with any such goose gyblets or stinking garbadge, as the Jygs of Newsmongers, and especially such of you as frequent Westminster hall, let them be circumspect what dunghill papers they bring thether: for one bad pamphlet is inough to raise a dampe that may poyson a whole Terme, or at the least a number of poor Clyents that have no money to prevent il aire by breaking their fasts ere they come thether. Not a base Inkdropper, or scurvie plodder at *Noverint* but vailes his asses eares on everie poast, & comes off with long Circumquaque to the Gentlemen Readers, . . .

From his *Terrors of the Night* entered June 30, 1593:

> . . . A long time since hath it [this manuscript] line suppressed by mee: untill the urgent importunitie of a kinde frend of mine (to whom I was sundrie waies beholding) wrested a Coppie from me. That Coppie progressed from one scriveners shop to another,& at length grew so common, that it was readie to bee hung out for one of their signes, like a paire of indentures. Whereupon I thought it as good for mee to reape the frute of my owne labours, as to let some unskilfull pen-man or Noverint-maker startch his ruffe & new spade his beard with the benefite he made of them. . . ."[40]

The following passage comes from Thomas Nashe's introduction to Robert Greene's *Menaphon* (entered 1589, printed 1590), will be quoted at length for its importance, has interlinear explanation as a result of its complexity and punning, and employs the derisive plural. Having punned on the bird and the writer named Martin, he continues:

> . . . But least I might seeme with these night crowes, *Nimis curiosus in aliena republica*, I'le turne backe to my first text, of studies of delight; and talke a little in friendship with a few of our trivall translators.[41] It is a common

> practice now a days amongst a sort of shifting companions, that runne through every arte and thrive by none, [teacher, translator, clerk, copyist, apprentice, playwright, poet, actor, etc.] to leave the trade of *Noverint* . . .

That is *Noverint universi.* . . . ("Know all men by these presents. . . ."); a Latinism for a scrivener or copyist who does up last testaments and wills, hence possibly a pun on the first name of the only dramatist of the period named Will.

> ". . . whereto they were borne . . ."

Shakespeare's father was a Justice of the Peace, an afeeror for the court, judge of the Stratford Court of Record, a Deputy for the High Bailiff, etc.

> . . . and busie themselves with the indevors of Art, that could scarcelie latinize their neck-verse if they should have neede; . .

This, as is Jonson's later accusation of Shakespeare's small Latin and less Greek, is a University man's scorn.

> ". . . yet English *Seneca* . . ."

Shakespeare obtained his Seneca for *Titus* and *Hamlet* from Jasper Heywood's *Thyestes*; refers to Seneca (II. ii. 419) and Hercules in *Hamlet*; and alters his source in Belleforest where King Hamlet dies in the story to the use of the ghost as a messenger, a Senecan device; likewise, has (until the end) the deaths take place offstage, except for Polonius behind the arras. Shakespeare takes the cannibalistic feast at the end of *Titus* from *Thyestes*.

". . . read by candle light. . ."

The author was a copyist during the day.

> . . . yields many good sentences, as *Blood is a beggar* [a line dropped from an early version because of this mocking] and so forth. And if you entreat him fair in a frosty morning [opening scene of Shakespeare's *Hamlet*], he will afford you whole *Hamlets*, I should say handfulls of tragical speeches. But o grief! *tempus edax rerum* [a

> quotation from *The Troublesome Reign of King John* said by Friar Lawrence], what's that will last always? The sea exhaled by drops will in continuance be dry and Seneca let blood line by line and page by page, at length must needs to die to our stage: which makes his famisht followers to imitate the Kidd [i.. e. goat] in Aesop, . . .

The whole phrase (". . . makes his famisht followers to imitate the Kidd . . .") means that authors, like Shakespeare in his *Titus Andronicus* and *Hamlet*, will imitate Thomas Kyd's *The Spanish Tragedy* in the tradition of blood revenge tragedy with plays-within-plays scenes and based upon Heywood's translations of Seneca.

> . . . who enamored with the Fox's newfangles, forsook all hopes of life to leap into a new occupation; . . .

The followers of Kyd have also left the trade of noverint and leapt to that of a dramatist.

> . . . and these men renowncing all possibilities of credit or estimation, to intermeddle with Italian translations: wherein how poorelie they have plotted (as those that are neither provenzall men, nor are able to distinguish of Articles) let all indifferent Gentlemen that have travailed in that tongue, discerne by their twopenie pamphlets: & no mervaile though their home-born mediocritie be such in this matter; for what can be hoped of those, that thrust *Elisium* into hell, . . .

King Hamlet's ghost is allowed to wander back to earth for a period of time and yet he has experienced hell-fires.[42]

> . . . and have not learned so long as they have lived in the spheares, the just measure of the Horizon without an hexameter [possibly Shakespeare's early bad dramatic poetry]. Sufficeth them to bodge up a blanke verse with ifs and ands, & other while for recreation after their candle stuffe, having starched their beardes most curiouslie, to make a peripateticall path [from Westminster[43]] into the inner parts [Inns of Court] of the Citie [London], & spend two or three howers [pun on whores?] in turning over French *Doudie*, . . .

This is again one of those loaded phrases which reads in this case to mean both to discuss inferior French literature and perhaps to do some whoring.

> . . . where they attract more infection in one minute, then they can do eloquence all dayes of their life, by conversing with anie Authors of like argument.[44]

This sounds something like intellectual gatherings at the Inns of Court or the later sessions which were said to take place after the performances of plays the dramatists and aficionados of the plays from the Inns had with Sweet Will at the Mermaid Tavern with Jonson, John Marston of Middle Temple, Dekker, Heywood, Chettle, and others from time to time.

Few, if any, contemporary scholars will accept this passage as an allusion to Shakespeare and yet it is strikingly parallel to the first generally acknowledged reference to Shakespeare in London by Robert Greene (edited by Henry Chettle) in 1592, undoubtedly attacking Shakespeare for copying others' history plays in his *Henry VI*[45], and Kyd's *Spanish Tragedy* in *Titus* and *Hamlet.*

> . . . there is an upstart crow [Nashe. ". . . But lesste I might seeme with these night crowes, . . ."], beautified with our feathers, that with his *Tiger's heart wrapt in a player's hide* [parody of a line from both *Henry VI Part Three* and its first version *The True Tragedie of Richard Duke of Yorke*] supposed he is as well able to bombast out a blank verse as the best of you; and being an absolute *Johannes fac totum* [Jack-of-all-trades], is in his own conceit the only shake-scene in a country.
>
> (*Epilogue* to *Greene's Groats-worth of Wit.*)[46]

In the above passage, the pun in "shake-scene" on Shakespeare's last name is more obvious than in "Noverint", a pun on his first name (i. e. copier of *wills*; Will the copyist); *Johannes fac totum* equally parallels Nashe's, those who "run through every art and thrive by none"; and, of course, "bombast out a blank verse" is virtually identical with Nashe's "to bodge up a blank verse with ifs and ands." But the significance is clear: *the person Greene is describing in his upstart crow reference is identical with those Nashe attacked in his noverint passage.* Greene's "Upstart crow" indicates that Shakespeare has done what Nashe accused him of, having decided "to leap into a new occupation" above his class, profession, and background by being neither a writer, poet, gentleman, barrister, nor an Inns of Court man, nor a University man to recommend him. This must have both pleased Shakespeare with signs of recognition of his patient merit but also displeased him in recollecting his father's inability to achieve the stature of Gentleman and his own fears of failure, or of not having this man's art or that man's scope. "Crow" could be a pun on "crowner's law" (country lawyer); or on being a copyist, scrivener, inkdropper, or lawyer's clerk covered with ink; or most likely a general pejorative epithet for those in black legal garb and noverints who smell dead flesh and come with their fees and their copies of last wills and testaments as suggested by Voltore, 'Vulture,' an advocate in Ben Jonson's *Volpone* and echoed by Corvino and Corbaccio; both 'Crows.'

Greene's vituperation against Shakespeare was to be taken back by Henry Chettle, his editor. In doing so the first portrait from life of Shakespeare emerges. It suggests interesting connections between his biography and his art, which produced the personality his contemporaries took him to be. There was intense internal striving on Shakespeare's part during these years from between 1585 and 1595; of his successes close to failure, of love and admiration close to hate, fear, and disappointment in his life, easily determined from his sonnets. His art, however, allowed him to project these upon his protagonists and antagonists so that he did not succumb to his father's decline nor his relative's oblivion. This projection allowed the elements to be so mixed in him as to make him balanced and not cantankerous as were Jonson and Marlowe, a man after other men's and women's hearts and not his own nor despairing, as were Webster and Marston, nor light and frolicsome as Dekker and Heywood. This is what Henry Chettle saw when he described Shakespeare to defend him against Greene's attack in a prefatory address to his *Kind-Heart's Dream* in December of 1592.

> With neither of them [Marlowe and Shakespeare] that take offense was I acquainted, and with one of them [Marlowe] I care not if I never be [Kit was reputed to be an atheist and a homosexual]. The other [William Shakespeare], whom at that time [earlier in 1592] I did not so much spare as since I wish I had, for that as I have moderated the heat of living writers, and might have used my own discretion (especially in such a case, the author [Robert Greene] being dead)—that I did not, I am as sorry as if the original fault had been my fault [it could possibly have been as editor], because myself have seen his [William Shakespeare's] demeanor no less civil than he excellent in the quality [i. e. acting] he professes. Besides divers of worship [Earl of Southampton, William Hatcliff, Lambarde or members of the Inns] have reported his uprightness of dealing, which argues his honesty, and his facetious [i. e. witty] grace in writing, that approves his art.[47]

After much obscurity and much dealings with the law, Shakespeare finally enters the scene with full lights up, a charming fellow respected by his colleagues in their writings, and by the jurists, who call for his plays. He is seen as civil in demeanor, excellent as an actor, upright and honest with respect to business affairs, the gentry and patrons, and is skillful as a poet and dramatist.

III

Shakespeare's Autograph in a Law Book

. . . the air of being in a legal neighbourhood . . . There was a little tottering bench of shabby old volumes, outside the door, labelled 'Law Books, all at 9d.' Some of the inscriptions . . . were written in law-hand . . . A little way within the shop-door lay heaps of old crackled parchment scrolls and discoloured and dog's-eared lawpapers.

Charles Dickens. *Bleak House* (Chapter v)

1. *Current Opinion on Shakespeare's Legal Background*

THE INTERPRETATION proposed by the previous chapter, that Shakespeare was a noverint, or solicitor's clerk, should not be regarded as either farfetched or as merely in the category of such other surmises as those which have him as a soldier or a sailor. The evidence for a brief legal internship of some kind is far stronger than that for any other proposal. It is an idea which has been held by many major and minor writers, critics, editors, biographers, and jurists on the basis of less information and more scattered data than are now available. Not only must the new information be examined, but the old claims reviewed, in order to establish both how widespread this concept has been and how logical it now appears, particularly since the most recent scholarly biography dismisses the notion.

At many points, S. Schoenbaum's *Shakespeare's Lives* deserves to be regarded as a classic of scholarly compilation in the field of Shakespearean biography. However, in the particular area of Shakespeare's personal legal experience, and of the previous biographers' comments upon it, Schoenbaum expresses attitudes of disbelief. Schoenbaum regards the claim of Shakespeare's legal experience despite its numerous proponents, as nonviable (in each case treating the evidence piecemeal and not as a whole.) Nor does he examine the Shakespeare autograph in the Lambarde law book at the Folger Library in Washington, D. C., although he cannot help but be aware of its existence. He even devotes a chapter to one of the signature's claimants (J. Q. Adams) without mentioning his work on the autograph. Schoenbaum holds to the view that whoever writes about Shakespeare writes about himself, and for the most part he is correct. But his own scholarly "life" (or lives) of Shakespeare amounts to a history of Shakespearean biographical scholarship, very significant in its own right, but not a biography. His thesis of personal projection leads him to dismiss most theories of Shakespeare's legal background on the grounds that those holding the opinion had legal careers. Yet few are in a better position than lawyers to discern the evidence and put forth the claim. Castigating others for their biases, Schoenbaum is severe in this regard on his own idol, Edmond Malone, accusing him of falling into the trap of identification, claiming Shakespeare as a lawyer because Malone himself was one. But careful critical examination, while often most valuable in allowing him to destroy popular myths (the deer-stealing episode, Shakespeare's holding horses before the theatres as his first job, the gift of £1000 from the Earl of Southampton, John Shakespeare's being a butcher, and William a butcher's apprentice), has not served him well in the matter of Shakespeare and the law. He treats this claim as having no more significance than those for Shakespeare the sailor, the soldier, the mender of plays, the horse-holder, and as less significant than the assertion that Shakespeare was a schoolmaster. Yet there is a great deal of evidence for this claim of legal background for the dramatist, as it is the purpose of this book to show.

In addition to its dismissal at Schoenbaum's hands, the belief that Shakespeare had legal experience has had a considerable degree of opposition throughout the scholarly community, a fact which may have made Schoenbaum feel he could dismiss it with safety. The difficulties producing this opposition result from an unfortunate conflict of elements. Shakespearean scholars, for the most part, are not sufficiently versed in the legal knowledge of Shakespeare's day, nor do they wish to burden themselves with so laborious a task. Unfortunately, those writers who are equipped with such legal background are usually lawyers who, as amateur Shakespeareans, often make serious errors concerning the dating of the plays, biographical facts, content of the plays, and are not adequately furnished with those techniques of literary criticism which impress professional scholars. Besides, as has been noted, such lawyers and jurists are fair game for the accusation that they are attempting to flatter themselves by trying to make Shakespeare one of their own. Furthermore, the arena has been badly muddied, even bloodied, by some lawyers and others who have misused legal evidence (in disregard of hard biographical data) to support Bacon as the author of the plays; when, as will be subsequently noted, Bacon's legal writings were probably as much influenced by Shakespeare, as the other way around.

To counter the Baconians, the "Stratfordians" (proponents of Shakespeare as the author of the plays) were not content merely to stand on the biographical data, which is adequate enough to dismiss Baconist theory. They attempted, as a means of countering Bacon the lawyer, to belittle the obvious legal evidence, undermining its authenticity by saying Shakespeare's knowledge was, in contrast with other dramatists of his period, neither accurate nor broad. One who followed this line was James G. McManaway, also one of the uncoverers of the Shakespeare autograph in the Folger. His belief in Shakespeare's scanty connection with the law of his day, a theme he supported in a Folger pamphlet used to counter the Baconists' claims, fed McManaway's disbelief in the genuineness of the evidence before him. This, in turn, has kept him from making any claim about, or analysis of, the signature he helped uncover in 1938.[1] Also, some critics correctly reject the idea of Shakespeare's ever having been a "lawyer" (or as the English would say, a barrister) because he would not have had the educational, social, or financial background for it. But they overlook or underestimate the categories of noverint, lawyer's clerk, or scrivener which would have produced much of a lawyer's knowledge, but would have been arrived at by another route. And as to a claim that Shakespeare's legal knowledge was scant and undistinguished when compared with that of some other dramatists, it must be admitted that certain of these, as members of the legal societies (John Marston, Francis Beaumont, and possibly John Webster); or as university men (Christopher Marlowe, Ben Jonson); or as having connections with the law trade as scriveners or associates of the Inns of Court (Thomas Kyd, Thomas Heywood) were obviously known to be directly connected with the law. However, let us note a most significant fact. This is that Shakespeare, presumed to have no such connection, is as accurate, as rounded, and as concerned about the law (before, above, and beyond his own personal litigations) as any of these others. This cannot be safely ignored and must be accounted for. Scholarship, then, has arrived at a very unproductive impasse. To bolster the claim of Shakespeare as author of his own plays against the jurist Bacon, the "Stratfordians" find themselves ignoring, or having to disclaim, Shakespeare's widespread legal knowledge and involvement in the people, places, and issues of the jurisprudence of his day. Denying this influence upon him draws a curtain across what might have brought him to write plays, the circumstances under which he did some of his writing, what caused him to put legal terms, concepts and problems in his plays, and what prompted him to give social and political purposes to his works.

2. *Scholars Viewing Shakespeare as a Lawyer*

UTILIZING Schoenbaum's survey and O. Hood Phillips' recent *Shakespeare & the Lawyers* (London, 1972) summarizing what lawyers' various opinions have been concerning law in Shakespeare, one can more easily encompass the arguments regarding Shakespeare's legal experience put forth by scholars in the past from the eighteenth-century Edmond Malone to our contemporary Anthony Burgess, as well as the assertions made by numerous jurists from Lord Campbell in Malone's time to Mark Edwin Andrews, a contemporary Houston lawyer. We are thus helped to recover from scholarly neglect evidence worthy of closer scrutiny. On occasion lawyers have sided with those critics who deride the thought of any extensive legal experience on Shakespeare's part. Sir Dunbar Plunket Barton who was a Bencher at Gray's Inn and Judge of the High Court of Justice in Ireland (*Shakespeare's Use of Legal Language*, London, 1929) and George W. Keeton who was Dean of the University of London Faculty of Law (*Shakespeare's Legal and Political Background*, London, 1930, revised and expanded considerably in 1968) are two who are cautionary about Shakespeare's knowledge as being anything other than pedestrian, out of date, and sometimes wrong. Barton makes some good points and concludes that 1) it is doubtful whether there are a half dozen real references to legal maxims in the whole of the thirty-seven plays; 2) legal metaphors abounded at the time as cliches; and 3) the Latin law phrases Shakespeare quotes are trivial. Keeton, despite his own 417- page analysis of legal concepts, trial scenes, and juridical puns, states in his preface:

> In the author's opinion, Shakespeare's legal knowledge differed little from that of other writers of his time, but

> his observation was closer and more accurate, and there were prominent lawyers of his day—notably Sir Edward Coke—who interested him greatly. The legal and political ideas which he incidentally expresses were part of the intellectual equipment of all educated men of his time, and his touch was sensitive. Beyond this, the author would not wish to go. (*p.* v.)

Keeton and Barton draw unwarrantedly conservative conclusions from their own data, whereas others on less information, analysis or professional background have asserted the conclusions Keeton and Barton withdrew from. Many others have gone significantly further. No one has been as emphatic as Mark Twain who staked his reputation on his premise that the author of the plays must have been a lawyer: he said he would ". . . stand or fall, win or lose, by the verdict rendered by the jury upon that single question."[2] The notion of Shakespeare's legal background and influence from the law took nearly two centuries to emerge, but it has been held ever since. The lack of overt contemporary evidence for this fact in the earlier centuries may simply be a result of its being a fairly normal background for nonuniversity writers, his family's legal and civic affairs were well-known, and his relationships to the Inns of Court were then obvious and assumed, although having since faded from our familiarity. The silence could have been a result of ignorance, lack of analytical skills, or presumption.

On November 29, 1790, the great Shakespearean scholar, Edmond Malone, a barrister who pursued his legal studies at the Inner Temple, published his *Shakespeare*. In it he states: "I believe, that on leaving school Shakespeare was placed in the office of some country attorney, or the Seneschal of some manor court."[3] Later on he says that Shakespeare was ". . . sufficiently conversant with conveyances to have taught others the forms of such legal assurances as are usually prepared by country attorneys; and perhaps spent two or three years in this employment before he removed from Stratford to

London." (I, ii, 180). This conviction on Malone's part, not easily won, finally brings him to revise his original reading of Nashe's noverint passage discussed in the previous chapter.

> In Kyd's *Spanish Tragedy*, as in Shakespeare's *Hamlet*, there is, if I may say so, a play represented *within a play*: if the old play of *Hamlet* should ever be recovered, a similar interlude, I make no doubt, would be found there; and somewhat of the same contrivance may be traced in *The* old *Taming of the Shrew*, a comedy which perhaps had the same authour as the other ancient pieces now enumerated.
>
> Nashe seems to point at some dramatick writer of that time, who had originally been a scrivener or attorney:
>
> "A clerk foredoom'd his father's soul to cross,
> Who *penn'd* a stanza when he should engross,"
>
> who, instead of transcribing deeds and pleadings, chose to imitate Seneca's plays, of which a translation had been published many years before. Our authour [William Shakespeare], however freely he may have borrowed from Plutarch and Holinshed, does not appear to be indebted to Seneca: . . .

Malone is overlooking the influence of Jasper Heywood's translation of Seneca's *Thyestes* upon Shakespeare's *Titus Andronicus*. This is perhaps because in Malone's day it was generally thought that someone other than Shakespeare wrote *Titus Andronicus*.

> . . . and therefore I [Malone] do not believe that he [Shakespeare] was the person in Nashe's contemplation [the noverint passage]. The person alluded to being described as originally bred to the law, (for the trade of noverint is the trade of an attorney or conveyancer . . .

At this point Malone has a footnote to explain "noverint," interesting for its embedded reference to *Titus Andronicus* linking it to noverints: "'The country lawyers too jog down apace,/Each with his *noverint universi* face' Ravenscroft's Prologue prefixed to *Titus Andronicus* [in 1687]. Our ancient deeds were written in Latin, and frequently began with the words, *Noverint Universi.* The form is still retained. *Know all men,* & etc."

> . . . I [Malone] formerly conceived that this circumstance also was decisive to shew that Shakespeare could not have been aimed at. I do not hesitate to acnowledge that since the first edition of this essay I have found reason to believe I was mistaken. The comprehensive mind of our poet embraced almost every object of nature, every trade, every art; the manners of every description of men, and the general language of almost every profession: but his knowledge of legal terms is not merely such as might be acquired by the casual observation of even his all-comprehending mind; it has the appearance of *technical* skill; and he is so fond of displaying it on all occasions, that I suspect he was early initiated in at least the forms of law; and was employed, while he yet remained at Stratford, in the office of some country attorney, who was at the same time a petty conveyancer, and perhaps also the Seneschal of some manor-court. (I, i. 306–307)

Malone appends twenty-six technical legal references from the works. Schoenbaum regards Malone's belief as speculation and dismisses it all with the statement, "Malone was not a barrister for nothing." (p. 179).

Schoenbaum says that Malone assigns too early a date to *Hamlet* on the basis of Malone's apparent misinterpretation of the noverint passage which Schoenbaum takes as alluding to a previous *Hamlet,* "perhaps by Kyd" (p. 169).

In addition to Malone, numerous other scholars have insisted that the noverint passage refers to Shakespeare, such as: Lord Campbell, Charles Armitage Brown, Charles Knight, Staunton, and Edward J. White.[4] Since the passage is in the plural, such critics as Arthur Freeman, R. B. McKerrow, and G. R. Hibbard believe it may refer to another or several other writers as well as to Shakespeare.[5] Freeman (p. 19) cites a playwright, Thomas Watson, who was living in Westminster as a noverint in 1579 and moves to St. Helen's Parish, Bishopsgate, in

1587, too early to be an author referred to by Nashe but perhaps one of a tribe of scriveners who became writers. Typical was Thomas Kyd, mentioned by Schoenbaum, who already lived on Lombard Street in the parish of St. Mary Woolnoth in the City of London. From the information provided by the Lambarde volume in the Folger, Shakespeare followed Watson's path a little later, coming from Stratford to live in Westminster by 1588, and eventually residing in St. Helen's Parish, Bishopsgate by 1593.

It is important to note that the belief in Shakespeare as a lawyer's clerk has not been restricted to barristers, lawyers, jurists, scholars, and critics, but has been held by artists and writers through the years. In Germany, Ludwig Tieck wrote a novella entitled *Dichterleben*, 1826 (translated as *The Life of Poets*, 1830) in which Shakespeare appears as a lawyer's clerk while writing *Romeo and Juliet*. William Watkiss Lloyd in his *Life of William Shakespeare*, for Samuel Weller Singer's edition of the *Dramatic Works* (1831), indicates he "is 'strongly confirmed' in his view that Nashe is lashing out at Shakespeare as the shifting companion who wrote an early version of *Hamlet*" and thus was a noverint. Victor Hugo, influenced by a medium who claimed to have communicated directly with the shade of Shakespeare, believed that after his marriage the latter became "clerk to an attorney" (*William Shakespeare*, trans. M. B. Andersen. [Chicago, 1887], pp. 10–11). One finds in Walter Savage Landor's creation entitled *Citation and Examination of William Shakespeare, Euseby Treen, Joseph Carnably, and Silas Gough, Clerk, before the Worshipful Sir Thomas Lucy, Knight, Touching Deer-Stealing, on the* 19*th Day of September in the Year of Grace* 1582: *Now First Published from Original Papers* (1834) that Shakespeare is portrayed as having been a conveyancer's clerk for over a year in an attorney's office before becoming a player. Charles Armitage Brown, the close friend of John Keats, in his *Shakespeare's Autobiographical Poems* (1838,

p. 254) from his extensive work on the sonnets, also positively concludes that Nashe's noverint passage refers to Shakespeare; hence that Shakespeare was a lawyer's clerk, and thus the author at the age of twenty-four of a first draft of *Hamlet.* In a fictional narrative entitled *The Youth of Shakespeare* (1839), the second volume of a trilogy by Robert Folkstone Williams, Shakespeare is depicted at the time of his wooing of Anne Hathaway as being employed as a lawyer's clerk. Schoenbaum (p. 343) applies his identification theory to John Payne Collier's *The Life of William Shakespeare* (1844) by asserting: "And, a lawyer himself [Middle Temple], he [Collier] accepts like other lawyers the barrister Malone's theory that the future playwright had employment for a time in an attorney's office after quitting the free school in Stratford." True, Collier was, unfortunately, a forger but not of Shakespeare's signature, as was William Henry Ireland (himself a solicitor's clerk). Emma Severn's novel *Anne Hathaway; or, Shakespeare in Love* (1845) depicts the young Shakespeare as he ". . . toils as a clerk in Swine Street [Stratford] for the venomous lawyer Jerry Leatherlands . . ." Charles Knight (*The Pictorial Edition of the Works of Shakespeare,* 1838–1841) in his Postscript to *Twelfth Night* says, "Shakespere knew the law of England better than his legal commentators." Nathaniel Holmes (1815–1901), Justice of the Supreme Court of Missouri, and afterwards Royall Professor of Law at Harvard University, in his *The Authorship of Shakespeare* (1866), although out to prove that only Bacon could have written these plays which evidence such learning, states that the author of the plays was a lawyer.[6]

Malone's position on Shakespeare's law experience is also supported by a major group, all members of the legal fraternity and writing close together: William L. Rushton's *Shakespeare a Lawyer* (1858); Lord Campbell's *Shakespeare's Legal Acquirements Considered* (1859); again Rushton in his *Shakespeare's Testamentary Language* (1869); and H. T.'s *Was Shakespeare a Lawyer?*

(1871). Rushton provides considerable data for his day, all tending to demonstrate how widespread was Shakespeare's knowledge of the laws of England. An even lengthier compilation comes from Lord Campbell, once Chancellor of England and author of *The Lives of the Chancellors.* Campbell acknowledges that Alexander Chalmers, Edmond Malone, and J. P. Collier have preceded him in his assumption concerning Shakespeare's technical knowledge of the law from personal experience and some kind of clerkship career.

Campbell sees in the compactness of Shakespeare's will not only evidence that the dramatist himself composed it but he also concludes from the language that Shakespeare had professional legal experience. He accepts the noverint passage as referring to Shakespeare, moving Schoenbaum (p. 463) to comment:

> In a pleasing fantasy Campbell sees Shakespeare as occupying a desk in the office of a prosperous country lawyer 'attending sessions and assizes,—keeping leets and law days,—and perhaps being sent up to the metropolis in term time to conduct suits before the Lord Chancellor or the superior courts of common law at Westminster . . .' [John Campbell, *Shakespeare's Legal Acquirements Considered*, London, 1859, p. 30]. Yet reality must at last intrude upon this idyll: Campbell has read Knight's popular Life, and he cannot ignore the biographer's devastating point about the absence from Warwickshire records of the poet's signature as a witness to deeds and wills.

Is this, however, any more logical than to conclude that Shakespeare read no books since his library or individual volumes have presumably not been found? Charles Knight and S. Schoenbaum both fall into the fallacy that to prove the nonexistence of a single body of data excludes the possibility of proving that Shakespeare's background existed from the presence of other areas of information.[7] Shakespeare may have witnessed documents in City of Westminster records that have not been searched. Schoenbaum continues: "Shakespeare could have obtained his legal knowledge (which is anyway less impressively technical than the author believes) in other ways." Unhappily, the "other ways" are not enumerated. Furthermore, since Campbell's analysis is admittedly far less thorough than the subsequent analyses of H. T., Edward J. White, and G. W. Keeton, no present-day authority would conceive of basing his arguments about Shakespeare's legal knowledge on Campbell's inadequate treatment of the topic. Again Schoenbaum: "Reason in the end prevails over desire, as Campbell settles for an agnostic position. (Others evinced less caution [but wider reasoning and closer analysis]—for example, 'H—T—,'who answers in the affirmative the question posed by his title, *Was Shakespeare a Lawyer?* (1871).)"

The 1871 volume dedicated to the Lord Chancellor by H. T., which Schoenbaum thus dismisses, confines itself in its close analysis only to *Measure for Measure* and *All's Well That Ends Well*. H. T. provides the first example of a mind approaching the question with a critical analysis and concluding that Shakespeare studied and worked with the law.

> The pages of Shakespeare's Plays are allowed to be strewed with references to English laws; but, on a careful examination, we have found that such references are far more numerous than has been usually supposed. In fact, the Poet's memory appears to have been full to overflowing of the principles and practice of Law, and of the quibbles and technicalities of the legal profession. Hence an interesting question has been raised as to whether Shakespeare had ever been engaged in the study or practice of English law. A little book on this subject was published by the late Lord Chancellor Campbell. In it his Lordship gave the results of his examination of twenty-three, out of the thirty-seven Plays which have been ascribed to our Great Dramatist. His judgment, delivered with the proverbial caution of a Scotchman, was, that no positive answer could be given to the question. We venture to think, however, that the trial was not satisfactorily conducted, in that the investigation was too cursorily made. His Lordship noted

> only such passages as, without study, would have suggested themselves even to a non-legal mind; whilst others were passed by.[8]

H. T. goes on to list the obvious and numerous references in *Measure for Measure*, but in order to give the case a real test, he cites passages from a less legalistically oriented work, *All's Well That Ends Well.* The following are some of his citations: the delivering up under wardship, derivation through inheritance, sharing by equal division, burial of person guilty of *felo-de-se* (self-murder), inhibitions in canon law, principal of a lean, non-inheritance of serfdom, abatement, accessory, congregated College, "ten groats is for the hand of an attorney" (lawyers' fees equalled 3s. 4d.), authentic fellows, heir, dower, misprison, contract, brief, warranted testimony, suffer question, ". . . reprieve him from the/ Wrath of greatest justice . . .," sworn, vowed, conditions, unsealed, "he will sell the fee simple of his salvation, the inheritance of it; and cut the entail from all remainders, and a perpetual succession of it perpetually [i.e. mortmain]." (IV, iii.), etc.

H. T. sees Shakespeare's legal knowledge as coming from a clerkship rather than from his father's litigations (which would have a relatively narrow scope) or from listening at Westminster (which would provide only a very superficial source for the use Shakespeare puts his knowledge of the law to in his plays). This compilation by H. T. suggests that Shakespeare must have had a deeper exposure to these terms provided by having been in such a situation as a tutor of writing (scrivener), or a law clerk (noverint), as well as through having pursued his father's litigations to save him lawyers' fees in Stratford, London and Westminster, and traveling expenses for messengers from Stratford, in addition to following his case, and others' cases in Westminster. Shakespeare's knowledge and reinforcement of interest in the law could well have come from several sources but it is difficult to make a convincing case that it was not technical, professional, pervasive and persistently employed.

In the twentieth century, support for the thesis of Shakespeare's legal experience continues to mount. From *Cassell's Illustrated Shakespeare* (London, 1913), edited by Dr. F. J. Furnivall and Mr. John Munro, comes this amusing declaration:

> Another tradition says that he was an attorney's clerk; and that he was so at one time of his life, I [Munro] as a lawyer have no doubt. Of the details of no profession does he show such an intimate acquaintance as he does of law; Shakespeare's knowledge of insanity was not got in a doctor's shop, though his law was (I believe) in a lawyer's office.
>
> (*p. xiii.*)

In the United States in the same year, Edward J. White brought out a second edition of his *Commentaries on the Law in Shakespeare.* White had already editied the *Third Edition of Tiedeman on Real Property.* He analyzes at length 511 different legal terms and concepts expressly stated in Shakespeare's plays, the long narrative poems, and the sonnets (he cites only eight, although there is scarcely a sonnet without at least one of the concepts he catalogs). This leads White to conclude that beyond a shadow of a doubt Shakespeare had a career as a lawyer's clerk or copyist and he presumes the passage by Nashe introducing Greene's *Menaphon* to be in reference to Shakespeare's having ". . . left the 'trade of Noverint' to become a dramatist."

> 'Noverint' was a well-known slang expression to indicate the business of a lawyer's clerk, or apprentice, so from this and other evidence, of his experience in a law office, prior to that year, he could well have read the case of Sir James Hales, published in 1578.
>
> (*p. xxxix*).

This case of *felo-de-se* appeared in Plowden's *Law Reports* and forms the basis for the argument concerning burial after suicide in the gravediggers scene of *Hamlet.*

As just indicated, H. T. noted previously that the concept of *felo-de-se* is mentioned in *All's Well That Ends Well.*

The most recent noted Shakespearean scholar and researcher of primary documents to insist on the claim of a clerkship for the dramatist is the respected Edgar I. Fripp. Fripp's most significant contribution is his edition of the *Minutes and Accounts of the Corporation of Stratford-upon-Avon and Other Records* 1553–1620. He presents his observations on Shakespeare and his use of law terms in *Master Richard Quiney* (1924). We shall quote Fripp at length for two reasons. First, to demonstrate the case for Shakespeare's legal background as it has been presented in the past, second, to note that Fripp's style unfortunately aids in the easy dismissal of his arguments. Fripp made pleasant reading out of what had been arrived at by the most laborious and meticulous kind of firsthand perusal of legal documents which themselves made rather dry reportage.

> That William Shakespeare was an attorney's clerk in his early manhood, as pointed out by Lord Campbell, can hardly be questioned. His legal terms are legion, are sometimes of a highly technical character, are frequently metaphorical, and, most convincing of all, are often wrought into the very fibre of his writing. When our attention has once been drawn to them it is difficult to get away from them. If they were not so obviously part of himself they might injure our pleasure in some of his finest passages. Second nature speaks in such lines as:
>
> Arms take your last embrace! and lips, O you
> The doors of breath, seal with a righteous kiss
> A dateless bargain to engrossing Death!
>
> (*Romeo and Juliet* v. viii. 113–115)
>
> What lover but a scrivener or lawyer's clerk would think in such a moment of the engrossing and sealing of a document? Or what perplexed philosopher but an attorney would bring in the term quietus from Chamberlain's accounts or Exchequer discharges when meditating suicide? Shakespeare was not on the lookout for a legal expression when he put on Dame Quickly's lips the pathetic words about Falstaff. 'A' made a finer 'end and went away an it

had been any Christian child; or when he gave to Quince as Prologue in "Pyramus and, Thysbie" the ridiculous legal tag, 'Our true intent is.' Equally undramatic but delightful to those who recognize it, and convincing to them of the author's early profession is such a phrase as that in the mouth of the servant in *Romeo and Juliet* (I. vii.), 'the longer-liver take all,' that is *diucius vivens*, the survivor, as in Robert Arden's deed of settlement, 17 July 1550, and Richard Hathaway's will, 1 Sept. 1581.

We need not claim for the Poet profound knowledge of the law. He was not a barrister nor a councillor. It is enough that he was an artist of consummate genius 'immured' for a period (to employ one of his own Latinisms) in a country attorney's office, and the facts demand no less. Only on the assumption of personal and expert acquaintance with the procedure of the Court Leet and the Court of record, the imposition of fine and punishment (by imprisonment, whipping, and sitting in the stocks, pillory, or cucking-stool), the issue of warrants by the Steward or town clerk, and their execution by the Serjeants-at-the Mace, the duties of Constable Affeeror, the phraseology and tautology of minutes and accounts, wills and inventories, lease and conveyances, the making of marks and signatures, the handling of paper and parchment, pen, ink, wax, and seal, can the phenomena which perpetually are present and even obtrude themselves in Shakespeare's earliest writings, be explained.

Such experience was less likely in the service of Thomas Trussil (a kinsman probably of Mary Arden), Walter Roche (late schoolmaster) or William Court (son of a former Steward), than of the Town Clerk and steward from 1571 to 1586, Henry Rogers. Shakespeare was probably in Rogers' office when on 11 Feb. 1580, after nearly two months' local talk, the body of Katherine Hamlet spinster was taken from her grave at Alveston, and Rogers as coroner held an inquest on the same and concurred with the verdict of the jury that her death by drowning in the Avon at Tiddington (about a mile from Stratford) on the 17 Dec., was *per infortuniam* (by accident) and not a case of *felo-de-se*: whereby she was entitled to Christian burial.

(*pp.* 41–45)

NATIONAL PORTRAIT GALLERY, LONDON

Chandos portrait of William Shakespeare, thought to be by Richard Burbage.

SHAKESPEARE'S BIRTHPLACE TRUST

Shakespeare's birthplace in Stratford-Upon-Avon, 1769

SHAKESPEARE'S BIRTHPLACE TRUST

Anne Hathaway's cottage

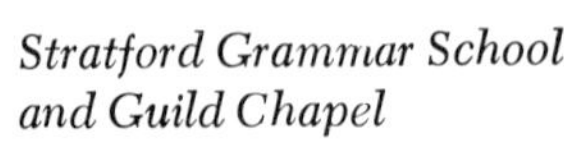

Stratford Grammar School and Guild Chapel

SHAKESPEARE'S BIRTHPLACE TRUST

New Place, Stratford residence Shakespeare purchased in 1597

BRITISH MUSEUM

Clopton Bridge on the road from Stratford to London

BRITISH TOURIST AUTHORITY

FOLGER LIBRARY

The Reading Room of the Folger Library

The Folger Shakespeare Library, Washington, D.C.

FOLGER LIBRARY

FOLGER LIBRARY

The Seventh Shakespeare signature

FOLGER LIBRARY

Shakespeare's Westminster address in the Folger's copy of Archaionomia

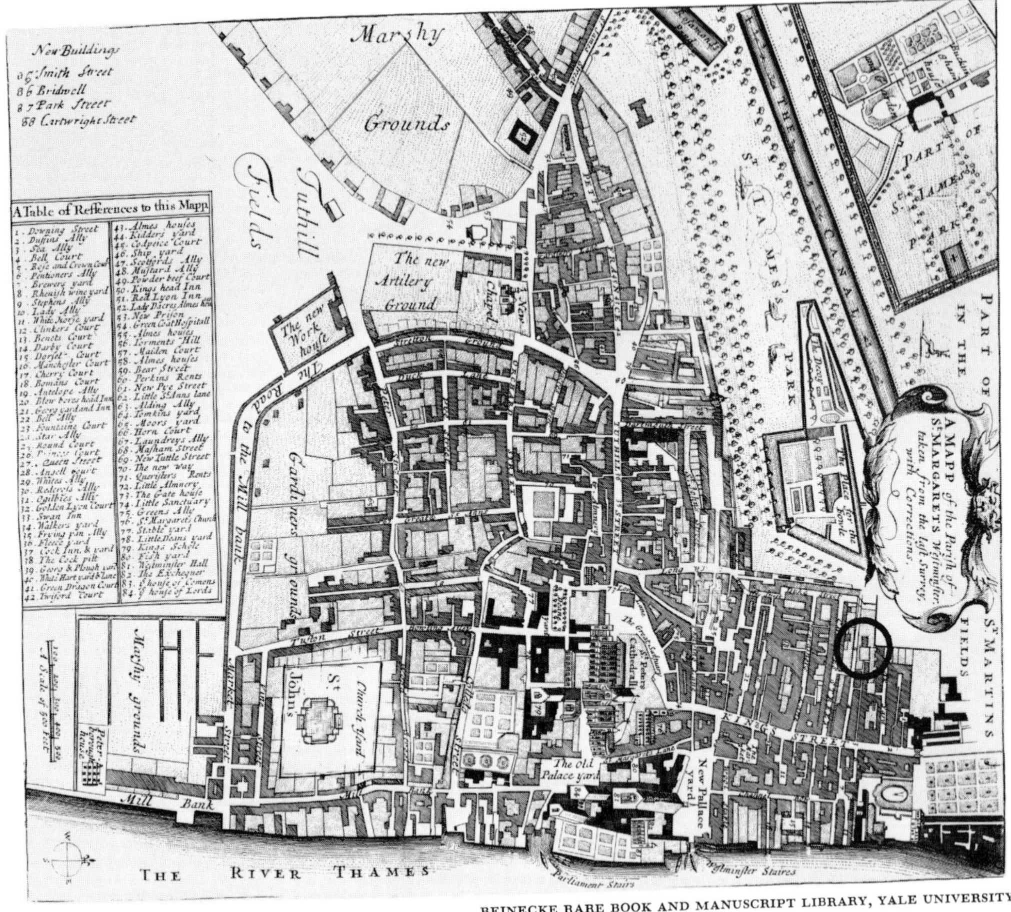

BEINECKE RARE BOOK AND MANUSCRIPT LIBRARY, YALE UNIVERSITY

Map of St. Margaret's Parish from Stow's Survey (1755) showing Rose and Crown Court (#5) running into Duke St. above Charles St.

City of Westminster and St. James' Park, 1660

Norden's map of Westminster, 1593

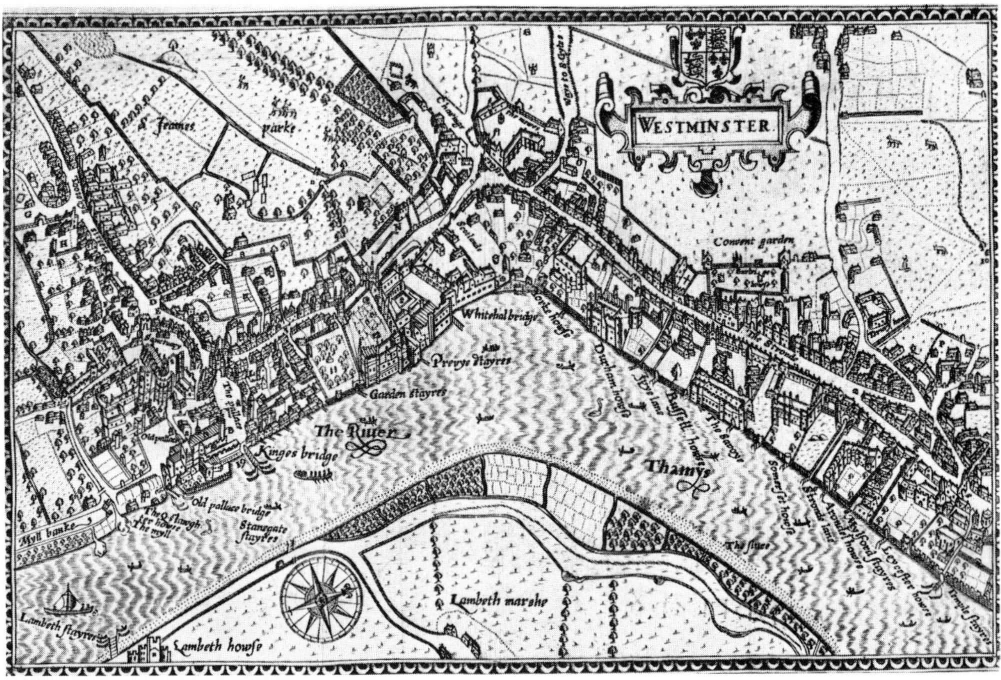

THE TRUSTEES OF THE LONDON MUSEUM

Westminster Palace Yard, hall on left, Abbey in background, in the time of Charles I

Westminster Hall by Samuel Ireland (1800), father of the famous forger of Shakespeare signatures

SAMUEL IRELAND

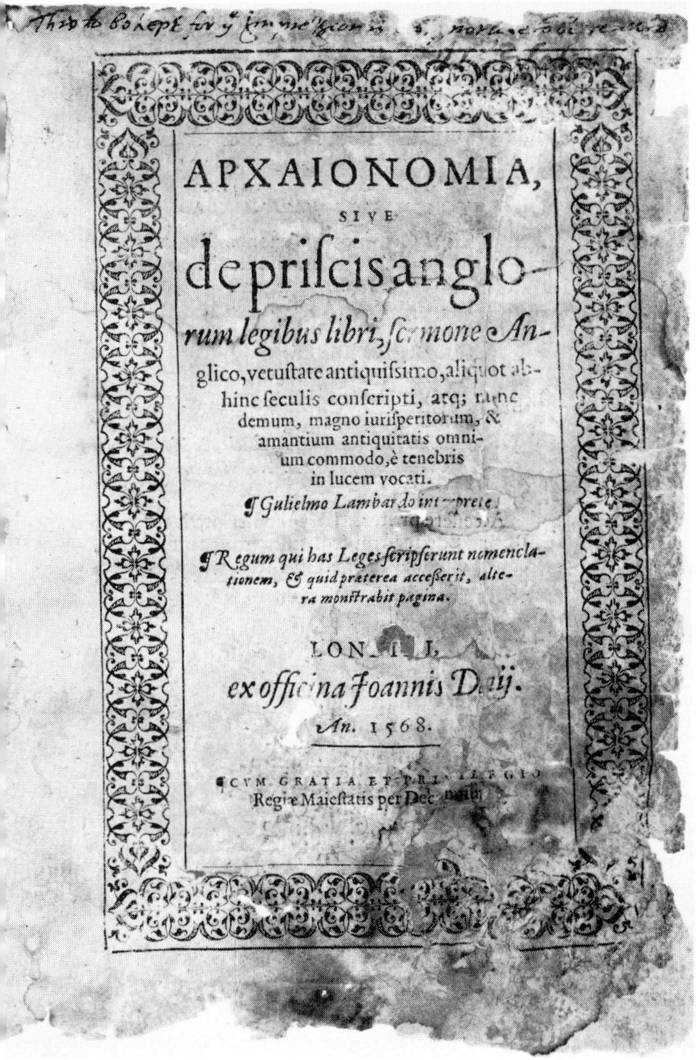

APXAIONOMIA,
SIVE
de priſcis anglo-
rum legibus libri, ſermone An-
glico, vetuſtate antiquiſsimo, aliquot ab-
hinc ſeculis conſcripti, atq; nunc
demum, magno iuriſperitorum, &
amantium antiquitatis omni-
um commodo, è tenebris
in lucem vocati.

¶ Gulielmo Lambardo interprete.

¶ Regum qui has Leges ſcripſerunt nomencla-
tionem, & quid præterea acceſſerit, alte-
ra monſtrabit pagina.

LONDINI,
ex officina Joannis Daij.
An. 1568.

¶ CVM GRATIA ET PRIVILEGIO
Regiæ Maieſtatis per Decennium.

Title page of Folger's William Lambarde's Archaionomia, *1568*

FOLGER LIBRARY

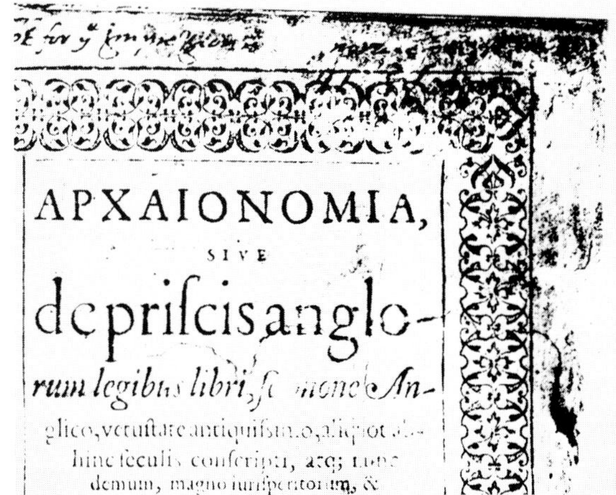
APXAIONOMIA,
SIVE
de priſcis anglo-
rum legibus libri, ſermone An-
glico, vetuſtate antiquiſsimo, aliquot ab-
hinc ſeculis conſcripti, atq; nunc
demum, magno iuriſperitorum, &

Area of Shakespeare's signature from front under ultra violet light

FOLGER LIBRARY

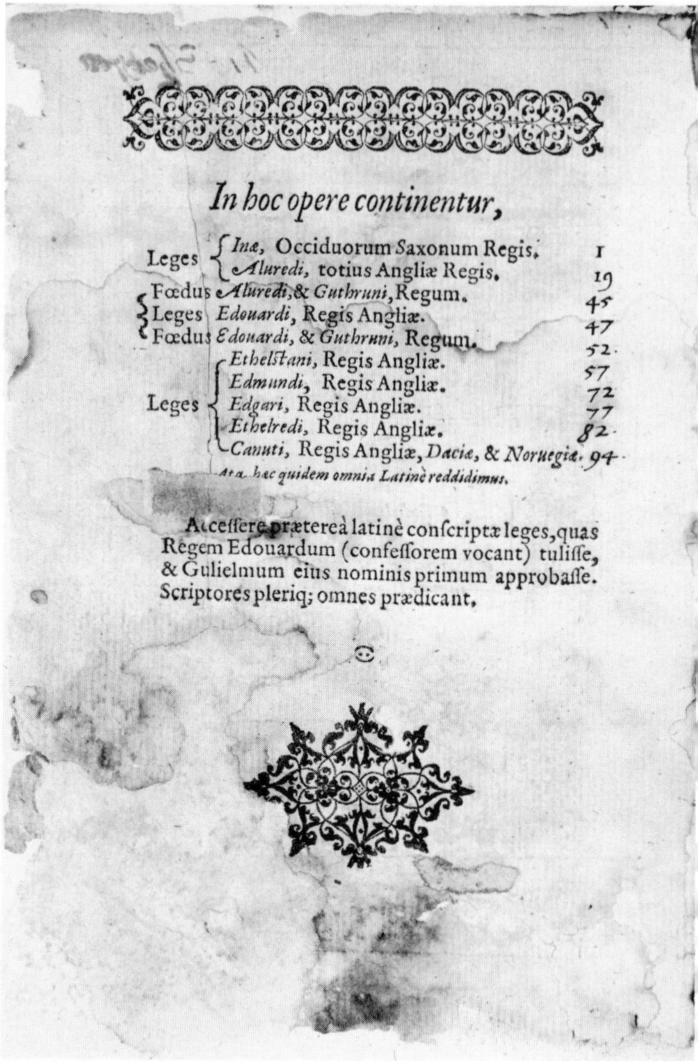

In hoc opere continentur,

Leges { *Inæ,* Occiduorum Saxonum Regis. 1
Aluredi, totius Angliæ Regis. 19

Fœdus *Aluredi,* & *Guthruni,* Regum. 45
Leges *Edouardi,* Regis Angliæ. 47
Fœdus *Edouardi,* & *Guthruni,* Regum. 52

Leges { *Ethelstani,* Regis Angliæ. 57
Edmundi, Regis Angliæ. 72
Edgari, Regis Angliæ. 77
Ethelredi, Regis Angliæ. 82
Canuti, Regis Angliæ, *Daciæ,* & *Noruegiæ.* 94

Atq; hæc quidem omnia Latinè reddidimus.

Accessere præterea latinè conscriptæ leges, quas Regem Edouardum (confessorem vocant) tulisse, & Gulielmum eius nominis primum approbasse. Scriptores pleriq; omnes prædicant.

Verso title page showing signature bleedthrough

FOLGER LIBRARY

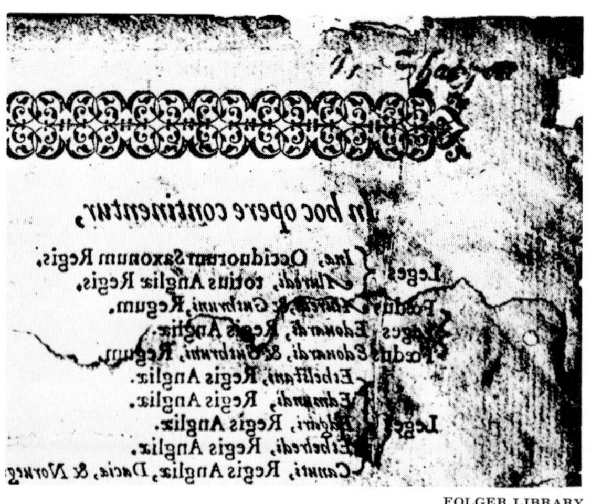

Mirror image of bleedthrough under ultra violet light

FOLGER LIBRARY

PUBLIC RECORD OFFICE, LONDON

Belott-Mountjoy Deposition signature of Shakespeare

Mortgage signature of Shakespeare

GUILDHALL LIBRARY, CITY OF LONDON

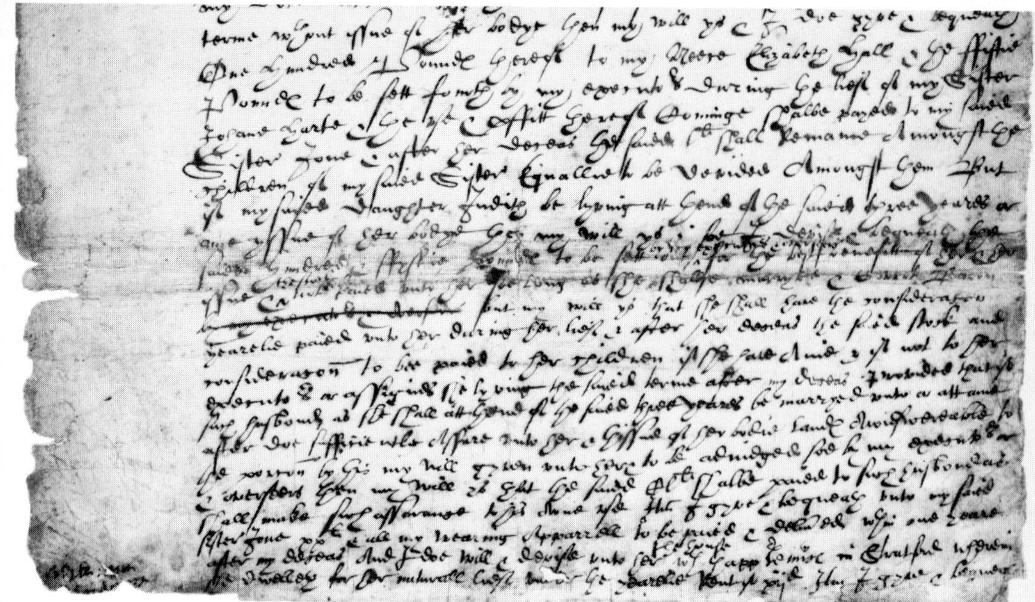

PUBLIC RECORD OFFICE, LONDON

Bottom portion of first sheet of Shakespeare's Will with a signature

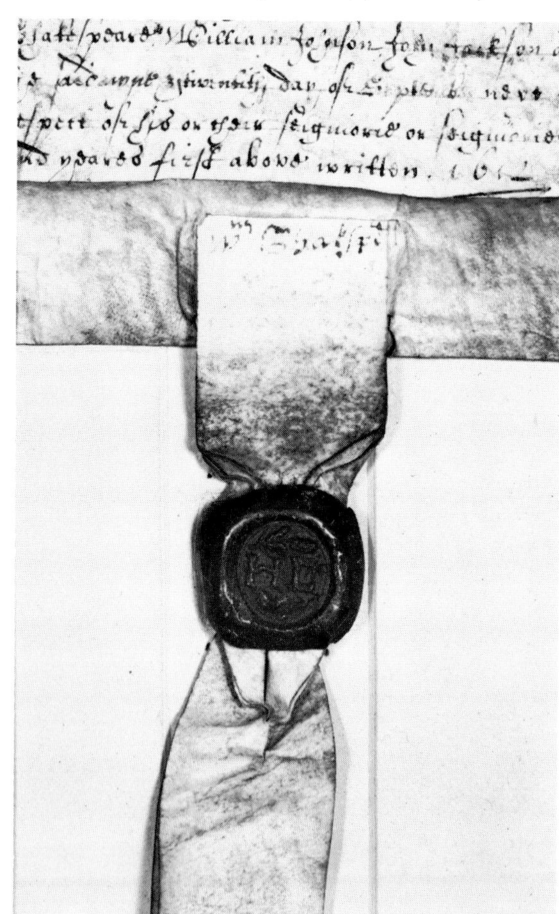

Mortgage Deed signature of Shakespeare

BRITISH MUSEUM

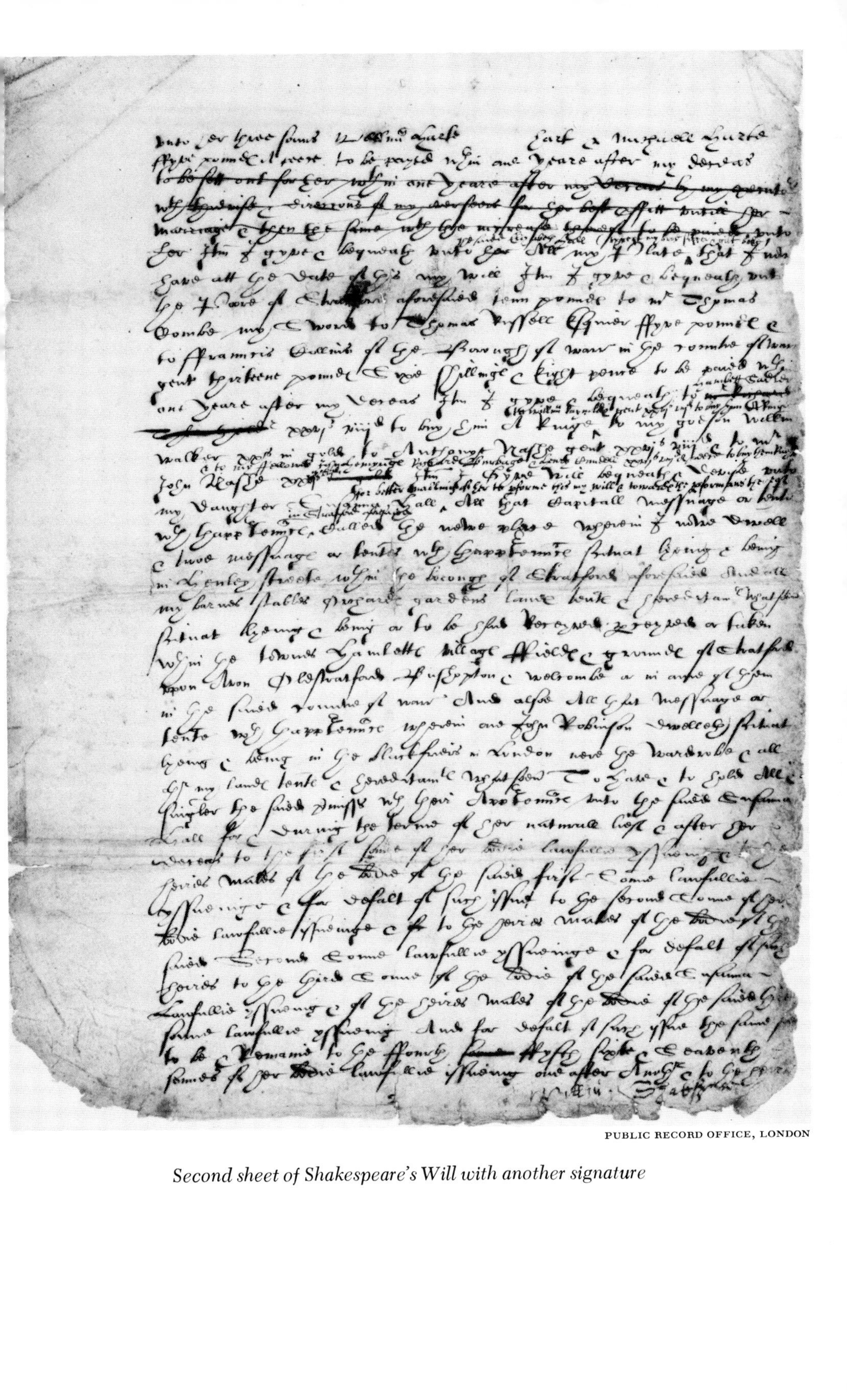

PUBLIC RECORD OFFICE, LONDON

Second sheet of Shakespeare's Will with another signature

SHAKESPEARE BIRTHPLACE TRUST

William Henry Ireland

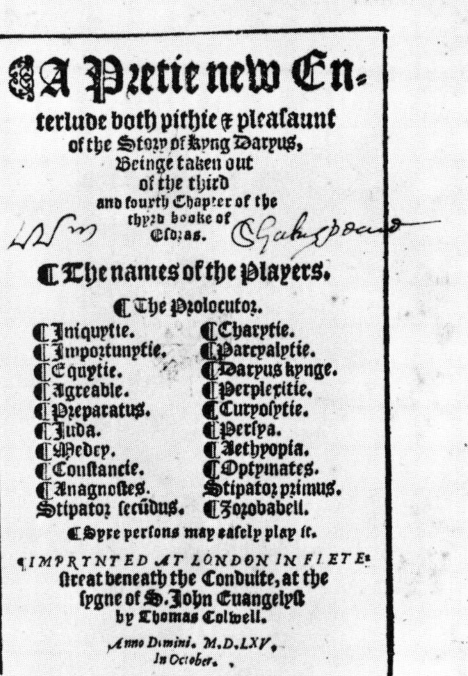

A Pretie new Enterlude both pithie & pleaſaunt of the Story of Kyng Daryus, Beinge taken out of the third and fourth Chapter of the thyrd booke of Eſdras.

The names of the Players.

The Prolocutor.

Iniquytie.	Charytie.
Importunytie.	Parcyalytie.
Equytie.	Daryus kynge.
Agreable.	Perplexitie.
Preparatus.	Curyoſytie.
Iuda.	Perſya.
Medey.	Aethyopia.
Conſtancie.	Optymates.
Anagnoſtes.	Stipator primus.
Stipator ſecũdus.	Zorobabell.

Syxe perſons may eaſely play it.

IMPRYNTED AT LONDON IN FLETE-ſtreat beneath the Conduite, at the ſygne of S. John Euangelyſt by Thomas Colwell.

Anno Domini. M.D.LXV. In October.

An Ireland forgery

HENRY E. HUNTINGTON LIBRARY AND ART GALLERY

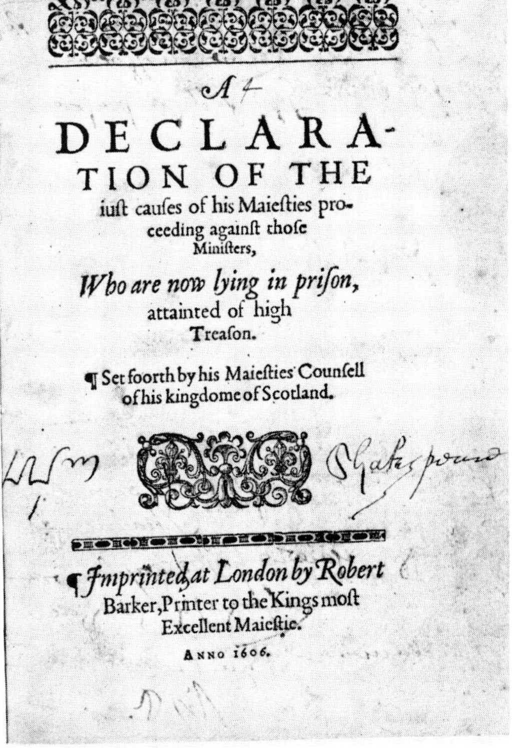

A DECLARATION OF THE iuſt cauſes of his Maieſties proceeding againſt thoſe Miniſters,

Who are now lying in priſon, attainted of high Treaſon.

¶ Set foorth by his Maieſties Counſell of his kingdome of Scotland.

¶ *Imprinted at London by Robert* Barker, Printer to the Kings moſt Excellent Maieſtie.

ANNO 1606.

Another of Ireland's characteristic forgeries

HENRY E. HUNTINGTON LIBRARY AND ART GALLERY

HENRY E. HUNTINGTON LIBRARY AND ART GALLERY

An obvious forgery (not by Ireland) in a law book

So by 1580, Shakespeare could have heard, or read about, or witnessed trials concerning *felo-de-se* in Stratford, or London. Fripp's own opinion on these matters appeared seven years after his death in his biography entitled *Shakespeare, Man and Artist* as seen through the press by F. C. Wellstood: "The future poet was 'most manifestly' trained in an attorney's office, probably that of Henry Rogers, the town clerk."[9] Fripp is the most insistent of scholars in his claim and yet, ironically, by pointing to still another source for *felo-de-se* in Stratford, in addition to the one in Plowden's *Reports*, he tends to weaken either as a primary source: i.e. Shakespeare could have heard about such a case from a source in Stratford or read about one in London. Thus the mere knowledge of *felo-de-se* does not prove him to have been a lawyer's clerk. On the other hand, the amount, diversity, and complexity of Shakespeare's legal knowledge was not so generally available as that regarding *felo-de-se*. Evidence presented in later chapters will suggest that although "We need not claim for the Poet profound knowledge of the law," we have grounds to do so if we wish. In support of this, and despite Fripp's weakness of presentation, his accumulation of learned opinion and of citations from the works is impressive.

In the highly respected work of E. K. Chambers, the assertion that Shakespeare was an attorney's clerk is viewed not so much with skepticism as with scorn for those who go beyond the evidence, as does Fripp on occasion. It is mainly through Chambers' caution (and Schoenbaum's criticism) that the idea of Shakespeare as the attorney's clerk has suffered eclipse. The idea has lost respect in the scholarly community. Yet the manner of its dismissal is no less assertive than some of the claims which Chambers and Schoenbaum attack:

> As with Shakespeare's general learning, so with his law. His writing abounds in legal terminology, closely woven into the structure of his metaphor. Here, again, the knowledge is extensive rather than exact. It is shared by other

> dramatists. Our litigious ancestors had a familiarity with legal processes, from which we are happily exempt. But many have thought that Shakespeare must have had some professional experience of a lawyer's office, although this was not the final opinion of the much-quoted Lord Campbell; and there are those who tell you by which Stratford attorney he was employed. This is only one instance of the willingness of conjecture to step in where no record has trod. On similar grounds Shakespeare has been represented as an apothecary and a student of medicine.[10]

Chambers is correct in noting that the legal terms permeate the plays by sheer quantity and depth of reference. That some of them from time to time are not exact is not necessarily due to the lack of Shakespeare's knowledge (and after all he is not in court) but is attributable to the character portrayed, and more likely than not the audience for whom the play is written, as Shakespeare frequently bothered to translate Latinisms in his text ("a phantasma, or a hideous dream." [*Julius Caesar* II. i. 65]) and explain that "water-thieves" are "pirates" (*The Merchant of Venice* I. iii. 22). The other dramatists using legal terms, sometimes with greater concentration and erudition (i.e. not translating the Latin title for a writ or a law phrase) were themselves either noverints, law students, university trained, or were writing specifically for a legal or academic audience. It can be observed in passing that Shakespeare's father's occupation and personal conduct of his affairs brought him up against the law quite often, but that does not show to what extent Shakespeare was involved in these legal actions nor explain the breadth and depth of his early and increasing legal knowledge. Of course if it is believed that his contact with his father's civil business, and personal, legal affairs was intimate enough to give him a background comparable to that of a lawyer's clerk, then the case is made from another route to the same effect, and well taken. If he merely researched the law to prepare himself for, say, *Merchant of Venice*, then his use of the variety of legal terminology would not be so pervasive in other plays. Lord Campbell's opinion is cited by Chambers as having changed, which is correct and understandable since it was originally based on very few, and relatively superficial, references to begin with.

What helped change opinions about Shakespeare's law background was the emerging notion by scholar-teachers and educators that Shakespeare taught school. But this is even less likely than his having been a solicitor's clerk, since his schooling, even if completed, would not qualify him for such a position. If a tutor (rather than a schoolmaster with a B. A. or M. A. from Cambridge or Oxford), he was probably not engaged by the gentry who would prefer someone from one of the Universities. Rather it would be his handwriting skills which would serve him, being a talent valued in a copyist, scrivener, noverint, or attorney's clerk. Careless conjecture has led holders of the opinion of a clerkship to become sitting ducks for the opposition, as the former claim without equivocation to know which office he worked in and when he was there.

Nonlawyers of that school of thought have often not had all the evidence at hand and have also weakened their case by citing as professional legalisms what could come from several, even relatively brief and superficial encounters and observations at the law courts or with Inns of Court students, or from a book, and have not employed the legal documents of the Shakespeare family, their complexity and their long-term influence. In a final comment on Chambers: by no means can one subscribe to his claim that "on similar grounds" Shakespeare could be represented as an apothecary, a student of medicine, a sailor or a soldier; which is not to say he could not have been any or all of these, but simply that there is no comparison between the body of evidence supporting a legal background and that supporting any other. Chambers' response has not suppressed completely the claim to a legal career, as it reappears with F. E. Halliday:

> If he [William Shakespeare] could not go to Oxford to be trained for one of the learned professions, he could begin more humbly in Stratford, perhaps as a clerk in a lawyer's office. There were plenty of possible openings: William Court was a lawyer, so was his former schoolmaster, Walter Roche, or his father might well have got him into the service of the town clerk, Henry Rogers.
>
> If Shakespeare did begin his career in this way, as an articled clerk to an attorney, it would account for his remarkable knowledge of law, legal terms and procedure. Of course, when he went to London he would pick up a good deal of legal jargon from the young men of the inns of court, but his knowledge seems to be something more professional than this, . . . The point need not be laboured, for there are few scenes in Shakespeare without some legal reference or image.[11]

Totally ignored by the scholarly community is E. B. Everitt's *The Young Shakespeare* (1954), which carefully provides photographic evidence of Shakespeare's law hand possibly present in a number of documents—conveyances, bonds, letters, play manuscripts, petitions, bills to Chancery, wills, etc. One reason for this treatment of Everitt may be because his case is incompletely researched and clearly overstated at points. But he is persuasive when he suggests that much attributed to the Stratford clerk Francis Collins (such as Shakespeare's will) is beyond Collins' writing skill. Everitt is helpful in introducing the possibility that Shakespeare's hand may be discoverable in more than one style with similar personal characteristics, and particularly that a body of his handwriting may be in law hand and hence mistakenly not considered that of the dramatist. Everitt also raises suggestive questions about plays written, and theatrical companies worked for, by Shakespeare during the silent years. He does this from documentary evidence regarding legal orthography, calligraphy, and the dramatist's early poetic style. He should not be overlooked, but one must treat his exposition with care.

To date the most recent references in passing to a period of Shakespeare's life at the law are those by Anthony Burgess, whose novel *Nothing Like the Sun* has Will Shakespeare a Gloucestershire tutor and then a lawyer's clerk. In his delightful biography, *Shakespeare* (1970), Burgess says: "Shakespeare, a great amateur of the law who had once, some of us think, been a near professional at it, had plenty of scope for litigation in his retirement." (p. 234). The remark is somewhat indicative of the general feeling, held by others, that Shakespeare mentioned law in his plays but was not personally involved with it to any great degree until after he stopped writing.

In Burgess we witness the revival of the conviction that Shakespeare was closely associated with law at an earlier period:

> There is a great deal about Shakespeare the lawyer's clerk, and the image of a young man with a beard and receding hair, scratching away at conveyances in dusty chambers, has assumed the status almost of a portrait from the life. The fact is that, though Shakespeare shows himself the Autolycus of most professions and trades, he exhibits in the legal department, more authority than is proper to a mere snapper-up of unconsidered trifles. Admittedly, he was a buyer of property and had the countryman's shrewd eye for sharp practice, but the flow of legal jargon in both the plays and the sonnets sounds as though it comes from the lawyer's, not the client's, side of the desk. (*p.* 50).

Thus many biographers have clung to the conviction of Shakespeare's legal experience. On the other hand, such scholars as Chambers and Schoenbaum have sought to eradicate this claim, using regretfully less evidence than the advocates. Yet it is this position of Schoenbaum's and Chambers' which has endangered the validity of any new evidence. Scholarship, which should carefully but fearlessly weigh the pros and cons of new documentary evidence, has actually been not only timid but even reluctant to advance new finds in this area for fear of adding fuel to an old controversy so poorly argued, yet still passionately maintained.

This is precisely the fate which has befallen the single most valuable object or article pertaining to Shakespeare outside of England. This is the Shakespeare autograph—only the seventh known—discovered by librarians at the Folger Shakespeare Library in Washington, D. C. in 1938. Although this extraordinary bit of faded writing has been known to scholars for some time, some strange reticence of scholastic perversity has prevented giving it consideration in print. Thus, once again, the data, in this case a primary artifact, supporting Shakespeare's legal interest and connections, although present for some time, has been virtually ignored by scholars, critics, and biographers. The implications of the Lambarde signature have not been pursued. It has been put to no biographical use to indicate Shakespeare's intellectual or personal concern about the law or legal figures. The finding, rediscovery and authentication of the only Shakespeare signature outside England, rescued from time, disbelief and neglect, is an account of great import.

3. *The Shakespeare Signature in the Folger Library*

RODERICK L. EAGLE, a contributor to the Francis Bacon Society's journal *Baconiana* since 1913, now residing in Falmouth, Cornwall, was walking by a junk shop in Perry Vale, Forest Hill, a southeastern suburb of London in 1915. In the window, otherwise filled with customary rubble, rubbish, and clutter of old tennis rackets, was a book in a vellum binding, considerably warped. Mr. Eagle decided to buy what was to be the oldest printed book among his antiquarian possessions. From the old woman who kept the shop, he purchased for 2s 6d. (about 60¢) a volume that turned out to be a copy of the first edition of William Lambarde's *Archaionomia* (the Greek title reads "ancient laws") printed in 1568. The book was the first printing ever of a text in Anglo-Saxon. The text was composed of old English laws compiled from a manuscript, and accompanied by William Lambarde's Latin translation. A signature of "W SHAKSPERE", with several water blotches and heavily creased, was just visible in the upper, right-hand corner of the title page. Roderick Eagle, an avid Baconian, was never particularly interested in the signature as he felt certain it was one of the numerous forgeries of the late eighteenth century. While recognizing that the dramatist's knowledge of law was remarkable, but believing that Anglo-Saxon laws could only have been of use or interest to the higher members of the legal profession, and that the legal Latin of Lambarde would have been too technical and difficult for Shakespeare, Eagle concluded that the autograph must be a forgery by a certain William Henry Ireland, who, while a conveyancer's clerk, had forged many documents supposedly pertaining to the dramatist and put his version of Shakespeare's signature in a number of old books. There was, however, additional writing. An address on the back of the vellum cover read "Mr. Wm Shakspeare lived at No. 1 Little Crown St. Westminster, N. B.— near Dorset Steps, St. James's Park." This Mr. Eagle correctly concluded, must have been written after the latter half of the eighteenth century, as no houses (or at least very few, and not with any regularity) were numbered before an Act of Parliament in 1765 ordering the numbering of locations to avoid confusion. The address tended to confirm Roderick Eagle's favoring an Ireland forgery, since Ireland was operating in the 1790's.

Mr. William T. Smedley, who was the Secretary and head of the Bacon Society at the time, was interested in the typography of the sixteenth century. To correct an error of statement about ornamental borders by Smedley which had been published, Roderick Eagle loaned Smedley the Lambarde volume around 1920. Eagle wrote at one time requesting the book's return, but Smedley never gave it back. Since Smedley was elderly and a very sick man, Eagle did not pursue the matter. Upon Smedley's death the executors included Eagle's Lambarde book containing the then completely obscured signature in a Sotheby's sale in 1938. The signature had faded from rubbing, and had been folded and crushed accordion-fashion several times.

The volume was tied up with three other books and advertised in a catalogue for a miscellaneous sale to be held on November 29, 1938. It was one of four books in item number 505, described as follows:

> James I. Apologie for the Oath of Allegiance,S.T.C. 14402; calf, 1609, . . . Heylyn (Peter) *Microcosmos*. . . , etc. (4).

At this point the narrative can be picked up from the last five pages of a lengthy article on other matters by Giles E. Dawson, paleographer of the Folger Shakespeare Library.[12]

> Since the Folger Library did not have a copy of Heylyn's *Microcosmos*, Dr. [Joseph Quincy] Adams [Director of the Folger] sent in a bid—a very small bid [of one pound], which represented what he thought the Heylyn item alone was worth.[13] The bid was successful, and in due course the four books arrived. The two unnamed volumes of the lot proved to be *Leycester's Commonwealth*, 1641, and William Lambarde's *APXAIONOMIA*, 1568. The latter was found in stiff vellum and was not in very good condition, the title page, for one thing, being dog'eared and crumpled. Upon careful examination, however, it proved to be by far the most interesting volume of the four. (*p.* 96).

A copy of *Archaionomia*, 1568, in better condition was already possessed by the Folger, and so this copy could have been discarded. Fortunately, the address on the back of the cover and some writing on the top portion of the title page were visible. It was decided that this copy of *Archaionomia* should be sent to the Library's binder in preparation for its placement on the shelf in the stacks. He ironed out the title page and thus revealed the writing in the narrow upper margin which read (prophetically): "This to be kept for the impression is [hole in page where the word "out" was probably written] nor like to be renew'd." The binder decided to send it back to the librarians for further investigation. In examining the returned volume, James G. McManaway, the curator of the Folger, noticed just beneath the words "nor like to be," partly in and partly above the upper right-hand portion of the ornamental border, a signature. When Giles E. Dawson entered the examination a moment later, McManaway tested his reaction by reading the signature as that of the British historian W. Slayter (1587–1647). At first perhaps half in jest, perhaps in amazement, perhaps in incredulity, Dawson suggested it appeared to him as "W. Shakspere." That moment, as far as it can be determined, was the first time anyone had identified to another person the signature as possibly being that of the dramatist. McManaway, Dawson, and Dr. Edwin E. Willoughby subjected the newly discovered find to careful paleographic study with the aid of magnifying glasses, ultraviolet and infrared light, and subsequent photographs and examination from enlargements.

The signature on the front had faded from wear since Eagle first saw it, but it was still fairly visible from the reverse side in the form of mirror-writing. Putting the back of the page up to a mirror, the signature plainly read "W Shakspere" with, as Dawson points out, enough space for an "m" between the first initial and the surname. Photographs under various light sources and blow-ups of these confirm the reading of the individual letters of the signature. A blotch from a water drop makes the end of the name difficult to decipher with the unaided eye: -ere, -ear, or -er? The enlarged photograph clearly favors the letters as -ere. This is the portion of Shakespeare's signature that is always the most difficult to read, and that Shakespeare frequently varied in its execution. It was for a time felt, and some still feel, that Shakespeare never spelled his name -eare, or -ear, for in the six known signatures it was Shakspē (in two),[14] or Shaksp, or as on the will, Shakspere (at least twice), but the third signature, on the final sheet of the will, now is generally believed to be "Shakspeare."

The library staff then turned to writing up, reporting and publishing their amazing literary find. Giles Dawson in his article admits:

> Some months before this paper was undertaken [in 1942] the MSS and books which it discusses were stored in an inacessible place [Converse Library, Amherst College, Amherst, Massachusetts] for the duration of the war, and I was forced to rely upon such notes and photographs as were available, and occasionally upon memory alone. (*p.* 77).

This is unfortunate, since Dawson's article describing the uncovering and initial surmises, written in 1942 and published in 1943, is one of only two in print,[15] and thus the only available information for anyone determining the claim for or against authenticity of the signature. The other article disclosing further examination and asserting authenticity, published subsequently in June 1943, is that of J. Q. Adams the Director and is dependent upon an earlier report by Dawson speaking for the members of the staff upon Adams' request about their findings. The notes Dawson made in preparation for this report became those upon which he based his article in 1942, without recourse to the volume itself. It is not clear whether or not J. Q. Adams' article in 1943, when it goes beyond Dawson in its own assertions, concerning the directive being possibly in Lambarde's hand and the presence of a "superscript m" (the former offered without substantiation, and the latter not present) is also based upon notes and photographs, as the volume had not been in the library since early 1942. This is important insofar as Adams introduces the feature of the "superscript m" which is not discernible in the book itself upon close examination.

Dawson omits at least four additional crucial features: three of these are visible in the photographs (although only one of these in the more frequently reproduced photograph from the back);[16] and the remaining characteristic of Shakespeare he does not discern and is usually absent from forgeries (particularly those of William Henry Ireland) is only visible if seen under a light source other than that employed by any of these earlier photographs. At least Dawson has warned his reader that he was not working with the original artifact; and his position is far more cautious in the setting forth of his data than is Adams. In fact, unlike the wording of Adams' article it is neither a claim for authenticity, nor does it purport to be a definitive examination. However, neither Dawson nor Adams, nor the other examiners followed up these reports. The reports will be examined subsequently in detail. Nor did they feel that they needed to open the question upon any additional findings, one way or the other, when the volume returned to Washington, D. C. after the war.

Ironically, one of the initial discoverers of the signature, James G. McManaway, has not committed his views to print although in reports on the library he has quoted J. Q. Adam's statement: ". . . there seems to be no reason to question its being the autograph of the poet."[17] Needless to say, the titles and placement of the two articles, report and subsequent passing references have managed to place all the information beyond the reach of any bibliographies, particularly since only one article's title bears the dramatist's name.[18] The one that does (Adams') is not in a Shakespearean, nor American, nor major journal, and the body of the other article (Dawson's) tends to deal with general and diverse topics; hence the data is virtually unknown to the Shakespearean profession.

Considering the implications of contacts, influence, interest, bodies of knowledge, and career background carried by the dramatist's signature in a Latin law book, little has been done to follow up on the autograph possessed by the Folger and very little has appeared in print, so little that to call it "disputed"[19] is to belie the fact that it has been virtually ignored. It has never been included in any study or reference as having any relevance to Shakespeare's biography, intellectual background, or his plays. The signature has not been contested with any thoroughness, and the only article purporting to approach a claim for authenticity is flawed in its assertions. The passing support in a note, article or report add up to mere agreements, sometimes on additional but unsatisfactory evidence; all will be analyzed subsequently.

The first mention of the signature in print is in a progress report by J. Q. Adams on the Folger for 1931–1941, published in 1942, (pp. 30–32) to the trustees of Amherst College who oversee the Library. This is expanded in Adams' article previously noted for the Rylands Library, which will be examined after looking at the article by Giles E. Dawson that preceded it. Dawson, in his attempt to find more corroboration for authenticity, was unable to find on any map a Little Crown Street in Westminster, or a Dorset Steps near St. James' Park, and so only uses the address as confirming the presence of the signature as early as c. 1785–1800, but that evidence does not rule out an eighteenth century forgery by, say, Ireland. Dawson goes on to examine the signature itself:

> The capital S and the h resemble those in one or two of the known signatures; the W, what we can see of it, follows the pattern of several of the six; and the whole is much more like Shakespeare's known signatures than any forgery I have ever seen or any of the *possibly genuine* signatures. I can say with confidence that it is not the works of William Henry Ireland. (*p.* 98).

Comparing this signature with the Ireland forgeries in the possession of the Huntington Library in California, I agree with Giles Dawson, as anyone would seeing them side by side, that the Shakespeare signature in Lambarde's book appears far more genuine than any of Ireland's, which are quite distinct unto themselves.

The Folger autograph, furthermore, is neither a copy of, nor similar to, the probably forged and incompletely formed signature in W. Hall's copy of Ovid's *Metamorphoses* (1502) and in Florio's translation of Montaigne's *Essays* (1603), both previous to their disclosure known to be in sources, or reading matter, associated with particular plays by Shakespeare. The Lambarde autograph resembles a composite, rather than a copy, of any one of the signatures already determined to be genuine. Its placement in the printed decoration was almost certainly done without the idea of drawing immediate attention to itself; and its being in a law book in Latin with a Greek title flies in the face of Ben Jonson's still widely accepted, however inaccurately interpreted remark that Shakespeare knew small Latin and less Greek. These factors tend to rule out a forgery. There is a logical connection between the Elizabethan writing or warning that this is a copy of a sparse edition and Shakespeare's feeling he should put his name in the book, to preserve it from loss. Dawson concludes, ". . . it is difficult to see how this signature can be the work of a forger in any period." (p. 99).

Possibilities for its presence, other than by authentic means, are equally ruled out:

> No one who for some unknown reason jotted Shakespeare's name down on a title page, at some time before 1800, could by accident have made it resemble so closely the dramatist's signature; nor could another person named W. Shakespeare have done so. (*p.* 100).

Dawson proceeds to his conclusion with dramatic understatement:

> The fourth possibility, the only one remaining, is that William Shakespeare wrote his signature on this title page, perhaps because he owned the book—a strange volume indeed for his library.

Not at all strange, as has been and will be shown, considering Shakespeare's connections with the law, his possible relations with Lambarde himself, and the nature of the volume's contents. All these link him to legal interests. But as for Dawson, all that he was prepared to say was that the only feasible explanation of the writing is that Shakespeare wrote his signature on this title page, adding ". . . we do not feel that actual proof can yet be brought forward. My own account of it has not been given with a view to persuading anyone that the signature is a genuine one . . ." In other words, Dawson can only say he finds it impossible to hold that the signature is a forgery of any kind, but the authentication must await "actual proof."

J. Q. Adams went further. He felt the evidence, particularly when amplified by scientific investigation and equipment, to be ultimately sufficient to claim that in all likelihood the signature was genuine. Adams, in his "Report on Progress" refers to the Lambarde book as ". . . a volume that seems to have come from the library of William Shakespeare." (p. 30). He states from his researches that the writing "This is to be kept. . . , etc" is "in a handwriting resembling that of Lambarde, . . ." (the Folger has become the main repository of important Lambarde manuscripts). The Italianate, Elizabethan hand in which the notice is written is close enough to that of Lambarde's to justify, but not guarantee, this claim on Adams' part. Adams indicates the address is untraceable, but continues to be very positive in his reporting:

> Though very faint because of the waterstain, the signature bore every indication of being authentic. After the bibliographers at the Library had subjected it to careful paleographical study and to close examination under ultraviolet and infrared light, and had reported favorably as to its genuineness, it was submitted to the experts at the United States Archives for a thorough study. With the cooperation of the Archivist, Dr. Connor, and of Dr. Tate, the distinguished authority on questioned documents, the signature was subjected, in the well-equipped laboratory of the Archives, to exhaustive microscopic, chemical, photographic, and other tests, and to a detailed comparison with the sig-

> natures of the poet accepted as genuine. At the end of several months of investigation, Dr. Tate reported that, after applying all the tests known to him, he could discover no evidence that the signature was not contemporary with the poet and hence what it purported to be, and that, after comparing its individual letters with those of the acknowledged signatures of Shakespeare, he believed it to be in all likelihood from the same hand. (*p.* 31).

J. Q. Adams continues and again goes beyond Dawson to state: "The fact, too, that no earlier reference to the volume is to be found is an argument in favor of the authenticity of the highly important signature it bears. Absolute certainty cannot now be established; but so far as modern science can tell, no reason exists to question the antiquity of the signature, and a paleographical study clearly points to its being a genuine autograph of the poet." Then Adams introduces an interesting interpretation of what is on the title page; assuming that the notice was written by Lambarde who was aware of the publication status of the edition, he says:

> One is tempted to ask: Did Lambarde present the volume to Shakespeare with the injunction to keep it since the edition was exhausted and not 'like to be reprinted [renew'd]'—a prediction that proved to be true?
> "*Report on Progress*" (*pp.* 31–32).

In June, 1943, Adams recounted the discovery in the *Bulletin of the John Rylands Library*. The editor of the *Bulletin* in some prefatory comments says,

> On looking up the Sotheby catalogue, which had proved so lucky for the Folger, we were struck by a fact which surely adds a piece of historic irony to the discovery. The Folger item comes from a lot described by the auctioneer as 'A very extensive collection of books designed to illustrate the Baconian theory of the authorship of Shakespeare's plays.' (*pp.* 234–235).

This lot came, of course, from the library of W. T. Smedley. If Smedley were indeed out to prove that Bacon

The view of all wch matter, beinge presented to her most
wise and princelie consideration of her matie, she was
pleased to demise these profites and Fines for other .5. yeares
to beggyn at the feast of the Annunciation 1590. in the 32th
yeare of her owne Reigne, for the yearely Rent formerly reser-
ved upo the leases to the Earle: Within the compasse of wch
.5. yeares (expired at the Annunciatio 1595.) there was advaun-
ced to her matie benefite by this Service, the whole Summe of
beyonde the auncient yearely revenewe, that
(before any lease) weare usually made of these Finances.
To the wch if there be added for the gayne
growen to her matie by the yearely encrease of 300li in Rent
fro the first demise to the Earle until the tyme of his death,
together wth the Summe of clearly wonne in
these first Termes bought of the Countesse; Then the whole
comoditie to her matie fro the first Institutio of this office
till thende of these last five yeares (expired at the Annunciation 1595) shall appeare to bee To the
wch Summe also, if fro wch the Earle and the
countesse Lessees hereby bee likewise adioyned, then the
whole profites, taken in these 29. yeares, that is, fro the first
demise to the ende of the last, for her matie, the Earle, and
the Countesse will amounte to

This Labour hitherto thus luckilie succeeding, the Deputies
in this Office, fynding by dayly proofe that it was wearysome
to the Subiect to travayle to dyverse places and therevt sundry
handes, for the pursuing of comon Seasures of Landes (eyther

William Lambarde's Italianate hand from a manuscript now at the Folger Library, Washington, D.C.

wrote Shakespeare's plays, a theory based chiefly upon the fact that their author must have had an erudite knowledge of English law, one can only imagine how he felt when Roderick Eagle lent him a law book with William Shakespeare's autograph in it!

Eagle never suspected the signature was genuine; Smedley knew of the Ireland forgeries and what they looked like. What would he be likely to do? Once he had the volume in his possession he 1] could have returned it to Eagle, releasing evidence of Shakespeare's advanced interest, or high-level, personal contact with English law for some "Stratfordian" to seize upon. Or, 2] he could have sought to expose it as some kind of forgery, say, by Ireland, which, however, unfortunately for the Baconian theory, it did not resemble, nor any forgery for that matter. Or, 3] he could claim that Mr. Eagle possessed an invaluable Shakespearean relic on the basis of its authenticity, but what would that do to his cherished Baconian theory? Or, 4] he could leave it hidden in his private library, perhaps carefully folding down the top right-hand corner of the title page in a series of accordion-type creases to keep the signature from view until he decided what to do with the evidence, hiding the signature: whereas the autograph was visible despite warping of vellum to Eagle. Or, 5] did he simply dismiss it out of hand, forgetting to return it, the volume becoming damaged in subsequent handling, obscuring the corner of the page? At any rate, between Mr. Eagle's nonbelief and Mr. Smedley's silence, the volume reamined unknown beyond these figures after its purchase in 1915 until its sale in 1938. The mystery still remains as to where it had been from Elizabethan times through the late eighteenth century, when the address was added, until 1915. A conjecture will be offered later suggesting how the volume might have remained in the Lambarde family from the sixteenth to the twentieth century.

Returning to Adams' article, the author, unaware of any previous owners of the valuable possession, focuses on the individual letters' placement and appearance within the signature. Adams errs in insiting that the blank space between the capital W or first initial and the capital S of the last name is for a "superior m" (p. 257). He believes that the Folger signature must match, or closely resemble, the signature on the tab to the seal of the mortgage-deed for Blackfriars (1613), which is the only genuine signature in which Shakespeare abbreviates his first name merely to a W and an m. The m, however, appears in the superscript position (W^m) because of the cramped space of the tab which also forced Shakespeare to abbreviate his last name. The signature is genuine, but the superscript m, hence, is abnormally in the superior location, meaning that *if Shakespeare's first name is abbreviated as* Wm, *the* m *does not have to be in the superscript position to make the signature genuine.* There is no evidence that Shakespeare ever signed his name with just a W. What Adams believes to be the superscript m in the Lambarde signature is clearly visible from the front as merely the flourish of the W, characteristic of Shakespeare. This flourish is not visible in the reversed photograph taken from the back of the title page. Adams' conviction that the signature is undoubtedly that of the dramatist, which goes beyond Dawson's cautious exposition of the problem of authentication, is based upon a misreading or misrepresentation of the evidence in the original. In fact, a proper reading of this critical area of the signature, as will be shown, finally completes the logical circle of evidence necessary to furnish the direct "actual proof" of authenticity from data in the signature alone; data which Dawson sought and Adams did not feel he needed to convince himself any more than he already was of the signature's authenticity. With the articles by Dawson and Adams as the only evidence for scholars outside the Folger, Dawson stepped back from any claim of authenticity in print, Adams moved into a position of strong assertion on false and partial evidence concerning a superscript "m," and all others remained silent.

No wonder there has been confusion, skepticism, and,

worse, a general lack of awareness in the profession of even the existence of what the majority of scholars who have come in contact with it believe could be the seventh known Shakespeare signature. With no knowledge of any evidence of immediate connections between William Shakespeare and William Lambarde, Adams nevertheless concludes:

> That the two men of letters in the small world of literary London knew each other is hardly to be doubted, and that Shakespeare was interested, as was Ben Jonson, in Anglo-Saxon law seems highly likely. We must be content, however, with the likelihood that here at least we have a volume that was once actually in the possession of the poet. (*p*. 259).

But no one has followed this up with research into Shakespeare's reasons for possessing the book; or when, how, or where he might have come in contact with its author.

There were several scattered commentaries upon Adams' article. Ambrose Heal of Beaconsfield in the British *Notes and Queries* for October 23, 1943 (p. 263) responded by providing the evidence that Little Crown Street in Westminster near Dorset Steps had existed and that the address was at least a genuine one after all, if not necessarily a genuine one for Shakespeare. Just after Ambrose Heal's note (pp. 263–264), there is one by Roderick Eagle, who rules "out any suggestion of there having been another William Shakespeare who had lived on the site of Little Crown Street, Westminster" because of the similarities between the Shakespeare signature in Lambarde and the genuine ones. But he persists in his belief that it is a forged copy of that of the Blackfriars mortgage-deed. He offers a fact in support of his opinion:

> I am informed by an expert in old manuscripts that the ink of Shakespeare's period contained size and would not, therefore, sink into the paper to the extent of necessitating the signature being photographed from the reverse side of the paper. This had to be done in the case of the alleged Shakespeare signature in the Folger copy of Lambarde's

'Archaionomia.' This being so, the inference is that the signature is a forgery in ink made to resemble that of the period, but not containing the ingredients formerly used.

The tests recognized, however, that the lack of size does not rule out the possibility that Shakespeare's ink was inadequately stirred, of different composition from the regular, or from the legal ink used in the Italianate hand on the same page; or that dampness, time and the condition of the paper and ink combined to produce the ink's sink-through. The fading from the front in all likelihood happened since 1800 when the person furnishing the address found the signature visible, and even possibly since 1920 when Eagle read the signature clearly. The testimony of the paleographical examinations by Joseph Quincy Adams, Giles E. Dawson, coauthor with Laetitia Kennedy-Skipton of *Elizabethan Handwriting 1500–1650* (1966), James G. McManaway, Edwin E. Willoughby, and the evidence from the National Archivist, Dr. Connor, and from Dr. Tate, after several months of applying exhaustive photographic, microscopic, chemical, and all the other laboratory tests known by him, all point in the same direction: no evidence was forthcoming which ruled out the conclusion that the signature was contemporary with Shakespeare's time, and was that of the dramatist. Clearly, in a matter of such moment, as new and more sophisticated methods of testing become available, they will be employed on the signature. But, until this happens, the present conclusions indicate that here, indeed, is William Shakespeare's seventh known signature.

In the April 21, 1945 *Notes and Queries* appeared a brief piece entitled "Shakespeare's Signature in Lambarde's APXIAONOMIA" (pp. 162–163) by Professor Frank Caldiero of New York. Caldiero states that the signature's ending in *-ere* assures him of its genuineness since Malone in 1796 said that that was how Shakespeare spelled his name most often, and never with an *a*; whereas what gave William Henry Ireland away was that he used such an *a*. Professor Caldiero was, however, incorrect in that the clearest signature on the Will is, in fact, spelled *-eare*.

In 1948, James G. McManaway quotes the general conclusions on the signature in a report on the Folger for *Shakespeare Survey* (p. 61). In the same journal for 1950, an article appears on a general topic concerning a paragraph in which seven sentences are devoted to the Folger Shakespeare signature in the Lambarde book. Despite its brevity, it is the only attempt to offer a criticism of any of the reports by the staff at the Folger. Charles J. Sisson in "Studies in the Life and Environment of Shakespeare since 1900" makes the following remarks with regard to the chief claimants for authentic signatures;

> There have been various attempts to add to the number of authentic signatures of Shakespeare by the discovery of books bearing his name in writing. There is little support for the signature in the Bodleian copy of Ovid's *Metamorphoses* (1502), but that in the British Museum copy of Florio's *Montaigne* (1603) is accepted by E. K. Chambers, though not by E. M. Thompson. A serious claim is made for a signature 'W. Shakspere' in a copy of William Lambard[e]'s *Archaionomia* (1568) purchased for the Folger Library in 1938. J. Q. Adams, in an article in the *Bulletin of the John Rylands Library*, XXVII (1943), maintained the authenticity of the signature. The signature is obscured by the ornament on the title-page over which it is written, and is best examined as an offset on the verso through a looking-glass. The excellent photograph here reproduced (see Plate IB) is thus made from the offset. A number of marked variations from any known signature or from normal Secretary hand causes doubts, after examination of the original, fortified by expert opinion of the reproduction, not least in respect of the *h* and of the style in general. It might perhaps even suggest a memoriter imitation of the Mortgage signature. The claim is, however, supported by the recency of the revelation of the signature in the process of ironing, as also by the references to Shakespeare (written in later) as resident in Westminster. (*p.* 4).

In answer to Sisson: Shakespeare's signatures vary from each other, and Shakespeare apparently did not bother to always follow normal Secretary hand (possibly contaminated by Chancery hand), thus the *h* in the Lambarde book is definitely that of the Deed and of the clearest signature on the Will; and Sisson is probably drawn to the Mortgage signature because of Adams' surmise concerning the superscript *m* in that document. Although the Lambarde signature does have a number of the Mortgage-Deed features, these are not exclusive to the Deed signature, being found also in several of the others.

Hereward T. Price accepts the signature as genuine and uses that fact to support his argument that Shakespeare's Latin was not small and that he had wide intellectual interests.[20] It is astounding to realize that Price is the only one to have used acceptance of the signature to make any comment whatsoever upon its implications for Shakespeare's plays, his life, or his thought.

Whereas one would think that much would inevitably have been made of the implications of the signature, we find only a single noncommittal reference upon its relationship either to Shakespeare or to a connection between Shakespeare and Lambarde. It appears in a chapter devoted to William Lambarde's time at Lincoln's Inn and to his writing of *Archaionomia*, in a full-length biography: *William Lambarde: Elizabethan Jurist 1536–1601* (Rutgers, 1965) by Wilbur Dunkel. This book was researched at the Folger, with acknowledgements to Giles E. Dawson and James G. McManaway. Here is Dunkel's passing reference to the Lambarde signature:

> A copy of *Archaionomia* in the Folger Shakespeare Library has the signature of William Shakespeare, believed by many scholars to be authentic. This is significant, as Shakespeare was not born until 1564 and thus was only four years old when *Archaionomia* was printed. This book apparently continued in esteem for many years, or why would Shakespeare have acquired it? But no arguments

> need to be advanced to support the continued use of this book even after the death of Lambarde, since the common lawyers in the seventeenth century avidly searched it for precedents which they evidently highly esteemed. (*p.* 35).

It was this reference which brought the Lambarde signature to my attention in the fall of 1969 at the Warburg Institute in London. I was on a sabbatical from Wesleyan University pursuing a study of primary documents which might have influenced Shakespeare's use and treatment of law in his plays. But it was not until the spring of 1971 that I was able to travel to the Folger to view the signature for myself, and no other references to the signature had come to my attention in the interim, basically due to the difficulty in tracing them. I possessed both the knowledge about Elizabethan treatises on law, Chancery, and equity which influenced the plays, and total ignorance of the fact that the signature existed in such scholarly limbo with regard to its authenticity. Upon seeing the signature, I already knew it could make sense that the volume had passed through Shakespeare's hands; as of yet I had not found the numerous points of contact possible between Shakespeare and Lambarde that this present book now discloses; the address was a complete puzzle to me. So I began the task of determining the authenticity to my own satisfaction, and then tracing and finding the various comments made about the signature in print.

I went to the Folger with one scribbled note of connection between Lambarde and Shakespeare which I had encountered in the Shakespeare text I use in my courses.[21] It came from Hardin Craig's edition of Shakespeare's plays:

> The subject of Richard II was a sore one with the queen herself. The note of a conversation with the queen by W. Lambarde, printed by Nichols, *Progresses of Queen Elizabeth* (ed. 1788), I, A-H, page 41, says,
>
> > Her majestie fell upon the reign of King Richard II, saying, I am Richard II, know ye not that? *W. L.* Such a wicked imagination was determined and attempted by

> a most unkind Gent. [i.e. Essex], the most adorned creature that ever your Majestie made. *Her majestie.* He that will forget God, will also forget his benefactors; this tragedy was playd 40tie times in open streets and houses. (*p.* 644).

Shakespeare's tragedy of *Richard II*, which in its fourth act depicts the dethronement of the head of state, was possibly rewritten for the occasion as the scene does not appear in the three earlier quarto editions of 1597 and 1598 (2); it was performed at the Globe upon request and payment of forty shillings over the usual fee by Sir Gelly Meyrick, a follower of the Essex faction, of which Shakespeare's patron was a leading member. The performance took place on a Friday, two days before the Essex rebellion, which was plotted for Sunday noon on February 8, 1601 in London as the crowds came from St. Paul's Cathedral. So it was to William Lambarde, in private audience on August 4, 1601 and reported in his diary, that Queen Elizabeth made her only known reference to William Shakespeare.[22] Perhaps this is merely coincidental, or perhaps she knew that Lambarde, whom she appointed Keeper of the Rolls in the Tower of London on January 21, 1601, had dealings or associations with the author of the play performed before the uprising. The repression of the uprising had produced severe punishments which Shakespeare and his players barely escaped; Shakespeare's patron, the Earl of Southampton, went to the Tower for his part in the attempted uprising. Furthermore, Shakespeare had lavishly praised Essex in *Henry V* (1599):

> How London doth pour out her citizens!
> The major and all his brethren in best sort,
> Like to the senators of the antique Rome,
> With the plebians swarming at their heels,
> Go forth and fetch their conqering Caesar in:
> As by a lower but loving likelihood,
> Were now the general of our gracious empress,
> As in good time he may, from Ireland coming,

Bringing rebellion broached on his sword,
How many would the peaceful city quit,
To welcome him!

(Prologue. Act v. 24–34.)

The actors, through the testimony of Augustine Phillips, a member of Shakespeare's company, made excuses at the trial on February 19, 1601, where Lambarde may have been one of the advisers to the attorneys who conducted the prosecution before a court of peers from the high courts. Phillips said the play was regarded by Shakespeare's group "to be so old and so long out of use [although it had just gone through three quarto editions, two in one year!] that they shold have small or no Company at yt."[23] The court acquitted the actors of any charge of treason, and confined and executed their betters.

Shakespeare's connection with the Essex affair was all too obvious through his praise of the Earl in *Henry V* and his authorship of the deposition scene in *Richard II*. The awareness of Shakespeare's partisanship was something that reached as high as the Queen herself and to the hierarchy of the judicial system, as exemplified by William Lambarde's knowledge that Elizabeth could thus play upon. This being the case, the question that invites itself is how did Shakespeare escape punishment, or even investigation? Who in Court and the courts was running successful interference for him, protection that clearly did not reach to Shakespeare's fellow players on the one hand, or to Shakespeare's patron (the Earl of Southampton) on the other? It is not likely that any help from the Essex faction would serve him in the matter; nor, perhaps, would the opposing party, represented so vehemently in prosection by Bacon, have any reason to belittle the various personages touched by such a treasonous business. Most likely the moderating limitation on the range of prosecution and investigation to prevent counter reactions would come from more neutral parties. Lambarde remained judiciously aloof from such political matters, as Dunkel says in his biography; he did not seek favor, was independent (p. 173), and did not join factions, remaining friends with Egerton, Burghley, Cobham and others during the various political and legal disputes of the time. And so a likely quarter from which such neutral help might have been obtained, or offered, would have been William Lambarde, who could have befriended Shakespeare by the time of the Essex trials as a result of his contacts in the Office of Alienations or Chancery.

Lambarde may have acted as an intercessor between Shakespeare and the nobility earlier. In fact, along with being virtually the Lord Keeper's (Sir Thomas Egerton's) deputy, Lambarde's closest association was with William Brooks, Lord Cobham (Dunkel, pp. 19, 82–88, 157–158 and 161–163). Lambarde was Cobham's executor. Cobham was briefly the Lord Chamberlain (p. 158) succeeding Lord Hunsdon as the official patron of Shakespeare, who was a member of the Lord Chamberlain's Servants. Lord Cobham's famous ancestor was Sir John Oldcastle, Lollard martyr in 1417 under Henry V. Originally Falstaff in Shakespeare's three plays about Henry IV and Henry V had not been "Sir John Falstaff" but rather "Sir John Oldcastle." Someone had relayed the offense this might cause Lord Cobham when Shakespeare published the Quarto of the first part of *Henry IV* in 1598. Shakespeare humorously has Ford, when he tricks Falstaff, take on Cobham's surname of Brook in *Merry Wives of Windsor* (II.ii.160). The change from Oldcastle came just as Shakespeare had his case in Chancery (1597–1599) where Lambarde was in office. Shakespeare removes again, and apologizes for, any confusion between the two Sir Johns in the Epilogue to the second part of *Henry IV* when it is published in 1600 the year between Essex's violent return from Ireland in 1599 and his abortive uprising and trial in 1601.

> One word more, I beseech you. If you be not too much cloyed with fat meat, our humble author will continue the story, with Sir John in it, and make you merry with fair Katharine of France; where, for any thing I know,

> Falstaff shall die of a sweat, unless already a' be killed with your hard opinions; for Oldcastle died a martyr, and this is not the man. My tongue is weary; when my legs are too, I will bid you good night: and so kneel down before you; but, indeed, to pray for the queen. (11.28–38)

Possibly, after initial contact as a result of the Queen's Bench suit (1588–1590) or the Chancery case opening in 1597, Lambarde and Cobham (as Lord Chamberlain in 1598) had prevailed upon Shakespeare to remove the satirical implications from the two parts of *Henry IV* (in 1598 and 1600) and perhaps the Lambarde and the Cobham family moderates could cite this favor and cooperation to protect Shakespeare against official allegations and suspicions. Thus the Queen at her private audience with Lambarde in 1601 may have been offering her references to Shakespeare's participation in the Essex business as a warning, or simply chiding Lambarde, for some part in covering for the famous playwright. No matter what the interpretation of the Queen's remark, it is at least a remarkable, although fortuitous, association between Lambarde and Shakespeare, particularly in comparison to the more direct ones offered at the Inns of Court, courts in Westminster, Office of Composition for the Alienations of Fines, Chancery, and the theatres, which will be documented in subsequent narration in the following chapters.

4. *A Proof of the Authenticity of the Folger Signature*

AT THE FOLGER, STC 15142 (i.e. William Lambarde's *Archaionomia*, 1568, of which the Folger has another, cleaner copy) was brought to me by Mrs. Laetitia Kennedy-Skipton Yeandle of the staff. I examined it, first at my reader's place and subsequently under the ultraviolet light, with Mrs. Yeandle's guidance and observation. None of the photographs of the signature in print are with the benefit of ultraviolet, or infrared light; Dawson admits that his article in 1942 is not based upon having the book in hand and he says merely that there is a space for an *m*; Adams' report (1942) and article (1943) are based upon Dawson; Adams by surmise identifies the signature most closely with that of the Mortgage-Deed having a superscript *m* and concludes 1) that the signature must have been present between 1765 and 1800 to warrant the numbered address in an eighteenth century hand, 2) that nothing from various tests rules out the ink, or characteristics of the hand, from being of Shakespeare's time, 3) that the signature can not be a deliberate nor unintentional forgery, and 4) that while believing in its authenticity, all which remains to be provided is direct, scientific, logical, or corroborating proof that the autograph is genuine. These were the critical circumstances in which the signature existed at the moment when I came upon it.

Close examination of the title page from the front, as opposed to photographs from the back, reveals three short, parallel lines slightly slanted to the right between the W and the S, indicating an ^{m} was placed there, but *on the line*, i.e. in a normal position. The presence of these lines, or at least two of them, is further confirmed by their being accompanied by quill scratches, or tears, in the printed border with which they intersect showing up as white dots in the print, and black lines under the ultraviolet light source. So the *m* is not that of the Mortgage-Deed, in fact of none of the signatures in its placement; but Shakespeare is not cramped in the Lambarde signature as he completes his surname, and evidenced by the Mortgage-Deed signature he would on an occasion abbreviate his first name as simply W with an *m*. Although he may have, there is no evidence that he ever made the abbreviation with just a W. For further confirmation of the presence of the *m* in the regular position, there is a feature far more visible because it can be seen in the photographs from the back, but it has received no previous comment. A short dash appears in a horizontal position between the W and the S. This is Shakespeare's horizontal bar, an acknowledged indication of an abbreviation taking place in his first or last name. We know this from the Belott-Mountjoy Deposition signature which many of the Lambarde signature's features resemble. The first name in the Deposition signature, which he signed May 11, 1612, appears as Willm.

Under ultraviolet light, upon the original page, or by juxtaposing from the front taken under different light sources, one sees superimposed on the printed line of the ornamental border a dot in the middle of the final swirl of the W. The swirl was what Adams mistook for the "superior m." The dot is a paramount personal characteristic of at least three of Shakespeare's signatures, not discernible in two, and faintly present in the Mortgage-Deed, looking with deliberation for it, as it is not an outstanding feature recommending itself to a forger if he were copying it. In other words, if to create the Lambarde signature a forger were copying the Mortgage-Deed, as it is thought by some to resemble most, there would be no dot.

Thus the Lambarde signature, containing no possible errors in spelling or abbreviation; possessing the regular (almost modern) *a* from at least three of the signatures, the particular slant and hook on top and curl on bottom of the *h* from at least two, and the extremely complicated S from at least four, has above all: 1) the W with its swirl and ornamental dot; 2) the abbreviated first name with the most crucial line above the lower case letters of the abbreviation, and 3) the state of the S exclusive to the Belott-Mountjoy Deposition. *This closes the logical circle because the Belott-Mountjoy Deposition signature was not discovered until* 1910 *and the Lambarde signature had to have been written by* 1800. Charles William Wallace and his wife Hulda Alfreda discovered the Belott-Mountjoy documents in the Public Records Office in 1910.

The Shakespeare signature was placed in the Lambarde volume after the Elizabethan Italianate hand and before the eighteenth century hand giving a Westminster address for William Shakespeare.[24] An expert forger, let alone William Henry Ireland, could not have had the information before 1910 to produce a composite (rather than a direct copy of any one signature) containing no errors and a number of features by chance only to be confirmed by the discovery of a genuine signature in the future. A forger working between 1910 and 1915 (when Roderick K. Eagle came across the volume in Perry Vale) would have had to have been doubly clever to be minutely accurate about Shakespeare's signature and have been equally versed with eighteenth century style of hand, content of ink, characteristics of calligraphy, numbering of streets, and obscure addresses. Coupled with this far-ranging expertise he would have to know that Shakespeare would have associations with Lambarde strong enough to override the dramatist's supposed deficiencies in 1] Anglo-Saxon, 2] Latin, 3] Greek, and 4] English law.

The Folger signature is neither sketched nor obviously done with meticulously clear imitation, but in continuous bold strokes and is of the proper height.[25] Its boldness suggests an uncramped situation and also a young hand. The six previously authenticated signatures are known to have been written between 1612 and 1616 because they appear on legal documents dated in his life. *Thus the Lambarde signature is probably the earliest known Shakespeare autograph.* It could have been placed in the book c. 1588–1590 or c. 1597–1601, when connections between Shakespeare and Lambarde were strongest. This would bring it, for confirmation purposes, closer than the others to Shakespeare's generally accepted hand in the manuscript of *The Boke of Sir Thomas More* (1591–92).

There are several facts suggesting the signature is not a forgery. A forger would have placed the signature in the margin, or in an open space for visibility (as in the non-Ireland ones at the Huntington); or, if he placed it on the border to camouflage his errors, he was defeated by the clear view obtainable from the reverse. A forger did not benefit monetarily, nor could he do so academically, since the book is not regarded as a source of any of the plays.

There is evidence providing support for why a genuine signature could be in the volume. A reason for Shakespeare's bothering to put his name in *this* book at all (since no genuine, complete signature exists in any book) may be found in the presence of the directive on the copy already referred to, and believed by Adams to possibly be in Lambarde's own hand: "This to be kept for ye impression is [out] nor like to be renew'd." This statement appears in the top margin, thus predating Shakespeare's signature, and forcing it out of its logical location to the upper right-hand corner, but lower than the previous writing and written across the ornamental border. Two interpretations of this directive are possible. Lambarde, or someone with considerable interest in, and knowledge about publishing, is either warning that the book must not be lost, since it cannot be replaced by another copy of subsequent editions, or asking that the book be returned to its owner. Renaissance readers of rare volumes would sometimes sign them not as owners but as having read a book owned by someone else. Shakespeare placed his signature in the book by William Lambarde because he did not want to lose it, since it would not be replaced, or perhaps because he had to return it to someone, possibly the author himself. He put it in the border to minimize marking the book up, but still facilitating someone's returning it to him if it were misplaced, thus avoiding any loss to himself or possible embarrassment between himself and Lambarde, his social superior.

A reasonable speculation is that the volume might have been returned to William Lambarde and remained in his private library, until sometime before 1915, where such a similar volume (warped vellum cover) remained until the library was broken up in 1924. If this is entertained as a possibility, then the information about Shakespeare's address could have been inserted between 1776 and 1796 by a member of the Lambarde family from some legal source, or possibly even from the private judicial papers of their famous ancestor. If indeed Shakespeare had to return the volume, then it might have been to Lambarde's private library at Lincoln's Inn, then Shakespeare may have come in contact there with other books and manuscripts Lambarde had in his possession pertaining to law and literature. For his early plays, Shakespeare was doing reading in his primary sources during the time of the litigation over Asbies. In order to prepare his history plays, he was reading through Saxo Grammaticus, Holinshed's and Hall's English *Chronicles*, Francois de Belleforest and French chronicles for *Love's Labour's Lost* and *Hamlet.* His short *Comedy of Errors* demanded several sources: Plautus' *Menachmi* was certainly before him to be translated from, and probably with the aid of Ariosto's *Suppositi*, translated and put into dramatic form in *Supposes* by George Gascoigne who had it performed at Gray's Inn. These materials, in turn, became sources for some of the plot elements in the various versions of *The Taming of the Shrew.* Inns of Court plays and entertainments, particularly from Gascoigne (whose *Jocasta* may have influenced Shakespeare's incest-motif in *Hamlet* and early passages of *Pericles*) and the *Gesta Grayorum* revels from Gray's Inn had formative impact upon *Love's Labour's Lost*, *Comedy of Errors*, and *Taming of the Shrew*, as they would his *Twelfth Night* which was performed later in Middle Temple.

Shakespeare was reading John Gower's *Confessio Amantis* for *Comedy of Errors*; Ovid's *Metamorphosis* for *Venus and Adonis*, and *A Midsummer Night's Dream*; and Ovid's *Fasti* for his *Rape of Lucrece*: for *Two Gentlemen of Verona* he was reading Sir Thomas Elyot's *The Boke of the Governour* (which contains a discussion about equity) and John Lyly's *Euphues*, the latter also doing him considerable service for the language style of *Love's Labour's Lost* (Lyly's grandfather was the author of Shakespeare's Stratford Latin grammar text.) He was consuming a number of leading English authors such as Lyly; Sir Philip Sidney's *Arcadia* for *The Two Gentlemen of Verona.* Edmund Spenser's *Faerie Queene* for his early version of *King Lear*, and Geoffrey Chaucer's *Knight's Tale* for *Midsummer Night's Dream* and later *The Two Noble Kinsmen*, perhaps in collaboration with Francis Beaumont from the Inner Temple, and Chaucer's *Legend of Good Women* for *Rape of Lucrece.* Of course Sir Thomas North's (a member of the Inns of Court) translation of Plutarch was an early member of Shakespeare's reading list affecting *Titus Andronicus, Rape of Lucrece, Midsummer Night's Dream*, and possibly *Timon of Athens.*

These are numerous and expensive books for Shakespeare to have possessed. William Lambarde, on the other hand, had a library comparable to the above list. Shakespeare could well have borrowed a copy from the library from time to time as possibly indicated by the signature in *Archaionomia.*[26] The following are just a few items that remained from Lambarde's library, and which Shakespeare might have found of interest, when this library was broken up by Hodgson and Co. in a London sale in 1924.[27] In 1581, William Lambarde purchased his copy of Amyot's French translation of Plutarch's Lives (1574) and he later also picked up North's English translation of Amyot published in 1595 by Shakespeare's Stratford friend Richard Field, who had just published the dramatist's two long narrative poems. Lambarde possessed collections from Cicero: *Ciceronis Epistolae* (1578) and *Rhetorica* (1544); plays by Plautus (*Plauti Comediae*), editions of Chaucer by Speght, Ariosto's *Orlando Furioso* (English translation by John Harrington, member of Lincoln's Inn), a source for *As You Like It*; works by Sir Thomas More (*Utopia*, 1518), an influence upon the *Thomas More* play and *Tempest*; Erasmus, Petrarch (sonnets), Dante (Bardolph's nose?), and Virgil (*Eclogues* in the pastoral comedies and *Aeneid*, 1560, having an influence upon the heroic works of Shakespeare). Lambarde had copies of his works such as *Archaionomia*, 1568, *A*

Perambulation of Kent (1576, revised in 1596), his edition of Fitzherbert on English law (1567); and volumes on manners, government, history, linguistics, law, philosophy and mathematics, such as: Drodorus Siculus's *Historia Graece* (1539), Walder's *Lexicon Graecum* (1539), *Caesaris Commentarii*, 1578 (*Lord Say*. "Kent, in the Commentaries Caesar writ./ Is term'd the civil'st place of all this isle:" *Henry VI, Part Two* IX. vii. 65–66.).[28] Justinian's *Institutiones* (1553) Baldassare Castigliano, *Il Cortegiano* (Castiglione's *Courtier*, 1557); works by Duns Scotus (1497, and 1515) and Euclid (1516).

Shakespeare sets several plays in Athens, and refers to Aristotle, Caesar, Cicero, Aeneas, classical law, mathematics, etc. Naturally, recourse to Lambarde's library was not indispensible for this. Nevertheless, this suggests that a history-hungry writer like Shakespeare would have found such a library irresistible and might well have sought avidly to avail himself of its literary riches.

* * *

We know of William Lambarde's long association with Lincoln's Inn during the very time Shakespeare was first in London and was reading manuscripts from that Inn. We know Lambarde managed the Revels there and that on several occasions Shakespeare's plays were included in the Revels at the Inns of Court. We know the jurist attended plays at several theatres and particularly at Paris Garden, where the Swan Theatre was located, and that Shakespeare's plays were done at the Swan, the most important of these being *The Merchant of Venice*. We know that in the 1924 sale of the Lambarde family library there was a copy of *Archaionomia* in a similar cover and condition as the one which Roderick L. Eagle obtained in 1915. In that sale there was also a manuscript copy of Beaumont (of the Inner Temple) and Fletcher's sequel to William Shakespeare's *The Taming of the Shrew*. William Lambarde maintained his interest in the theatre from the time of his law student days until his death. As already mentioned, it is to him that the Queen made her only known reference to Shakespeare, the year before Lambarde died.

But the most probable contact between William Shakespeare and William Lambarde would have taken place while the former was a litigant and the latter an officer of the court in Westminster Hall (1588–1590; 1596; 1597–1599). It has been the purpose of this chapter to present the arguments for the authenticity of the seventh Shakespeare signature discovered in a copy of William Lambarde's *Archaionomia*, 1568, now in the possession of the Folger Shakespeare Library. And this evidence supports the case for Shakespeare's surprisingly learned and intimate contact with English law and certain of the prominent figures in jurisprudence of his day.

As we have seen, numerous writers, biographers, scholars, jurists, and critics of the past have, with varying amounts of evidence, come to the conclusion that Shakespeare was a noverint or lawyer's clerk during his so-called lost years. Furthermore, none of these conclusions had the benefit of today's knowledge concerning the Lambarde signature. As for that signature, many paleographers, bibliographers, bibliophiles, librarians, curators, and scholars have concluded that that signature is genuine even though some of those scholars had not had all the supporting evidence which has now been brought to light. Finally, none of these concluded that its presence offered any evidence of Shakespeare's relationship to English law. There is today not only more data supporting the signature's authenticity, but the analysis of the Belott-Mountjoy Deposition signature, discovered after 1800 in 1910, with the Lambarde signature dated as prior to 1800, helps provide further proof of the authenticity of the Lambarde signature. J. Q. Adams asserted the signature was genuine on a misreading of the evidence and has since admitted that "absolute certainty cannot now be established"; and Giles E. Dawson said his account did not have the purpose of "persuading anyone that the signature is a genuine one" but he saw no evidence for its being a forgery of any kind. An article of mine ("The Seventh Shakespeare Signature," *Shakespeare Newsletter*, May 1971 and "Shakespeare Signature in the Folger," *Shakespearean Research and Opportunities*, Nos. 5–6, 1970/71, pp. 110–117) concludes that we must now, upon the evidence, presume the signature to be genuine. As part of an article in *The New York Times* (August 19, 1971, p. 40) reporting my claim to the further authentication of the signature, the director of the Folger, O. B. Hardison, said at that time, "It's an intriguing situation. It is up to the scholarly world to examine the pros and cons in perspective." (The statement reappeared in the *Folger Library Newsletter* in December, 1971 and *Amherst: The College and its Alumni*, Fall 1971.) After the interview with *The New York Times*, Dr. Hardison said that ". . . new details increased the probability that this might be a true signature. I think it's a genuine 16th century signature." (*Washington Post* editorial August 20, 1971). On March 31, 1973, Dr. Richard Schoeck of the Folger staff, and a specialist on the Inns of Court and Renaissance jurisprudence, announced to a meeting of the first annual Shakespeare Association of America, in a paper entitled "Shakespeare and the Law" presented at the Folger, that Shakespeare's autograph in the Library's copy of Lambarde's *Archaionomia* was "probably genuine." The past chapter of this book has been written to persuade the reader and Shakespearean scholars that the signature is, indeed, a genuine one and biographers of the dramatist and commentators about his use of law cannot now ignore it except at their peril. This ensuing biography provides more connections between Lambarde and Shakespeare that were not known until the possibility was entertained by the existence of the autograph, which corroborates the genuineness of the signature. The remarkable fact is that they have remained dormant for four centuries and that upon assuming the signature to be that of the dramatist they become apparent. There is now more justification than ever to maintain that Shakespeare had extensive legal knowledge and interests; and extensive contact with figures in the legal profession, in Chancery, in high judicial positions, and in the Inns of Court. In the following chapters we shall explore how these contacts and interests affected his plays and his thought. The biographical and paleographical evidence for some kind of a legal career for the dramatist has been presented. Now we shall observe how this background structured themes in his works, affected his personal concerns, and how, to a degree little recognized, he was able to utilize these intimate preoccupations, and his artistic and professional skills to produce legal, political, and social change. It is precisely this latter aspect of the study which will force us to reevaluate Shakespeare as a thinker, as a family man, and as an author who, from design, worked to control and alter the context of his society.

IV

Shakespeare's Plays:

MERCY AND EQUITY *v.* LAW AND JUSTICE

KENT: Will you lie down and rest upon the cushions?
LEAR: I'll see their trial first. Bring in the evidence.
[*To Edgar*] Thou robed man of justice, take thy place;
[*To the Fool*] And thou, his yoke-fellow of equity,
Bench by his side. [*To Kent*] You are o' th' commission,
Sit you too.
EDGAR: Let us deal justly.

Lear III. vi. 36–42

1. *Shakespeare and the Inns of Court*

IT HAS BEEN demonstrated that Shakespeare's considerable interest in the law must be regarded with a new seriousness, and that this interest extended over the years to form a profound background for his plays and to become one of the most pervasive preoccupations in Shakespeare's personal life. It was not merely an interest in legal matters to provide the surface of theatrical vocabulary needed to please and flatter the lawyers in the audience, but rather had a design to impress them with something more. Shakespeare's involvement reached beyond the depiction of trials and the characterization of robed men to commissions and courts struggling with the vital and critical notions of the relationship of justice and equity to the law. In Chapter II, passages and references from the plays were employed as additional evidence of Shakespeare's legal transactions affecting his life. The methodology and subject of examination will be reversed to achieve a different, but allied, purpose. Presuming upon the documents and interpretations of Shakespeare's biographical record, with their indication of a depth of experience, knowledge, and interest in the law, this chapter will indicate how these legal moments from his life influenced his literary works. By exploring this influence and the use he puts it to, more crucial and precise meanings can be discerned behind the better-known and important plays coming from Shakespeare's mature period. Even from this distance in time an analysis can sometimes suggest what the dramatist was attempting to do with his works and the purpose he put them to in the legal society of his day and on occasion before the head of state.

Unlike Ben Jonson, Kit Marlowe and other Elizabethan dramatists who were university men, Shakespeare was not. Accordingly while a number of writers were members of the Inns of Court (such as John Marston, Francis Beaumont, John Webster, John Ford, John Donne, and others), Shakespeare was not. This makes it all the more remarkable that Shakespeare's considerable and impressive contacts with the training schools for lawyers is of the same magnitude if not greater than those for Jonson (who, it is said, helped his father lay the brick wall at Lincoln's Inn), Marston, Kyd, Heywood, Marlowe, Beaumont, Fletcher, Ford, Webster and Donne. Almost everyone would agree that the sonnets are addressed to a member of Gray's Inn, either William Hatcliffe, the Earl of Southampton, or the Earl of Pembroke. *Venus and Adonis* and *Rape of Lucrece* are dedicated to the Earl of Southampton. One of the first recorded performances of a play generally acknowledged to be by William Shakespeare is that of *The Comedy of Errors* when it was done at Gray's Inn in 1594. In 1602 *Twelfth Night* is performed in Middle Temple Hall. Sometime early in his career, as early as 1587 or 1588 if one follows Hotson; or 1589, or 1590 says the noverint passage; or 1592 declares the "upstart crow" and "Shake-scene" of the affronted Robert Greene; or from 1592 to 1594 by virtue of the Dedications of the narrative poems to the Earl of Southampton; and certainly by Christmas of 1594 with the performance of his *Comedy of Errors*, Shakespeare had turned to the Inns of Court for a number of artistic needs. There he sought patronage from Hatcliffe or either of the Earls for his poetry; and possibly he found recommendations for plays, masques or entertainments for private occasions, or revels from members. He looked for audiences and places for production in Lincoln's Inn, Gray's Inn, and Middle Temple revels; for friendship from students, lawyers, jurists and nobility who were members, for intellectual discussions from dramatists, poets and other close acquaintances at the Inns, John Marston and Shakespeare's cousin Thomas Greene at Middle Temple, and John Donne at Lincoln's Inn. There he reveled in ambrosial subject matter for his plays in Clement's Inn and Middle Temple; technical talk, and research material in manuscripts, literary volumes, and law books in the private libraries. He acquired legal knowledge from chats, moot courts, and from the writings of such jurists of the Inns as West, Lambarde, Bacon, Hake, Ashe, and others.

A number of possible direct connections between Shakespeare and the Inns of Court can be catalogued, and the sheer weight of it suggests the ease he had, in gaining entrance through personal relationships to the societies where his works were performed, read and admired under the exceptional favor sufficient to evidence that his entry, by whatever means, was most favorably achieved. He had his plays preferred over Ben Jonson's for performance there, as when *Twelfth Night* was selected over *Cynthia's Revels*, and his pieces sent up for Christmas season performances at the Royal Court four and six at a time to Jonson's one or two, and an occasional play by Marston or Beaumont.

The connections may have found their initiation early

and as far away as Stratford. There the residence of New Place, which Shakespeare purchased in 1596, was situated in virtually a legal "district," as far as Stratford was concerned. William Court, one of Shakespeare's father's Stratford lawyers, and Walter Roche, who left a teaching position the year Shakespeare entered the School to become a lawyer, lived across the street; Shakespeare rented rooms to Thomas Greene while he was town clerk, and New Place, itself, was purchased from the son of the Inner Temple lawyer who had lived there, William Underhill. William Underhill Jr. in 1588 had entertained the Stratford town recorder, Mr. James Dyer. James Dyer in 1580 is listed in Westminster in Hilary Term as recording the Wilmecote Fine on Asbies. Shakespeare's cousin, Thomas Greene, and his friend John Marston, the dramatist, became associated with Middle Temple and, at the exchange of festivities around Christmas time, the Templers collaborated with Gray's Inn.

Whatever John Shakespeare's London attorney's associations were with the Inns, Shakespeare would have benefited from them during the Lambert case from 1588 to 1590, which is the most obvious contact for an early introduction to the societies. Shakespeare later bought land from a William Combe, and his nephew John Combe left £5 to Shakespeare in his will. William Combe was admitted to the Middle Temple in 1571, became Reader there in 1595, and served as counsel for Stratford in 1597. Combe, Greene, and Marston would have been the most intimately associated with the Stratford dramatist amongst many providing support for the performance of Shakespeare's plays at Middle Temple.

The most intriguing and closest of the personal legal contacts between Will and the Inns was that furnished by Thomas Greene. Thomas Greene always claimed to be Shakespeare's cousin and possibly was by marriage.[1] He was from Warwickshire. His father had business with the Stratford Corporation, and with the Marstons in Coventry. Thomas stood surety for John Marston's entry into Middle Temple in 1594 and the Marstons for him in 1595. He had started out in Staple's Inn. He rented the rooms from Shakespeare in New Place by 1609 and named his children for the Shakespeares, Anne in 1603/4 and William in 1607/8. His brother, John Greene, was born in 1575, settled in Stratford, was of Clement's Inn, and was acting as an attorney by 1599. The Greene brothers from Stratford were associated, from 1574 to 1602 at least, with Middle Temple and Clement's Inn and these, out of the thirteen or fourteen major and minor Inns of Court, are the two of the three Shakespeare mentions in the texts of his plays, the third being Gray's Inn, where *Comedy of Errors* was done.

Thomas Greene became solicitor for Stratford in 1601, was called to the bar in 1602, and from 1603–1617 held the position of Town Clerk, succeeded by Francis Collins who had been the clerk for Shakespeare's will the year before. He moved out of New Place when Shakespeare retired and by 1611 was residing in St. Mary's House near the Stratford Parish Church. Greene prosecuted at least one case and handled and was partner to several other legal and business transactions as William Shakespeare's attorney in Stratford. Later in his life, Thomas returned to London where he was selected a Reader of Middle Temple in 1621, then Master of the Bench, and finally elected to the illustrious office of Treasurer. There are numerous ties between Greene and Shakespeare from 1594 to 1616 which necessitate no further search for the source of enthusiasm over the selection of *Twelfth Night* for Middle Temple entertainment in 1602, which happens to coincide with Greene's being called to the bar from that Inn.

To summarize, then, the most probable connection by 1594 for Shakespeare at the Inns of Court, at Middle Temple and possibly earlier at Staple's Inn, was his cousin Thomas Greene. Likewise, William Combe was there from April 1593 through May 1594; possibly Hatcliffe furnished such service in 1587 and 1588; perhaps

Lambarde presented such an opportunity between the court case and Lincoln's Inn in 1590 or 1591; and most probably before this his London attorney John Harborne from 1588–1590. Also from 1585–1597, by connections from Stratford men associated with the law such as Walter Roche, William Court, the Underhills and Humphrey Colles of Middle Temple, with whom Will later shares the income from a partial ownership of the town's tithes, Shakespeare might have been set up to advantage in his relations at the Inns.

The kind of relationship Shakespeare enjoyed existed between many writers and Inns of Court men as patrons of drama. This is indicated by Ben Jonson's dedication of his two *Every Man* humor plays to the Inns of Court, and by an epistle of Thomas Heywood's ushering in the 1633 Quarto of Christopher Marlowe's *The Jew of Malta*, performed at the Cock-pit theatre at Court in Westminster:

> *To My Worthy Friend, Master Thomas Hammon, of Gray's Inn*, etc.
>
> This play, composed by so worthy an author as Mr. Marlowe, and the part of the Jew presented by so unimitable an actor as Master Alleyn, being in this later age commended to the stage: as I usher'd it into the court and presented it to the Cock-pit, with these Prologues and Epilogues here inserted, so now being newly brought to the press, I was loath it should be published without the ornament of an Epistle; making choice of you unto whom to devote it; than whom (of all those gentlemen and acquainttances, within the compass of my long knowledge) there is none more able to tax ignorance or attribute right to merit. Sir, you have been pleased to grace some of mine own works with your courteous patronage. I hope this will not be the worse accepted because commended by me, over whom none can claim more power or privilege than yourself. I had no better a New Year's gift to present you with; receive it therefore as a continuance of that

inviolable obligement by which he rests still engaged: who, as he ever hath, shall always remain,

Tuissimus,
Tho. Heywood[2]

The legal language in the dedicatory letter is a device appropriate to the addressee, a member of Gray's Inn, as furnished by such phrases as 'tax ignorance', 'attribute right to merit', and 'inviolable obligement by which he rests still engaged'. It was in similar fashion that Shakespeare's early plays were preferred at the Inns, and at Gray's.

Two of Shakespeare's famous contemporaries in poetry were also associated with the legal institutions in London. John Donne was a member of Lincoln's Inn and Edmund Spenser was one of the Clerks of Chancery. In the spring of 1591, the poet John Donne enrolled first in one of the minor Inns of Court, Thavies Inn, after coming down from being earlier at Oxford until 1587, and then at Cambridge. The Inns of Court in London were known as the Third University, as indeed they were for Donne. His initial membership at Lincoln's Inn coincides precisely with the time Lambarde occupied rooms there, from 1591 to 1594. Donne returned in 1616 to become the Preacher for Lincoln's Inn until 1622. He had a reputation for being neat, a great visitor of ladies, and a frequenter of plays. In 1594, the year of *The Comedy of Errors*, Donne was absent from his duties, one of which was to be in charge of Christmas festivities, just as Lambarde had been for All Soul's Day, 1566, in the same Inn. John Donne subsequently left the Inns by June, 1594 to follow subsequently the Earl of Essex to the Continent. It is thought that since Donne's lyrics (songs and sonnets) were not published until 1633, two years after his death, that Shakespeare saw some of his lyrics in manuscript in Lincoln's Inn between 1591 and 1594; and since Shakespeare's "sugared sonnets among his private friends" mentioned by Francis Meres in 1598[3] were not published until 1609, it is thought that Donne must have read them, if previously, in manuscript also, in about 1594. The following sonnets have a relationship, probably Donne had read Shakespeare's.

CXLVI

Poor soul, the centre of my sinful earth,
[Thrall to] these rebel powers that thee array,
Why dost thou pine within and suffer dearth,
Painting thy outward walls so costly gay?
Why so large cost, having so short a lease,
Dost thou upon thy fading mansion spend?
Shall worms, inheritors of this excess,
Eat up thy charge? Is this thy body's end?
Then, soul, live thou upon they servant's loss,
And let that pine to aggravate thy store;
Buy terms divine in selling hours of dross;
Within be fed, without be rich no more:
So shalt thou feed on Death, that feeds on men,
And Death once dead, there's no more dying then.

William Shakespeare

X

Death be not proud, though some have called thee
Mighty and dreadful, for, thou art not so,
For, those whom thou think'st thou dost overthrow,
Die not, poore death, nor yet canst thou kill me.
From rest and sleep, which but thy pictures be,
Much pleasure, then from these, much more must flow,
And soonest our best men with thee do go,
Rest of their bones, and soules' deliverie,
Thou art slave to Fate, Chance, kings, and desperate men,
And dost with poison, war and sickness dwell,
And poppie, or charms can make us sleep as well,
And better than thy stroke; why swell'st thou then?
One short sleep past, we wake eternally,
And death shall be no more; death, thou shalt die.

John Donne

In about 1598, Donne became secretary of Thomas Egerton, the son of Sir Thomas Egerton, Lord Keeper of the

Great Seal of England under Elizabeth I and Lord Chancellor under James I. Another famous English poet of this time is related to Chancery and the Inns: On 22 March 1580–1, Queen Elizabeth granted to Edmund Spenser the office of registrar or clerk in Chancery. Spenser's *Prothalamion* describes in passing the Inns and Middle Temple:

> At length they all to merry London came,
> To merry London, my most kindly nurse . . .
> There when they came, whereas those bricky towres,
> The which on Thomas' broad aged back do ride,
> Where now the studious lawyers have their bowers
> There whylome wont the Templar Knights to bide,
> Till they decay'd through pride, . . .
>
> II. 127–136

Throughout Shakespeare's life, the Inns were the center of literary activity and associations in London.

There were (and still are[4]) four prominent Inns of Court, way stations to civil appointments to Court and the legal profession at the courts (then in Westminster): Lincoln's Inn, Middle Temple, Inner Temple and Gray's Inn. Numerous minor Inns prepared students for the major ones. Those most frequently referred to are: Clement's Inn, Thavies Inn, Furnivall's Inn, Staples Inn, New Inn, and so forth. Jasper Heywood, who was part of the literary movement of translators during the 1560s at the Inns of Court, listed the prominent Inns in his Prologue to his translation of Seneca's *Thyestes*. *Thyestes*' influence, complained of in Nash's noverint passage, reached to Thomas Kyd's *Spanish Tragedy*, and Shakespeare's *Titus* and *Hamlet*.

> But yf thy will be rather bent,
> a yong mans witt to prove,
> And thinkest that elder lerned men
> perhaps it shall behove,
> In woorks of waight to spende theyr tyme,
> goe where Minervaes men,
> And finest witts doe swarme: whome she
> hath taught to passe with pen.

In Lyncolnes Inne and Temples twayne,
  Grayes Inne and other mo,
Thou shalt them fynde whose paynfull pen
  thy verse shall florishe so,
That Melpomen thou wouldst well weene
  had taught them for to wright,
And all their woorks with stately style,
  and goodly grace t'endight.
There shalt thou se the self same North . . .

[That is, Sir Thomas North, the translater of Plutarch's *Lives*, which is a major source for at least seven of Shakespeare's plays.]

  . . . whose woorke his witte displayes,
And Dyall dothe of Princes paynte,
  and preaches abroade his prayse.
There Sackvyldes [*i.e. Thomas Sackville, Lord Buckhurst*]
  Sonnetts sweetely sauste
  and featly fyned bee,
There Nortons ditties do delight, . . .

Thomas Norton and Thomas Sackville, both of the Inner Temple, were the coauthors of the first regular English tragedy in dramatic form entitled *Gorboduc*, which is a source for *King Lear*. There were three Yelvertons at the Inns; one of them became a member of Parliament and another became Sir Henry Yelverton the Judge of the Court of Common Pleas in Westminster Hall under Elizabeth I.

  . . . there Yelvertons doo flee
Well pewrde with pen: suche yong men three,
  as weene thou mightst agayne,
To be begotte as Pallas was,
  of myghtie Jove his brayne.

Pallas, of course, is Pallas Athene, particularly as the female, moderating principle represented by Athene the equitable judge in Aeschylus' *Eumenides*. William Baldwin of Middle Temple supervised the collection of poems known as *A Mirror for Magistrates* whose depiction of Buckingham influenced Shakespeare's *Richard III* and whose general form of *de casibus*, rise and fall of great princes, affected the structure of Shakespeare's early history plays.

> There heare thou shalt a great reporte,
>   of Baldwyns worthie name,
> Whose Myrrour dothe of Magistrates,
>   proclayme eternall fame.
> And there the gentle Blundville is
>   by name and eke [*i.e. also*] by kynde [*i.e. nature*],
> Of whome we learne by Plutarches lore,
>   what frute by Foes to fynde,
> There Bavande [*i.e. William Bavande of the Middle Temple*] bydes, that turnde his toyle
>   a Common welthe to frame,
> And greater grace in Englyshe geves,
>   to woorthy authors name.
> There Googe [*i.e. Barnabe Googe*] a gratefull gaynes hath gotte,
>   reporte that runneth ryfe,
> Who crooked Compasse dothe describe,
>   and Zodiake of lyfe.
> And yet great nombre more, whose names
>   yf I shoulde now resight,
> A ten tymes greater woorke then thine,
>   I should be forste to wright.
> A pryncely place in Parnasse hill,
>   for these there is preparde,
> Where crowne of glittryng glorie hange,
>   for them a ryght rewarde.[5]

To this list of figures at the Inns in the 1550s and 1560s may be added the following dramatists, poets, and writers from Shakespeare's period: Henry Wotton (Middle Temple, 1595); John Davies (Middle Temple, 1588–1626); John Marston (Middle Temple, 1594–1606); Thomas Overbury (Middle Temple, 1597–1604); John Webster (Middle Temple, 1598); John Ford (Middle Temple, 1602–1617); John Manningham (Middle Temple, 1598–1622); John Pym (Middle Temple, 1602–1605); John Donne (Lincoln's Inn 1591–1594, 1616–1622); Francis Beaumont (Inner Temple, 1600–1602); Francis Bacon

(Gray's Inn, 1576–1626); Thomas Campion (Gray's Inn, 1586–1595); Thomas Lodge (Lincoln's Inn, 1578–1595); and John Harrington (Lincoln's Inn, 1581).[6] Connected to the Inns through their writings were Shakespeare, Christopher Marlowe, Ben Jonson, Fletcher, and Thomas Heywood.

This is quite an illustrious collection of literary artists. The Inns of Court were clearly places where literature thrived in plays patronized, translations made, and poetry read and written. William Prynne wrote in his *Histriomastix* (1633): "That Innes of Court men were undone but for Players; that they are their chiefest guests and imployment, and the sole business that makes them afternoons men: that this is one of the first things they learne as soone as they are admitted, to see Stage-playes." (Fol. 3v.)

They knew Shakespeare at the Inns of Court. John Davies (Middle Temple, 1588–1626) wrote in *Microcosmos* (1603):

> And though the stage doth stain pure gentle blood,
> Yet generous ye are in mind and mood.

"Two years later he again alluded to 'W. S.', this time as one of those stage players 'guerdon'd not to their desserts', and in 1610 he paid generous tribute 'To our English Terence, Mr. Will. Shake-speare', employing a regal reference that would occasion future conjecture."[7]

> Some say, good Will, which I in sport do sing:
> Hadst thou not played some kingly parts in sport,
> [*i.e. acted King Hamlet's ghost*]
> Thou hadst been a companion for a King,
> [*i.e. as the Prince of Purpoole to lead the entertainment for the Crown from the Inns of Court*]
> And been a King among the meaner sort.
> [*i.e. been the Christmas King of the revels at the Inns*].

John Manningham, a barrister of the Middle Temple, wrote in his diary in London on March 13, 1602 after *Twelth Night* was performed there:

> Upon a time when Burbage played Richard the Third there was a citizen grew so far in liking with him, that before she went from the play she appointed him to come that night unto her by the name of Richard the Third. Shakespeare, overhearing their conclusion, went before, was entertained and at his game ere Burbage came. Then message being brought that Richard the Third was at the door, Shakespeare caused return to be made that William the Conqueror was before Richard the Third. Shakespeare's name was William.[8]

And Shakespeare knew the Inns of Court, particularly Clement's Inn, the one his cousin John Greene had attended, and Gray's that had performed his *Comedy of Errors*:

> JUSTICE SHALLOW: . . . I dare say my cousin William is become a good scholar: he is at Oxford still, is he not?
>
> JUSTICE SILENCE: Indeed, sir, to my cost.
>
> SHALLOW: A' must, then, to the inns o' court shortly. I was once of Clement's Inn, where I think they will talk of mad Shallow yet.
>
> SILENCE: You were called 'lusty Shallow' then, cousin.
>
> SHALLOW: By the mass, I was called any thing; and I would have done any thing indeed too, and roundly too. There was I, and Little John Doit of Staffordshire, and black George Barnes, and Francis Pickbone, and Will Squele, a Cotswold man; you had not four such swing-bucklers in all the inns o' court again and I may say to you, we knew where the bona-robas were and best of them all at commandment. Then was Jack Falstaff, now Sir John, a boy and page to Thomas Mowbray, Duke of Norfolk.
>
> SILENCE: This Sir John, cousin, that comes hither anon about soldiers?
>
> SHALLOW: The same Sir John, the very same. I see him break Skogan's head at the court-gate, when a' was a crack not thus high: and the very same day did I fight with one Sampson Stockfish, a fruiterer, behind Gray's Inn.
>
> *Henry IV, Part Two*. III. ii. 10–36.

SHALLOW: I remember at Mile-end Green, when I lay at Clement's Inn,—I was then Sir Dagonet in Arthur's Show—there was a little quiver fellow, and a' would manage you his piece thus; and a' would about and about, and come you in and come you in: 'rah, tah, tah,' would a' say; 'bounce' would a' say; and away again would a' go, and again would a' come: I shall ne'er see such a fellow.

(II. 295–306)

FALSTAFF: This same starved justice hath done nothing but prate to me of the wildness of his youth, and the feats he hath done about Turnbull Street; and every third word a lie, duer paid to the hearer than the Turk's tribute. I do remember him at Clement's Inn like a man made after supper of a cheese-paring.

(II. 324–329).

What fond associations the Inns bring and here, in 1596 Shakespeare expresses a particular affinity to Gray's Inn, which had done his *Comedy* two years earlier and to Clement's Inn where his cousin was; he referred only once elsewhere to another Inn, Middle Temple, where his other cousin was to be and to its Hall, where *Twelfth Night* is performed in 1602. This reference is in *Henry VI, Part Two*. II. iii. in which the scene is set in Middle Temple Garden. Shakespeare's contact with the Inns of Court was not a one-time association. The dramatist's relationship was from at least 1594, if not as early as 1587/88, through 1602, and included Gray's Inn, Lincoln's Inn, Middle Temple, and Clement's Inn. This amounts to the influence of a place upon Shakespeare's work and thought —he definitely had an Inns of Court Period in his development.

2. Comedy of Errors *at Gray's Inn.*

WITH his literary fame assured, particularly at places like the Inns of Court by his preëminently successful *Rape of Lucrece* (May 9, 1594) and by having the Earl of Southampton as his acknowledged grateful patron of his work, access to dramatic presentation at Gray's Inn for Shakespeare would be easy to achieve. Possibly some of the members had seen previous works by Shakespeare commissioned by, and performed before, the Earl. Shakespeare had in his first draft of *Comedy of Errors* a play, with its two sets of twins and resulting mistaken identity, which would be naturally inviting for Gray's Inn. The play is based on Plautus' *Menaechmi*, which had also influenced Ariosto's *I Suppositi*, being the source for another historical, literary event at Gray's Inn. A member of Gray's Inn, George Gascoigne, in 1566 wrote *Supposes* (based on Ariosto), the first English comedy of distinction, and it was performed in Gray's Inn Hall. *Supposes* is used by Shakespeare as a source for his *The Taming of the Shrew*. The plots of all these roles are based upon the existence of twins, disguised servants and role changes. This has particular appeal to lawyers, barristers, attorneys, and students of the Inns because when prosecuting according to English or Anglo-Saxon law, as opposed to Continental or Roman law, the defense only has to establish in the mind of the jury "reasonable doubt" as to guilt, since the presumption is that the accused is innocent until proven guilty. In other words, the defense only has to put forth a substantial counter-hypothesis, all other things equal, producing the identical effect in the case by alternative means but ruling out their client as agent.

Hence, any reality can result from hypothesizing identical results from different premises or causes. Conclusion: The case proves to be that of mistaken identity; thus the client or supposed agent is declared innocent. A meaningful complement to all this exists in the fact that the several performances of *Comedy of Errors* in Shakespeare's lifetime, when it was done at the Inns in 1594 and much later again at Court in 1604, took place on Holy Innocents' Day, December 28th. This feast day celebrates the slaughter by Herod of the innocent children, among whom he thought might be the Christ-child, an ironic example of fruitlessly trying to eliminate any chance of mistaken identity. The plot device of the twins was such an obviously repeated success that Shakespeare reproduces the basic premise in *Twelth Night, or What You Will* for Middle Temple (February 2, 1602) which Manningham in his diary says reminded him of Plautus' *Menaechmi.* John Marston of Middle Temple was to get on the bandwagon too with his *What You Will* (c. 1601–1607) resembling *Twelth Night* and *Comedy of Errors.*

Somehow, the *Comedy of Errors* was preferred! The play was selected for the Christmas revels at Gray's Inn. The famous revels at the Inn during the holiday season of 1594/95 were the most elaborate ever recorded. The series of events included a masque by Francis Davison, at least one poem written for the occasion by the famous Elizabethan poet and musician Thomas Campion, a group of speeches by Francis Bacon and Shakespeare's *Comedy of Errors.* The text of the revels survives and is entitled "*Gesta Grayorum*, or the History of the High and Mighty Prince Henry, Prince of Purpoole. . . . Who Reigned and Died, A.D. 1594. Together with a Masque as it was presented . . . for the Entertainment of Q. Elizabeth. . . ." It was the custom to invite the Inner Temple to the revels at Gray's but it was so crowded that after attempting to be seated and creating a hubub the members of Inner Temple left. There was tilting, jousts and vaulting and ". . . after such sports, a Comedy of Errors (like to Plautus his *Menechmus*) was played by the players. So that night was begun and continued to the end in nothing but confusion and errors; whereupon it was ever afterwards called *The Night of Errors.*" Later a mock-arraignment was conducted to determine the cause of the mix-ups on the night when *The Comedy of Errors* was offered:

> . . . the Prisoner was freed and pardoned, the Attorney, Sollicitor, Master of the Requests, and those that were acquainted with the Draught of the Petition [the invitation of the Inner Temple to Gray's Inn], were all of them com-

manded to the Tower; so the Lieutenant took charge of them. And this was the End of our Law-sports, concerning the Night of Errors.[9]

In celebration of the newly restored friendship between Gray's and the Templars, a pageant was presented and those in attendance were the Right Honourable the Lord of the Great and Privy seals, Lord Ellesmere, Sir Thomas Egerton who had just managed to get his closest colleague, William Lambarde, appointed as one of his Masters of Chancery. Also in attendance was Shakespeare's patron of his narrative poems, the Earl of Southampton, and his friend, the Earl of Essex. In the audience, or participating in the processions were the Earls of Shrewsbury, Cumberland, Northumberland, and the Lords Buckhurst (Thomas Sackville of Inner Temple, one of the authors' of *Gorboduc*), Windsor, Mountjoy, Sheffield, Compton, Rich, Burghley, Mounteagle, and the Lord Thomas Howard; Sir Thomas Henneage and Sir Robert Cecil, with a great number of Knights and Ladies.[10]

Shakespeare knew that he would have such learned gentlemen as his patrons and auditors, so the text of *Comedy of Errors* was altered to speak to such ears. On the occasion of this newest and most exciting opportunity for his play, the author added to his earlier draft legal passages and two trial scenes which would be appropriate to his specific audience. This year, 1594, dates the beginning of Shakespeare's overt interest in legal equity. His case before Queen's Bench had ended in 1590 without it.

Equity is simply that which is fair and just, but more technically for sixteenth century England it is a system of jurisprudence chiefly associated with the high court of Chancery serving to supplement and remedy the limitations and inflexibility of the common law. Upon occasion, equity functioned to provide extraordinary relief, payment in kind as opposed to damages, overriding justice coupled with what might appear to be mercy. This fount of equity was found only in Chancery, presided over by the Lord

Chancellor or Keeper of the Great Seal and ruled by four Masters of Chancery such as William Lambarde and his close associate George Carew (Middle Temple, 1586).[11] The Lord Keeper (Egerton) attended *Gesta Grayorum* as did Sir Thomas Henneage, Master of the Rolls, the office later assumed by William Lambarde. It was not only up and coming law students who knew of Shakespeare's *Comedy of Errors*, but also the leading justices of the realm.

Shortly before, Shakespeare had interpolated legalisms in another play to delight the ears of famous members of the Inns. *Love's Labour's Lost*, full of legal jests and literary topicality, was probably revised earlier than the *Comedy of Errors* in the same year of 1594 to be performed before the Earl of Southampton in his London house, as G. P. V. Akrigg in his *Shakespeare and the Earl of Southampton* has shown (pp. 207–215). The play takes a passage from a work by William West of the Inner Temple.

> . . . mark the topicality for a Court of a Prince of Love and his fellow gentlemen-scholars in the philosophy of the law, of a scene laid in the court of a prince whose bookmates and fellow-scholars have sworn to keep the statutes of their fellowship: to study and see no women. Legal jests are thickly sown: "intituled, nominated, or called,' 'taken with the manner,' and 'in manner and form following'[12]

"And from West's *Symboleography* I [Leslie Hotson] added the *Quis*? . . . *Quando*? . . . *Ubi*? . . . *Quid*? etc. of an indictment for felony, so deliciously hit off in Armado's letter—'The time When? About the sixth hour . . .' and so on, indicting the rational hind Costard of crime with the female Jacquenetta."[13] Hotson goes on to propose 1588/9 for the date of the play as somehow a part of William Hatcliff's festivities when he was Prince of Purpoole at Gray's Inn. However West's *Symboleography* was not published until 1591 and with revisions and additions again in 1594; possibly Shakespeare read it in manuscript in Inner Temple. However, in all probability the dramatist added legal passages from Inns of Court writers, particularly William West, to his first drafts of *Love's Labour's Lost* and *Comedy of Errors* in 1594 to be in both cases performed privately before members of Gray's Inn.

1594 marked a year in which several of Shakespeare's plays work with the concept of equity paralleling the similar explosion of the subject matter into a number of treatises, in print, being revised, in manuscript and in preparation. One of these in new printing was the highly influential William West's *Symboleography*, a word for the legal documents or instruments representing conveyance deeds, indentures, etc., done at Middle Temple Gate and had added to it in this year of 1594, before *Comedy of Errors* was performed, "another Treatise of Equities, [on] the jurisdiction and proceedings of the high Court of Chauncerie." From time to time, West cities passages from Christopher St. Germain's *Doctor and Student*, a debate between a doctor of divinity and a student of laws which was so popular that an edition had come out every few years since 1528. Furthermore, some of these editions had been printed at Middle Temple. Shakespeare's fellow dramatists, Ben Jonson and John Marston, read *Doctor and Student* as they take a word from the treatise and use it respectively in *Every Man Out of His Humour* (III. iv), dedicated to the Inns of Court, and Marston's *Satires* (III. viii), written in his rooms at Middle Temple.

The word picked up, misspelling and all, is "synderesis". Marston writes "returne sacred Synderesis,/ Inspire our trunckes," and Jonson mocks it in a list of inkhorn terms as "the soules Synderisis". *Synteresis* is Greek for the mystical bond between the body and the soul, the flesh and the spirit; and in *Doctor and Student* signifies the spark of life which *Equitie* (the bond) gives to the *Law* (the flesh) and *Justice* (the spirit of the law) making a living legal system out of the bare bones of the letter of the law. William West, quoting Christopher St.

Germain's *Doctor and Student* says in his 1594 edition:

> . . . equitie may mitigate *Rigorem iuris* [rigorous justice], which equitie is no other thing, then [sic] an exception of the law of God, or of the law of reason, from the general principles of man's positive law, not agreeing with them in some particularity, which exception is inwardly imployed in every general ground or maxim of the Law.
>
> (*Section* 29c)

The concept of mercy accomodating man's written laws to human necessity is precisely the subject of the first scene in *The Comedy of Errors*. The Duke of Ephesus, Solinus, explicates the legal situation which Aegeon, a merchant from Syracuse, has created by his entering Ephesus: "I am not partial to infringe our laws, [your Duke having] seal'd his rigorous statutes with their [i.e. Ephesians'] bloods, /Excludes all pity from our threatening looks. /Therefore by law thou art condemn'd to die." Aegeon pleads for equity from natural law arguments: ". . . the world may witness thay my end /Was wrought by nature, not by vile offence, . . ." and feels his search for his family led him into a "merciless" predicament. The Duke speaks of the conflict between his personal empathy and his official duty: ". . . we may pity, though not pardon thee."

> . . . were it not against our laws,
> Against my crown, my oath, my dignity,
> Which princes, would they, may not disannul,
> My soul should sue as advocate for thee.
> But, though thou art adjudged to the death
> And passed sentence may not be recall'd
> But to our honour's great disparagement,
> Yet I will favour thee in what I can.
>
> (*cf.* ll. 4–150)

West goes on from the earlier passage to indicate that clemency is only proper to a Prince, one who legislates as well as judges.

The Duke grants Aegeon one day in which to obtain the 1,000 marks' ransom. Finally in the last scene, Solinus is so moved by the circumstances that have united Aegeon's family against all odds that he refuses to accept the offer of even a few ducats.

> ANTIPHOLUS OF EPHESUS: These ducats pawn I for my father here.
> DUKE: It shall not need; thy father hath his life.
> (V. i. 389-390)

The Duke is following West's observation:

> Wherefore in some cases it is necessary to leave the Words of the Law, and to follow that reason and Justice requireth and to that Intent Equity is ordained; that is to say, to temper and mitigate the rigor of the Law. (*p.* 53)

The Comedy of Errors dramatizes a court of equity where the ruler suspends the law, taking the nature of the circumstances into consideration. The play is also similar to *Doctor of Divinity and Student of Laws* insofar as the Roman Law (*lex scripta*) is mitigated by Christian theology appropriate to Solinus (Solon representing the lawgiver) ruling mercifully over the Ephesians, subjects of St. Paul's Epistle.

During this time of producing plays for private performances and works for the nobility (*Venus and Adonis*, *Rape of Lucrece*, *Love's Labour's Lost*, and *Comedy of Errors*), Shakespeare was commissioned to do *A Midsummer Night's Dream* for a wedding in a great house. A number of possibilities have been offered for the time of 1594 to 1596. Chief of these are: the marriage of the third earl of Bedford to Lucy Harrington on December 12, 1594; that of the Earl of Derby to Elizabeth Vere, daughter of the Earl of Oxford, on January 26, 1595; or that of Rt. Hon. Thomas son of Lord Berkeley, to Rt. Hon. Elizabeth, daughter of Sir George Carey, on Februay 19, 1596. The Queen would have been present upon these occasions and the latter wedding would have the further connection of including the son of the Sir Henry Carey, who was Shakespeare's players' patron until his death on July 23, 1596.

For whichever of these weddings, Shakespeare once

again addresses in *A Midsummer Night's Dream* a noble audience, perhaps including juridical figures, and his judicial personage engages in the same action as the Duke of *Comedy of Errors.* Theseus relinquishes "the sharp Athenian law" upon Hermia when he discovers the lovers in such concord, against the will of her father. The dramatist had obtained legal audiences and they were to watch his authority figures mitigate the law to achieve justice. These plays were trial runs for a program of broadsides to the law students, lawyers, attorneys, barristers, judges, Masters of Chancery, Chancellors and Monarchs with the theme of equity jurisdiction over common law in England that the noverint-turned-dramatist was to promulgate in his works for, at first, an educational purpose and, finally, for the purpose of reform as his plays became a sophisticated mirror for magistrates.

3. *The Merchant of Venice*

SHAKESPEARE had just anatomized authority, inheritance, legitimacy and justice in the *Henry IV* plays in 1596, and done vignettes of the judicial system: from Monarch to the Lord Chief-Justice of the King's Bench,[14] to the country justices Shallow and Silence, and even to the sheriff's officers, Fang and Snare; all were preserving the Elizabethan order against riotousness and rebellion at various levels of the politic's hierarchy. In these plays the author is worried about whether there is or "... there's no equity stirring:" (*Henry IV*, Part I, II. ii. 106.)

In *The Merchant of Venice* (1597) Shakespeare turned to study the technicalities of legal procedure. When he comes to writing his most obviously legalistic play, a number of biographical events between 1594 and 1597 have taken place touching Shakespeare's legal background and personal matters of inheritance. *The Merchant of Venice* is partly about the game of winning an inheritance by the Christians with someone providing the bankroll:

the loss of a daughter and a fortune by Shylock, with a mercantile setting; a court of law attempting to mitigate cutthroat competition and the aggrandizing spirit. Shakespeare, himself, has personally at the law, sought to mitigate threats of personal injury; lost an offspring who would have inherited his estate; and attempts to set up for himself an expanded inheritance. William Lambarde may have been a witness of both the legal action and the artistic product in this period.

William Lambarde (1536–1601) moves through several offices relating to Shakespeare's litigations up to a moment when it is possible to place him in the audience of *Merchant of Venice.* He had published *Archaionomia* in 1568 and had, since 1590, been working at Lincoln's Inn on a manuscript of the history of the high court of Chancery to which Shakespeare may have had access. The manuscript was entitled *Archeion* and published in 1591 with a letter of dedication to Sir Robert Cecil dated October 22, 1591. He accepted the position of deputy of Lord Burghley (William Cecil) in the Office of Composition for the Alienations of Fines in October 4, 1589, a general interest he maintained throughout his subsequent appointments. He was made Master Extraordinary of Chancery June 1592 and was assigned to the Office of Alienations. Four significant cases (in *Acta Cancellaria*) between December 4, 1595 and July 15, 1600 indicate he was consulted for major decisions.[15] The Keeper, Egerton, Lord Ellesmere, made Lambarde Keeper of the Records of the Rolls Chapel on May 26, 1597, and Master Ordinary December, 1597; and shortly before his death the Queen appointed him, upon the Lord Keeper's recommendation, Keeper of the Records of the Tower on January 21, 1601. In 1595 Lambarde is the most active Master of Chancery and the Lord Keeper relies upon him heavily.

On August 11, 1596, Hamnet Shakespeare dies at the age of ten and is buried in Stratford. He is survived by his dark-haired twin sister, Judith and the golden-haired, older sister Susannah. The loss of the only son is keenly felt and in all probability reflected by remarks about Prince Arthur who dies as a child in *King John* (1596):

CONSTANCE: If thou . . . wert grim,
Ugly and slanderous to thy mother's womb,
Full of unpleasing blots and sightless stains,
Lame, foolish, crooked, swart, prodigious,
Patch'd with foul moles and eye-offending marks,
I would not care, I then would be content,
For then I should not love thee, no, nor thou
Become thy great birth nor deserve a crown.
But thou art fair, and at thy birth, dear boy,
Nature and Fortune join'd to make thee great:
Of Nature's gifts thou mayst with lilies boast
And with the half-blown rose.

(III. i. 43–54

PEMBROKE: O death, made proud with pure and princely beauty!
The earth had not a hole to hide this deed.
BIGOT: Or, when he doom'd this beauty to a grave,
Found it too precious-princely for a grave.
SALISBURY: Kneeling before this ruin of sweet life,
And breathing to his breathless excellence
The incense of a vow, a holy vow,
Never to taste the pleasures of the world,
Never to be infected with delight,
Nor conversant with ease and idleness,
Till I have set a glory to this hand, ...

(IV. ii. 35–36, 37–40, 65–71)

CONSTANCE: Young Arthur is my son, and he is lost . . .
If I were mad, I should forget my son . . .
'O that these hands could so redeem my son . . .'
And, father cardinal, I have heard you say
That we shall see and know our friends in Heaven:
If that be true, I shall see my boy again;
For since the birth of Cain, the first male child,
To him that did but yesterday suspire,
There was not such a gracious creature born.
I shall not know him: therefore never, never
Must I behold my pretty Arthur more.

PANDULPH: You hold too heinous a respect of grief.
CONSTANCE: He talks to me that never had a son.
KING PHILIP: You are as fond of grief as of your child.
CONSTANCE: Grief fills the room up of my absent child,
Lies in his bed, walks up and down with me,
Puts on his pretty looks, repeats his words,
Remembers me of all his gracious parts,
Stuffs out his vacant garments with his form;
O Lord! my boy, my Arthur, my fair son!
My life, my joy, my food, my all the world!
(III. iv. 46, 57, 71, 76–81, 88–97, 103–104.)

He knew whereof he spoke. From this point Shakespeare lacked an immediate male heir, which was to disturb him greatly.

On October 20, 1596, after a twenty-year hiatus, an application for a Grant of Arms to Shakespeare's father was responded to in a rough draft drawn up in Herald's College, London. It indicates that just before his decline, John Shakespeare in the 1570s had property valued at £500. Undoubtedly the application comes from William Shakespeare's assistance and insistence, like other actors in court, to have heraldic honors. In a complex psychological move, not entirely from filial gratitude, William knows he will lack an extension of himself with the loss of his son and so he establishes his own future inheritance by rebuilding his father's position. As Prince Hal says, "And pay the debt I never promised, /By how much better than my word I am." (*Part One*. I. ii. 232–233).

William Camden confirms and presents the heraldic honors in 1599, only a year or so before John Shakespeare's death. This authorizes him to impale the Arden arms, ironically after he has lost the Arden inheritance. Upon receipt of this John can be titled "Gentleman" and William can receive his title by inheritance. Shakespeare will "gentle" his own condition (*cf. Henry V*. IV. iii. 56–67). At least the grant had not come in the fashion ridiculed by the Fool in *Lear*: ". . . he's a mad yeoman that sees his son a gentleman before him." (III. vi. 10–15).

In the Court of Queen's Bench in Westminster, during Michaelmas term (October 9–November 29) of this same year (1596) there appears an "Entry of a Writ of Attachment issued out of the Court of King's [Queen's] Bench on behalf of William Wayte for the arrest of William Shakespeare, Francis Langley [manager of The Swan Theatre built 1594/95 in Paris Garden, Southwark on the Surrey side of the Thames from London], Dorothy Soer and Anna Lee."

> Be it known that William Wayte seeks sureties of the peace against William Shakespere, Francis Langley, Dorothy Soer wife of John Soer and Anna Lee for fear of death and so forth. [Writ of] attachment to the Sheriff of Surrey.[16]

The litigation involves William Gardiner, a judge of the local Southwark court. It appears that Gardiner had to suppress the theatres, and used his stepson as an agent. Above all Langley resisted and Shakespeare was also implicated. Langley had entered for a similar writ against Wayte. There is no evidence of either writ being served, nor of Shakespeare having to give his sureties to the very court to which his father had lost his with such disastrous consequences sixteen years previously. At any rate, it was a close call and not the kind of activity expected from Sweet William, Gentle Will, but there may be something more here than meets the eye at first. A trade, his quality, was at stake if the theatre was closed and he had moved to live close by it.

The court action against him, and possible impending financial crisis that might have originated the controversy recapitulated too closely the fearful abyss into which his father had fallen. The threat emerged just as Shakespeare was attempting to restore his father, in order to reestablish his origins and secure himself. Furthermore, the recent loss of his son, and its accompanying grief just as he is asserting his patrimony could give vent to a combativeness that was usually under the control of his art.

ROYAL SHAKESPEARE THEATRE COLLECTION, STRATFORD-UPON-AVON

The Flower Portrait of William Shakespeare

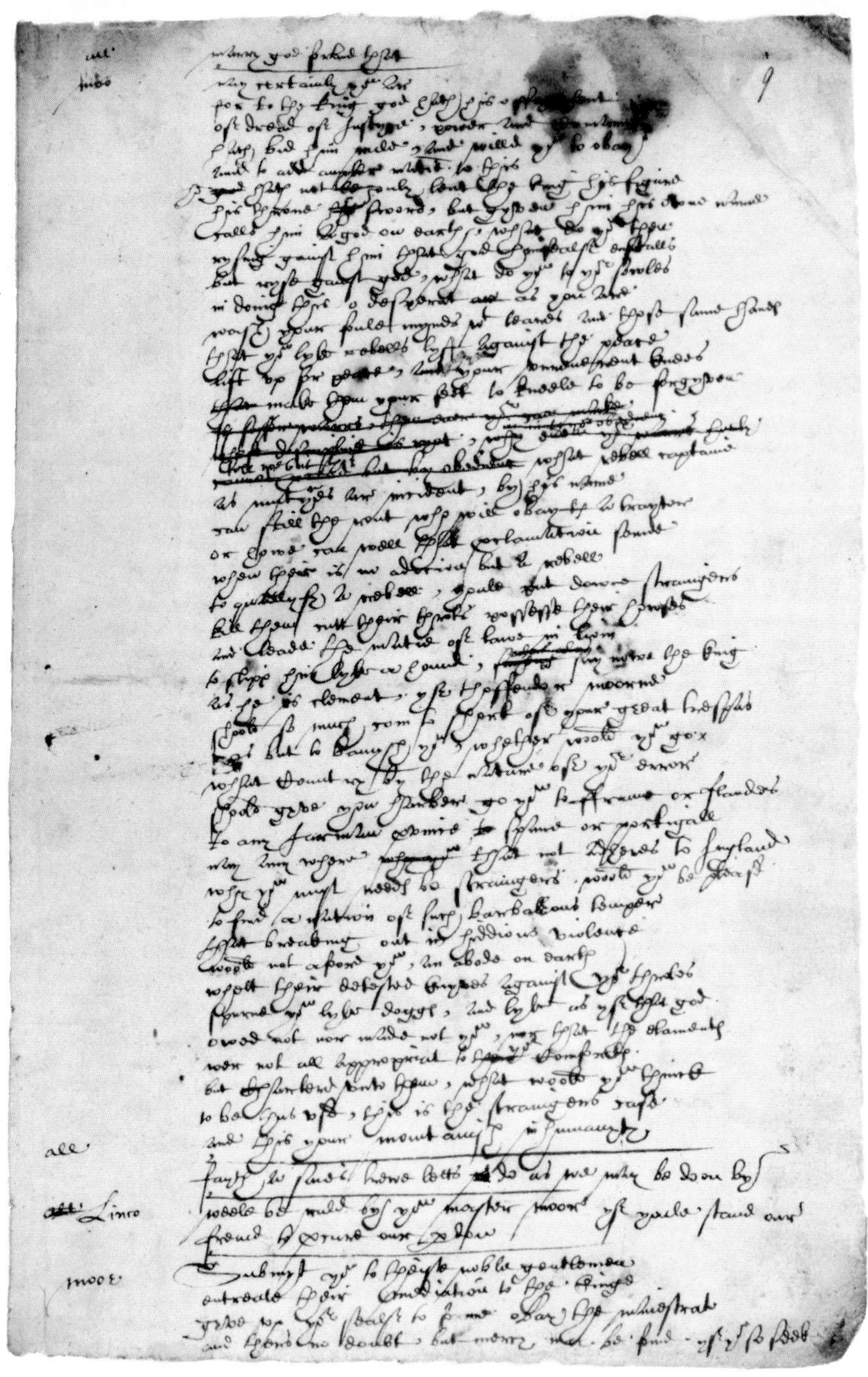

BRITISH MUSEUM

Believed to be Shakespeare's hand in a scene of the Thomas More *play.*

SHAKESPEARE BIRTHPLACE TRUST

Mary Arden's home in Wilmcote

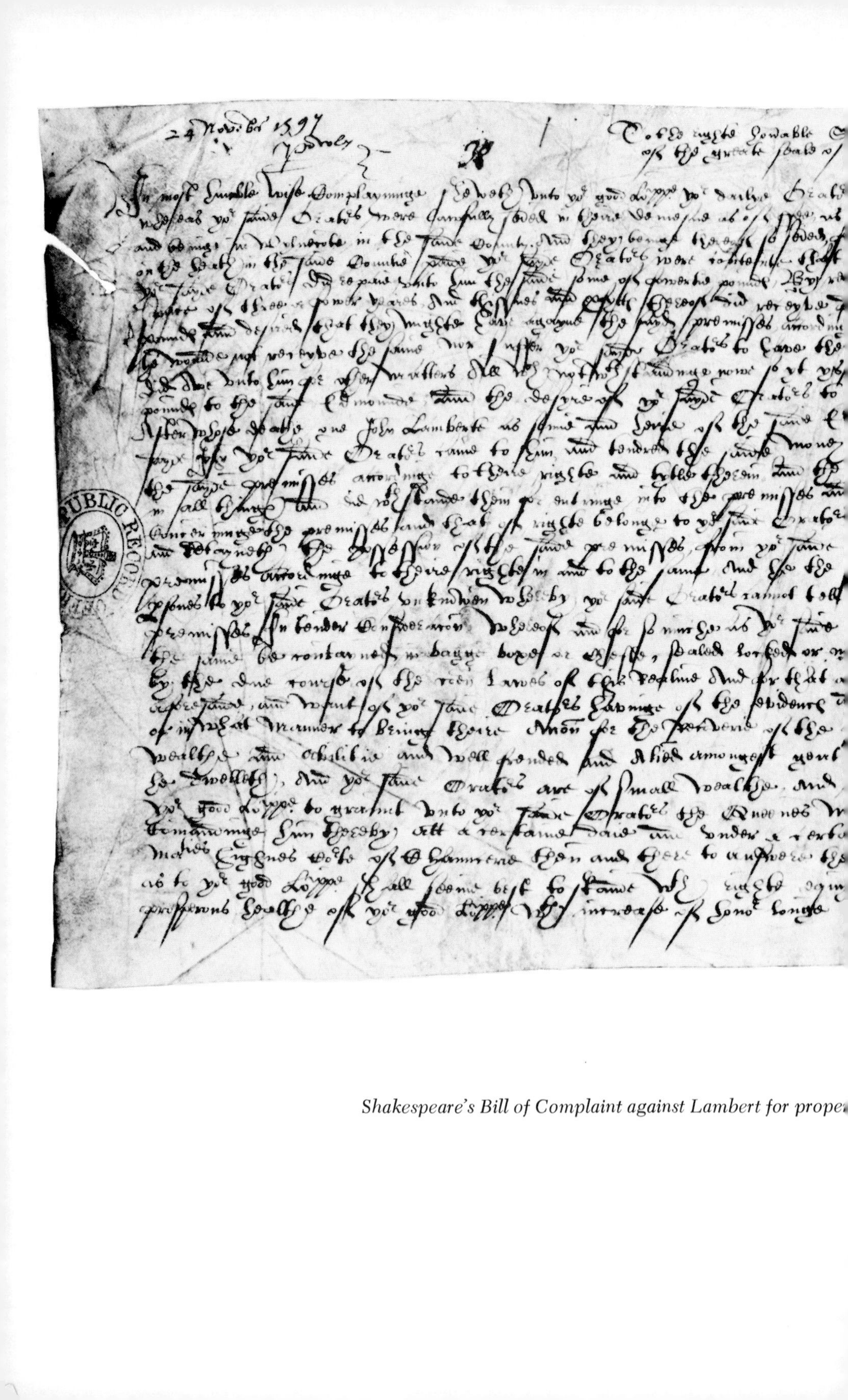

Shakespeare's Bill of Complaint against Lambert for prope

PUBLIC RECORD OFFICE, LONDON

Wilmcote, addressed to Sir Thomas Egerton in Chancery.

Possibly Henry Wriothesley, 3rd Earl of Southampton (Shakespeare's patron) by Nicholas Hilliard

FITZWILLIAM MUSEUM, CAMBRIDGE

Possibly William Hatcliff, thought by some to be the "W. H." of the Sonnets

VICTORIA AND ALBERT MUSEUM

SAMUEL IRELAND

Gray's Inn where Hatcliff and Southampton were members, and where Comedy of Errors *was put on in 1594.*

NATIONAL GALLERIES OF SCOTLAND, BY PERMISSION OF THE MARQUESS OF LOTHIAN

John Donne, poet, preacher and a member of the Inns of Court

SAMUEL IRELAND

Lincoln's Inn Gate where John Donne and William Lambarde had rooms (1591-1594).

SAMUEL IRELAND

Temple Church of the Inns of Court where John Donne preached (1616-1622).

SAMUEL IRELAND

North front of Middle Temple Hall where Twelfth Night *was performed in 1602.*

SAMUEL IRELAND

Southwest view of Hall of Middle Temple where John Marston and Shakespeare's cousin were members.

SAMUEL IRELAND

Clement's Inn where Shakespeare's cousin went, and which is referred to in Henry IV, Part 2.

SAMUEL IRELAN

Inner Temple where Francis Beaumont was a member (1600-1602).

Print depicting performance similar to ones held in Inns of Court.

Interior of Middle Temple Hall looking southeast.

NATIONAL MONUMENTS RECORD, LONDON

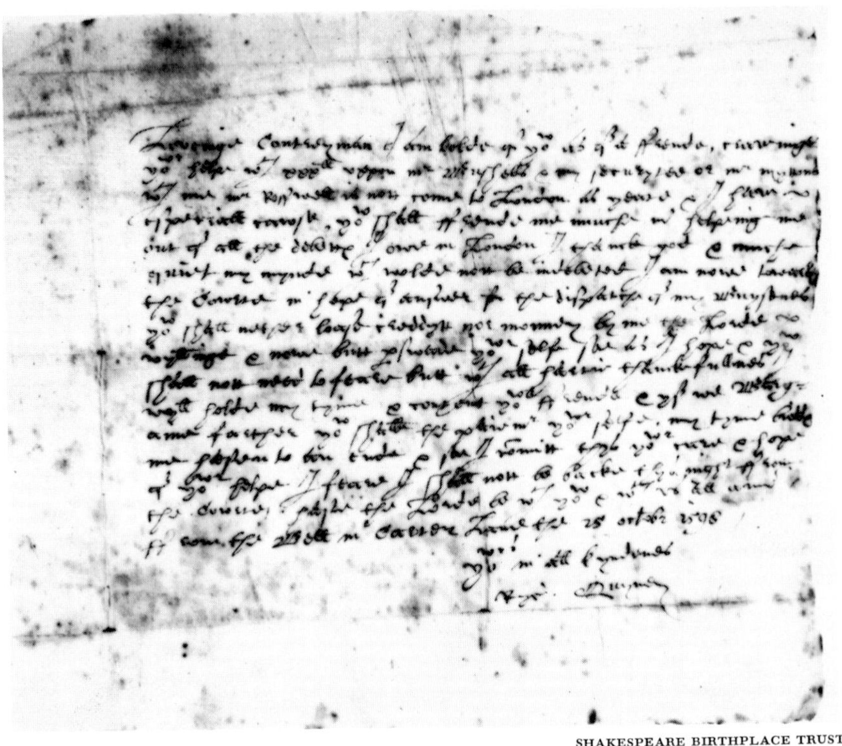

SHAKESPEARE BIRTHPLACE TRUST

Letter of Richard Quiney (whose son Thomas married Judith Shakespeare) requesting to borrow £30 from Shakespeare in 1598.

Third sheet of Shakespeare's last testament with a third signature

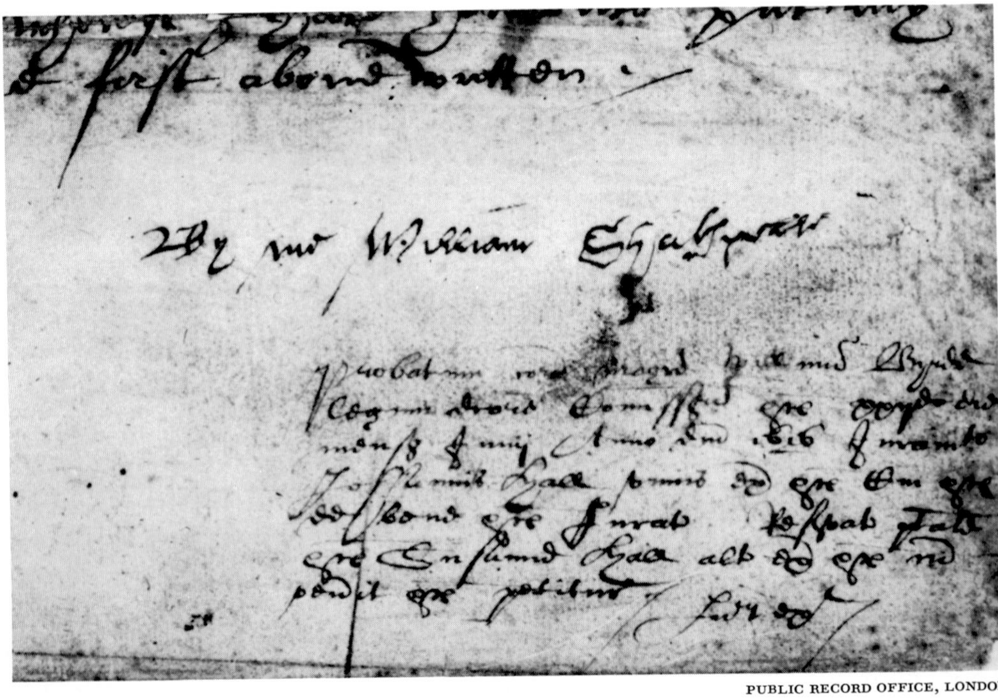

first above written

By me William Shakspeare

PUBLIC RECORD OFFICE, LONDON

Supposed painting of Thomas Nash of Lincoln's Inn and his wife, Shakespeare's granddaughter (daughter of Susanna Hall, Shakespeare's eldest daughter)

SHAKESPEARE BIRTHPLACE TRUST

Hall's Croft where Susanna Shakespeare lived with her husband, Dr. John Hall.

SHAKESPEARE BIRTHPLACE TRUST

FROM THE GORHAMBURY COLLECTION, BY PERMISSION OF THE EARL OF VERULAM

Sir Francis Bacon by Paul van Somer. Bacon was a member of Gray's Inn and participated in the revels.

HOLY TRINITY CHURCH, STRATFORD-UPON-AVON

Shakespeare's monument in the Stratford Parish Church

NATIONAL PORTRAIT GALLERY, LONDON

Edmond Malone, the biographer of Shakespeare, by Sir Joshua Reynolds. Malone was the first biographer to suggest that Shakespeare had a legal background.

Shakespeare was to be reminded by Ben Jonson of this episode of the warrant for sureties against life and limb by Shakespeare, himself, being an actor in *Every Man In His Humour* (1598). There Roger Formal (a clerk, the justice's novice, a proper fine penman) is told by Justice Clement to make out a series of warrants to keep the peace; these are bandied about, and the cause of much confusion. Warrants such as Shakespeare used in *Comedy of Errors* had been served against his father, by his father, and now in 1596 against Shakespeare himself.

The Masters of Chancery were at this time receiving unregulated tips of 2s., rather than the recent 4d., for *supplicavits*, or writs to justices of the peace requiring them to find a person to keep the peace.[17] Since one of the litigants was William Gardiner, a Justice of the Peace for Surrey, action may have been attempted by Langley and Shakespeare to obtain their writs to keep the peace from Chancery rather than Queen's Bench (common law) on the grounds that one had to obtain a superior jurisdiction over Gardiner, a judge of the local Southwark court and a person of power, influence, and wealth. Wayte was a ne'er-do-well and Gardiner had been a notorious litigant in Chancery.[18] As Master of Chancery, William Lambarde may have already been advising the lower court what he would hand down within the year as an opinion:

> It was one thing to regulate a trial in order to secure impartiality, but it was now quite a different matter to initiate a bill in Chancery solely on the grounds that the defendant was powerfully aided in the county. Whatever Chancery had once done, Lambarde gave it as his opinion in 1597 that reasons of this kind were insufficient by themselves to maintain a cause in Chancery and that the parties should proceed at common law. [Rumney *v.* Wentworth (1597)][19]

As one of the regulators of Chancery and advisors for Queen's Bench, and a Justice of the Peace for Kent, Surrey's neighboring county, Lambarde may have had an interest in the case, since it also involved the broader issue of the attempt by the Privy Council in July 1596 to suppress theatres emerging in the suburbs, as in the liberties of Surrey that were beyond the City's jurisdiction.

At least the information Leslie Hotson has uncovered on the matter of these actions indicates that in 1596 Shakespeare is once again involved with Queen's Bench in Westminster and at this time is associated with the Swan in Paris Garden. In this same year of the applications for the issuances of warrants, William Lambarde publishes his revised edition of *A Perambulation of Kent*, originally printed in 1576. He adds to his 1596 version in his account of the pilgrimages to Boxley, where those who visit the shrine do not get off scot-free, the following passage:

> . . . no more than such as goe to Parisgardein, the Bell Savage, or Theatre, to beholde Beare baiting, Enterludes, or Fence play, can account of any pleasant spectacle, unlesse they first pay one pennie at the gate, another at the entrie of the Scaffolde, and the thirde for a quiet standing.[20]

This has the sound of a personal complaint. How remarkable to have such direct information that this Master of Chancery attended plays in Surrey Bankside. William Lambarde saw Interludes in Paris Garden, Surrey by 1596 where Shakespeare was living, writing and performing in the Liberty of the Clink. William Shakespeare was in Court of Queen's Bench in 1596, and later in Chancery located in Westminster Hall where Lambarde worked; and Shakespeare's signature is in Lambarde's book.

Therefore, in addition to possibly meeting at the Inns of Court festivities such as the revels of Gray's Inn or in discussions in rooms at Lincoln's Inn, Shakespeare could have encountered Lambarde in Westminster Hall, or Lambarde could have met Shakespeare at the Swan. Shakespeare's company is acting at the newly constructed Swan in Paris Garden, Southwark in 1596 and it is in this year that the *Merchant of Venice* is thought to have been performed. It is reasonable to assume Lambarde would not pass up seeing *The Merchant of Venice*. Around this time (1596–1597) the chances for Shakespeare and Lambarde meeting are very high indeed, as they also are for 1588–1591 at Westminster, 1594–1595 at the Inns, and 1597–1599 in Chancery.

It is at least Mark Edwin Andrews' belief, in his helpful study of *The Merchant of Venice*[21] that the play was not only influenced by Shakespeare's thorough familiarity with English jurisprudence, but that the play in turn ultimately affected Egerton as Lord Chancellor, Sir Francis Bacon, and other judicial figures in their thoughts about Chancery and equity. Production of the play clearly affected King James, as he later asked for two performances of *The Merchant* within three days. To these judicial figures can now be added Egerton's right-hand man, William Lambarde who was a frequenter of the plays at The Swan.

In *The Merchant of Venice*, William Shakespeare is not just dramatizing a generalized court scene and sentimentalizing about mercy; rather, he is presenting Chancery procedure and advocating that it be used precisely along its theoretical lines, so as not to abrogate the common law of Queen's Bench and Common Pleas, and thus becoming merely a rival court. William Lambarde was referring to Chancery in his manuscript of *Archeion* as the "Gate of Mercie" and he championed reform from within in order to preserve its unique jurisdiction. In *Merchant*, Shakespeare puts to obvious use his readings in William West's *Symboleography* and Christopher St. Germain's *Doctor and Student*. The "mercy" of the high Court of Chancery's equitable decisions by the Lord Chancellor is not to be confused with the simple clemency or empathetic pity of Solinus in *The Comedy of Errors* and Theseus in *A Midsummer Night's Dream*, nor the somewhat easy piety of Germain's *Doctor and Student*, for William West says:

> There is a difference between Equitie and Clemencie: for Equitie is alwaies most firmly knit to the evil of the Law which way soever it bends, whether to clemency, or to severity.[22]

Seemingly extraneous, Biblical directives are most apparent in the Duke of Venice's "How shalt thou hope for mercy, rendering none?" (IV. i. 88). These, however, are also present in, and involved by, Germain:

> . . . thou do to another as thou wouldst should be done to thee . . . that in every general Rule of the Law thou do observe and keep Equity.[23]

This, in turn, serves an institutionalized, judicial function in the procedure of Chancery, which as a Court of Conscience operates *in personam*, upon oath, to insure that the plaintiff has come before the Bench "with clean hands." Observe in the familiar passage, operating at the same time, Portia's, and of course Shakespeare's, precise sense of how equity accomplishes justice, how Chancery has a remedial function over the strictures of the common law, how a person within an institution can reflect the hope that the application of its system can transcend the system's own limitations to achieve the idealized purpose for which the institution was constructed:

> PORTIA: The quality of mercy is not strain'd
> It droppeth as the gentle rain from heaven
> Upon the place beneath: it is twice blest;
> It blesseth him that gives and him that takes:
> 'Tis mightiest in the mightiest: it becomes
> The throned monarch better than his crown;
> His sceptre shows the force of temporal power,
> The attribute to awe and majesty,
> Wherein doth sit the dread and fear of kings;
> But mercy is above this sceptred sway;
> It is enthroned in the hearts of kings,
> It is an attribute to God himself;
> And earthy power doth then show likest God's
> When mercy seasons justice. Therefore, Jew,
> Though justice be thy plea, consider this,
> That, in the course of justice, none of us
> Should see salvation: we do pray for mercy;
> And that same prayer doth teach us all to render
> The deeds of mercy. I have spoke thus much

To mitigate the justice of thy plea;
Which if thou follow, this strict court of Venice
Must needs give sentence 'gainst the merchant there.
SHYLOCK: My deeds upon my head! I crave the law,
The penalty and forfeit of my bond.

(IV. i. 195-206).

Portia speaks of the power which resides in Chancery. The Lord Chancellor was regarded as the Keeper of the King's Conscience, regulating the monarch's justice with his mercy exercised as equity in Chancery. The Chancellors used to hold high ecclesiastical office, as did Thomas-à-Becket who was also Archbishop of Canterbury in the time of Henry II; or they had a very independent religious consciousness, as did Sir Thomas More under Henry VIII. In Elizabeth's reign, they were secular jurists, but had to uphold their moral obligations; under King James, Sir Francis Bacon was impeached by Parliament upon the charge of accepting bribes.

Portia's speech is mirrored by a clerk of Chancery in his own famous work. Edmund Spenser was granted by Queen Elizabeth the office of clerk in Chancery and he wrote in 1596, the year of *The Merchant of Venice*:

Most sacred virtue she [Justice] of all the rest,
Resembling God in his imperiall might;
Whose soveraine powre is herein most exprest,
That both to good and bad he dealeth right,
And all his workes with Iustice hath bedight.
That powre he also doth to Princes lend,
And makes them like himselfe in glorious sight,
To sit in his owne seate, his cause to end,
And rule his people right, as he doth recommend.

Some Clarkes doe doubt in their devicefull art,
Whether this heavenly thing, whereof I treat,
To weeten *Mercie*, be of Iustice part,
Or drawne forth from her divine extreate
This well I wote, that sure she is as great,
And meriteth to have as high a place,

Sith in th' Almighties everlasting seat
She first was bred, and borne of heavenly race;
From thence pour'd down on men, by influence of grace.

Who will not mercie unto others shew,
How can he mercy every hope to have?
To pay each with his owne is right and dew.
Yet since ye mercie now doe need to crave,
I will it graunt, your hopelesse life to save;
With these conditions, which I will propound:
First, that ye better shall your selfe behave
Unto all errant knights, whereso on ground;
Next that ye Ladies ayde in every stead and stound.[24]

Equity and mercy as attributes of Chancery are very much in the legal wind of London in 1596 with Germain's *Doctor and Student*, West's *Symboleography*, Lambarde's *Archeion*, Spenser's *Faerie Queene*, and Shakespeare's *Merchant of Venice*.

Portia's famous "Quality of mercy" speech is not just an idealistic invocation but a reminder that it is a Court of Equity which has been convened where, as she says, "mercy seasons justice" and one can come "to mitigate the justice of [the] plea." As St. Germain recognizes, "Equity is a right Wiseness that considereth all the particular circumstances of the Deed the which also is tempered with the Sweetness of Mercy." He continues:

> If thou take all that the words of the Law giveth thee [which is the 'rigorous course' (IV. i. 8) of Shylock's action upon the due and forfeit of his bond (l. 35)], thou shalt sometime do against the law. (*p.* 52)

Portia's ruling of a pound of flesh only, and no blood as the award to be taken from Antonio by Shylock is a severely precise reading of the letter of the law—the reverse of what is expected when one seeks leniency, a loose interpretation, or a moderated sentence. This is a dramatic and legalistic triumph of Shakespeare's design to illustrate how Chancery should fulfill the instruction that "Equity followeth the Law in all particular cases where Right and Justice requireth, notwithstanding the general Rule of the Law be to the contrary."[25] The very terms of the bond were instructive in the debate between law and justice as Shakespeare would have read in West and was picked up by later writers on equity from Gray's Inn, such as Thomas Ashe:

> For it is to bee understood that the law hath two parts, *Carnem* & *Animam*: the letter resembleth the flesh [and that was Shylock's due], and the intent and reason the soule [equity is the spirit of the law].[26]

Not only does Portia speak to legal theory but to Shakespear's biographical past. William's father loses Shakespeare's estate which he was to inherit from his mother, and Portia, symbolically reverses the condition by functioning as a female mercy-figure employing equity to restore what was forfeited by a bond.

Shakespeare, at the end of *Merchant of Venice*, manages during Shylock's remaining life to provide for both Antonio and Shylock as well as preserve the corpus of the estate for the ultimate use and benefit of Shylock's heirs. *Shakespeare* v. *Lambert* discloses that John Shakespeare had failed to do this for his son, and hence his residual interest was not recognizable in common law before the Court of Queen's Bench. Only a court of equity, such as Chancery might provide, could establish and recognize an instrument for such use.

> NERISSA: Ay, and I'll give them [comforts] him [Lorenzo] without a fee
> There do I give to you and Jessica,
> From the rich Jew, a special deed of gift,
> After his death, of all he dies possess'd of.
> (v. i. 290–293)

This legal construction is precisely what Shakespeare knows to set up in his own will for not only his two daughters, but his grandchild and in hopes of a grandson or great grandson, yet (but never) to come.

> . . . unto the said Susanna Hall for and during the term of her natural life, and after her decease to the first son of

> her body lawfully issuing and to the heirs males of the body of the said first son lawfully issuing, and for default of such issue to the second son of her body lawfully issuing and to the heirs males of the body of the said second son lawfully issuing, and for default of such heirs to the third son of the body of the said Susanna lawfully issuing and of the heirs males of the body of the said third son lawfully issuing; and for default of such issue the same so to be and remain to the fourth, fifth, sixth and seventh sons of her body lawfully issuing, one after another, and to the heirs males of the bodies of the said fourth, fifth, sixth, and seventh sons lawfully issuing in such manner as it is before limited to be and remain to the first, second, and third sons of her body and to their heirs males. And for default of such issue the said premises to be and remain to my said niece [granddaughter] Hall and the heirs males of her body lawfully issuing; and for default of such issue, to my daughter Judith and the heirs males of her body lawfully issuing. . . .

Had Hamlet lived, this verbal search would not have been necessary to establish Shakespeare's line of inheritance. Time will reveal why Susanna was preferred, not merely as the eldest daughter, and will give significance to the phrase "lawful issue" for both Susanna and Judith. The technicalities Shakespeare had to be aware of in not only his own court case, but also in the *Merchant of Venice*, and in his Last Will and Testament, as the result of the creation of a use after a use, and of the Trust are explicated with detail in Mark Edwin Andrews' informative work.[27]

4. *William Shakespeare in Chancery.*

CHANCERY and equity were mainly concerned with property, conveyance, use, inheritance, and things held in trust. Shakespeare makes a major purchase in 1597, so that finally he possessed a separate residence of his own to replace what he might have had in Asbies. The transaction is in keeping with his acquiring an estate for himself, and replacing his father's losses; looking after the rest of his family, and toward the family's future since no son will. Shakespeare senses the burden from both sides of time (. . . nothing 'gainst Time's scythe can make defence /Save breed, to brave him when he takes thee hence. Sonnet XII.): He will not inherit, and will have no male inheritor.

IV

Unthrifty loveliness, why dost thou spend
Upon thyself thy beauty's legacy?
Nature's bequest gives nothing but doth lend,
And being frank she lends to those are free.
Then, beauteous niggard, why dost thou abuse
The bounteous largess given thee to give?
Profitless usurer, why dost thou use
So great a sum of sums; yet canst not live?
For having traffic with thyself alone,
Thou of thyself thy sweet self dost deceive.
Then how, when nature calls thee to be gone,
What acceptable audit canst thou leave?
  Thy unused beauty must be tomb'd with thee,
  Which, used, lives th' executor to be.

VI

Then let not winter's ragged hand deface
In thee thy summer, ere thou be distill'd:
Make sweet some vial; treasure thou some place
With beauty's treasure, ere it be self-kill'd.
That use is not forbidden usury
Which happies those that pay the willing loan;
That's for thyself to breed another thee,
Or ten times happier, be it ten for one;
Ten times thyself were happier than thou art,
If ten of thine ten times refigured thee:
Then what could death do, if thou shouldst depart,
Leaving thee living in posterity?
  Be not self-will'd for thou art much too fair
  To be death's conquest and make worms thine heir.

Shakespeare leaves his parents and sister in the double house on Henley Street, and from William Underhill, whose father was a member of Inner Temple, he purchases on May 4, 1597, New Place, the second largest house in Stratford.

The Concord of Fine and Foot of Fine indicating the conveyance is recorded in the Court of Common Pleas, Westminster.[28] William Underhill, the son of the owner, held the legal office of the Queen's Escheator for the counties of Warwick and Leicester, so legal offices and connections continue to run in the Underhill family. Shakespeare's new residence places him among a whole packet of lawyers living all within a block of each other, Walter Roach, William Court, the Greenes, and the Underhills. The Combes were at the College on the way to the Church.

Evidenced by his plays' texts, audiences and successes, Shakespeare has at this time the legal knowledge, acquaintances, and financial where with all to reopen the case over Asbies that has rankled so long. The property was alienated in 1578; the mortgage became due in 1580; the Stratford agreement for compensation for the Shakespeares' residual title was reached in 1587; the breaking of which resulted in the case in Court of Queen's Bench from 1588 to 1590, and then the matter was dropped. Now in 1597, Shakespeare's father has his coat of arms pending, and his own house liberated from Will's immediate family. The restoration process is going well and so, as a part of this campaign, the dramatist turns to the reclaiming of Asbies, or to gain at least restitution for the loss. During or just after, this new court case opening in Chancery, that gate of mercy, that fount of equity, Shakespeare writes *As You Like It*, in which Orlando complains to his younger brother, Oliver, who is keeping his inheritance from him:

> . . . obscuring and hiding from me all gentleman-like qualities. The spirit of my father grows strong in me, and I will no longer endure it: therefore allow me such exer-

> cises as may become a gentleman, or give me the poor allotery my father left me by testament; with that I will go buy my fortunes.
>
> (I. i. 71–77)

The plot includes two sons keeping property from their respective brothers. The second pair is made up of Duke Senior having been exiled from his rule by Frederick. At the end of the play the second son of Sir Roland tells Duke Senior of Duke Frederick's reformation from his evil ways:

> His crown bequeathing to his banish'd brother,
> And all their lands restored to them again
> That were with him exiled. This to be true,
> I do engage my life.
> DUKE SENIOR: Welcome, young man;
> Thou offer'st fairly to thy brothers' wedding:
> To one his lands withheld and to the other
> A land itself at large, a potent dukedom.
>
> (V. iv. 169–175).

John Shakespeare's estate of Asbies was being withheld from Shakespeare by his father's brother-in-law's son.

Shakespeare reopens his case in Westminster Hall through a recently selected London attorney by the name of J. Stovell who, like his father's attorney John Harborne, is never mentioned by Chambers, Eccles, nor Schoenbaum. This time, on November 24, 1597, the suit is entered in Chancery where William Lambarde is Master, particularly of alienations, within whose jurisdiction this litigation falls. The plea is against John Lambert, the son and heir of Old Edmund, and instituted in the names of John and Mary Shakespeare. At this time, John was not attending civic meetings, nor going to church, nor showing up at courts, nor pursuing any trade; he was accruing debts, and was not apparently receiving any income from holdings, although he is able to maintain the property and dwelling on Henley Street. William could maintain him from his earnings, and probably did if the Stratford rumors are correct concerning Shakespeare's expenses there.

The dramatist is not mentioned in the Chancery documents, which has resulted in their unwarranted neglect by scholars. He was referred to in the papers on the case in Queen's Bench and it is clearly his financing, interest, concerns, expectations, and presence which stands behind the new court action.

The Bill of Complaint follows:

> To the right honorable Sir Thomas Egerton, knighte, lorde keper of the greate seale of England.

The chancery bill is addressed to the man who had attended the revels at Gray's Inn in 1594 when *The Comedy of Errors* had been a bone of contention in a mock trial; Sir Thomas was also Lambarde's closest mentor.

> In most humble wise complayninge, sheweth unto your good lordshippe your dailye oratours, John Shakespere of Stratford-upon-Avon, in the county of Warwicke, and Mary his wief, ...

Since Mary and John Shakespeare held the main rights through inheritance and marriage, the claim is in their names. William had secondary rights as inheritor, but it had never actually passed to him. The expense of the case was undoubtedly borne by the dramatist; particularly evidencing the famous son's involvement are the significant attorneys and Masters who become enmeshed in the action. Something of a monetary advantage might be obtained by the success of the suit, either as an income for his father and mother, or as an addition to his estate, insofar as the lease given out for the use of the land had earlier been obtained at a very low rate and it was about to expire at which time it could be renewed. The new lease could provide a per-annum income that equaled the £40 mortagage that was being contested.

> . . . that wheras your saide oratours were lawfully seized [i.e. in the possession of] in their demesne as of fee, as in the rights of the said Mary, of and in one mesuage and one yarde lande with thappurtenances, lyinge and beinge in Wylnecote, in the saide county, ...

The Wilmecote property ("Asbies Estate") has been estimated, as the result of confusion in the titles and difficulty in locating the plot precisely, as ranging from 40 to 56 acres with a cottage to two houses with two gardens. There were probably some forty acres of land, some of it arable, and four acres associated with a dwelling house.

> . . . and they beinge thereof so seised, for and in consideracion of the somme of fowerty pounds to them by one Edmounde Lamberte of Barton-on-the-Heath . . .

This is Old Lambert from the village celebrated by Christopher Sly in the Induction of *Taming of the Shrew.*

> . . . in the saide countie [i.e. Warwickshire] paide, your sayde oratours were contente that he, the saide Edmounde Lamberte, shoulde have and enjoye the same premisses *untill suche tyme as your sayde oratours did repaie unto him the saide somme of fowertie poundes* [*Italics mine*];

The Shakespeares are making the claim that Asbies was mortgaged.

> . . . by reasone whereof the saide Edmounde did enter into the premisses and did occupie the same for the space of three or fower yeares, and thissues and profyttes thereof did receyve and take; . . .

This is inaccurate insofar as the period of Edmund Lambert's possession ran from the time of his paying John Shakespeare the £40 in 1578 until Edmund died in 1587, a period closer to nine years, rather than three or four. Either the Shakespeares were being forgetful or they were moderating the length of uncontested possession.

> . . . after which your saide oratours did tender unto the saide Edmounde the sayde somme of fowerty poundes, and desired that they mighte have agayne the sayde premisses accordinge to theire agreement; which money he the sayde Edmounde then refused to receyve, sayinge that he woulde not receyve the same, nor suffer your sayde oratours to have the saide premisses agayne, unless they would paye unto him certayne other money which they did owe unto him for other matters; . . .

Edmund had stood surety for John on several occasions and may have lost payments when John did not meet his obligations and these were still owed by John.

> . . . *all which notwithstandinge, nowe so yt ys;* . . .

In other words, the case is as it has been stated, that the Shakespeares are to have Asbies returned to them on their payment of £40 which they are now prepared to do. What has happened to the other debts is not clear; possibly paid or dissolved.

> . . . and yt maye please your good lordshippe . . .

This is addressed to Egerton the Lord Keeper and would be received by a representative, most likely in the Office of Alienations, one of the Masters (William Lambarde),[29] or his representative, or clerk.

> . . . that, shortelie after the tendringe of the sayde fowertie poundes to the saide Edmounde and the desyre of your sayde oratours to have theire lande agayne from him [i.e. in 1580], he the saide Edmounde att Barton aforesayde dyed [actually not so shortly after in April 1587, a good seven years later], after whose deathe one John Lamberte, as sonne and heire of the saide Edmounde, entred into the saide premisses and occupied the same; after which entrie of the sayde John your saide oratours came to him [i.e. in September of 1587, five months after Edmund's death] and tendred the saide money unto him, and likewise requested him that he woulde suffer them to have and enjoye the sayde premisses accordinge to theire righte and tytle therein and *the promise of his saide father to your saide oratours made,* . . .

Unfortunately, Edmund's promise to the Shakespeares had been a verbal one, between relatives who had had a number of unrecorded transactions. Chancery, however, could recognize such agreements between man and man (rather than man and property according to common law) in the matters of conscience, that is of things pertaining to oaths, faith, and trust. This was the crucial point in the *Shakespeare* v. *Lambert* case in Chancery and would have repercussions upon laws pertaining to mortgages today. The type of appeals invoked by Chancery are suggested by the Duke in the court of Venice. The lines are possibly written in 1596 within a year of the Bill of Complaint filed in 1597.

> Shylock, the world thinks, and I think so too,
> That thou but lead'st this fashion of thy malice
> To the last hour of act; and then 'tis thought
> Thou'lt show thy mercy and remorse more strange
> Than is thy strange apparent cruelty;
> And where thou now exact'st the penalty,
> Which is a pound of this poor merchant's flesh,
> Thou wilt not only loose the forfeiture,
> But, touch'd with human gentleness and love,
> Forgive a moiety of the principal;
> Glancing an eye of pity on his losses,
> That have of late so huddled on his back,
> Enow to press a royal merchant down
> And pluck commiseration of his state
> From brassy bosoms and rough hearts of flint,
> From stubborn Turks and Tartars, never train'd
> To offices of tender courtesy.
> We all expect a gentle answer, Jew.
>
> (IV. i. 17–34)

. . . which he, the saide John [Lambert], denyed in all thinges, and did withstande them for entringe into the premisses, and as yet doeth so contynewe still [i.e. from September 1587 to November 1597, another ten years]; and by reasone that certaine deedes and other evydences concerninge the premisses, and that of rights belonge to your saide oratours, are coumme to the handes and possession of the sayde John, [i.e. John Lambert possesses the symbolegraphia, or instruments of conveyance, indentures, leases, titles and deeds], he wrongfullie still keepeth and detayneth the possession of the saide premisses from your said oratours, and will in noe wise permytt and suffer them to have and enjoye the sayde premisses accordinge to their righte in and to the same; and he, the saide John Lamberte, hathe of late made sondrie secreate estates of the premisses to dyvers persones to your said oratours

> unknowen, whereby *your saide oratours cannot tell againste whome to bringe there accions att the comen lawe for the recovery of the premisses* [*Italics mine*]; . . .

The Shakespeares are employing a number of devices to ensure attention from Chancery. This one is essentially to request the right of discovery to obtain all instruments in the defendant's possesion in order to make their case better founded, perhaps strong enough to proceed at common law. Lambert might have served upon him a kind of injunction from Chancery against any further leasing or sale of the land until the matter were settled. These writs were not obtainable from lower courts, and sometimes amounted to a recognition of the complaint. The suit follows correct form by recognizing Chancery's appellate function, insisted upon by William Lambarde in his rulings and his writings, and dramatized by Portia's function as the learned Doctor advising the Duke in his court. Also the Shakespeares are not seeking damages but recovery of the property, Chancery can offer remedy in kind rather than just penalties.

> . . . in tender consideracion whereof, and for so muche as your saide oratours knowe not the certaine dates nor contentes of the saide wrytinges, nor whether the same be contayned in bagge, boxe or cheste, sealed, locked or noe, and *therefore have no remeadie to recover the same evydences and wrytings by the due course of the comen lawes of this realme*; and for that also, by reasone of the saide secreate estates so made by the saide John Lamberte as aforesaid and want of your saide oratours having of the evidences and wrytings as aforesaid, *your saide oratours cannot tell what accions or against whome, or in what manner, to bringe theire accion for the recoverie of the premisses att the comen law*; . . .

Pleadings in Court of Queen's Bench had to be precise according to form, but Chancery recognized the plea despite its form and with writs of discovery could help search out the right basis for a plea and advise or instruct the litigant on the proper form to proceed with at common law, "Have I not seen dwellers on form and favour

/Lose all, and more, . . ." (Sonnet CXXV). The Shakespeares were pursuing every possible ground to obtain action from Chancery.

The Bill of Complaint moves towards a close with several formulaic, but nevertheless pertinent, statements. John and Mary's declining personal situation in opposition to Lambert's makes the Chancery legal tag phrases speak to their case.

> . . . and for that also the sayde John Lamberte ys of greate wealthe and abilitie, and well frended and alied amongest gentlemen and freeeholders of the countrey in the saide countie of Warwicke, where he dwelleth, and *your saide oratours are of small wealthe* and verey fewe frendes and alyance in the saide countie, . . .

This is a patterned insistence upon their citizen rights in Chancery to appeal as poor and unable to get justice against a wealthy, powerful and well-friended antagonist.

> . . . maye yt therefore please your good lordshippe to grant unto your saide oratours the Queenes Majesties moste gracyous writte of subpena, . . .

This is a summons to appear in a court of conscience and be examined upon oath, *in personam* and not by attorney with instruments or affidavit as evidence.

> . . . to be directed to the saide John Lamberte, comandinge him thereby att a certaine daie, and under a certaine payne therein to be lymytted, personally to appeare before your good lordshippe in Her Majesties highnes courte of Chauncerie, then and there to answere the premisses; and further to stande to and abyde suche order and direction therein *as to your good lordshippe shall seeme best to stande with righte, equytie and good conscyence*, . . .

The reference invokes the specific virtues particular to Chancery pertaining to personal rights, things of conscience and matters of equity.

> . . . and your sayde oratours shall daylie praye to God for the prosperous healthe of your good lordshippe with increase of honour longe to contynewe.[30]

Thus, the Chancery Bill ends with the familiar tag of a complimentary, personal address to the Chancellor.

John Lambert is very much the Shylock of the Shakespeare Chancery case. As if it were Shylock responding with his,

> I have possess'd your grace of what I purpose;
> And by our holy Sabbath have I sworn
> To have the due and forfeit of my bond:
> If you deny it, let the danger light
> Upon your charter and your city's freedom.
>
> (IV. i. 35–39)

so John Lambert in November, 1597 enters his Reply, or Replication, to the Bill of Complaint.

> The answeare of John Lambarte, defendante, to the byll of complainte of John Shakespeere and Mary his wief, complainantes.
>
> -The said defendante, saving to himself both nowe, and att all tymes hereafter all advantage of excepcion to the uncertentie and unsufficiencie of the said complainantes byll, and also savinge to this defendante such advantage as by the order of this honorable courte he shal be adjudged to have, for that the like byll, in effecte conteyninge the selfe-same matter, hath byne heretofore exhibited into this honorable courte againste this defendante, . . .

Shakespeare was pursuing this with such intensity that there were two bills of complaint on the same case before Chancery and Lambert was complaining against the legal harassment.

> . . . whereunto this defendante hath made a full and directe answeare, wherein the said complainante hath not proceeded to hearinge; . . .

This previous Bill and Replication to the same are not extant, as they were voided during the pursuit of this Bill and Reply.

> . . . for a seconde full and directe answeare unto the said complainantes byll sayeth that true yt is, as this defendante

> verylie thinkethe, that the said complainantes were, or one of them was, lawfully seized in theire or one of theire demeasne, . . .

John Lambert is beginning his case at the point at which by the plaintiffs' own admission there is conveyance indisputable by law; the moment Mary received the land as her portion from the Ardens.

> . . . as of fee, of and in one messuage and one yearde and fower acres of lande with thappurtenaunces, lyeinge and being in Wilmecott, in the parishe of Aston Cawntloe, in the countie of Warwicke, and they or one of them soe beinge thereof seized, *the said complainante, John Shakespeare, by indenture bering date uppon or about the fowertenth daye of November, in the twenteth yeare of the raigne of our Sovereigne Lady the Queenes Majestie that now ys* [i.e. November 14, 1578], *for and in consideracion of the summe of fortie powndes of lawfull Englishe monney unto the said complainante paide by Edmunde Lamberte, this defendantes father in the said byll named, did give, graunte, bargaine and sell. . . .*

Here is the rub! Shakespeare is claiming the land was mortgaged to be recovered by payment of debt (fine and recovery), and now is willing to (even possibly pay the other debts) since the land is of value. Likewise, John Lambert is willing to forego the £40 mortgage payment and other debts, standing on the transaction as a sale, so that he can preserve its income for himself. Lambert continues, saying John Shakespeare did

> . . . sell the said messuage, and one yearde and fower acres of lande with thappurtenaunces, unto the said Edmunde Lamberte, and his heires and assignes, to have and to holde the said messuage, one yearde and fower acres of lande, with thappurtenaunces, unto the saide Edmunde Lamberte, his heires and assignes, for ever; in which indenture there is a condicionall provisoe conteyned . . .

John Lambert turns the legal document of alienation inside-out, making a strict reading of the indenture as a "sale," with the condition of redemption as an exception to the sale if, and only if, the fee is tendered on the *specific* day. Whereas Shakespeare's claim is that the alienation was a mortgage only to be forfeited if the exception to the usual payment procedure occurs, if for some reason the money for the mortgage is not tendered on the specific date. Lambert recognizes this provision, as he continues:

> . . . that, if the said complainante did paye unto the said Edmunde Lamberte the summe of fortie powndes . . .

The case rests, Lambert is saying, on whether the £40 were or were not, paid on the specific due date. On the other hand, the Shakespeares say the amount was "tendered" on that day. It could go hard for the Shakespeares insofar as they have admitted that the payment was not made. Nevertheless, they are in a court of equity and the judge can, when the case is brought to trial, act upon conscience, be merciful, and recognize unwritten promises and claims if witnesses can offer corroboration. The judge of Chancery might be as Antonio describes the Duke in his court:

> I have heard
> Your grace hath ta'en great pains to qualify
> His [*Shylock's*] rigorous course; but since he stands obdurate
> And that no lawful means can carry me
> Out of his envy's reach, I do oppose
> My patience to his fury, and am arm'd
> To suffer, with a quietness of spirit,
> The very tyranny and rage of his.
>
> (IV. i. 6–13).

> . . . [if the payment were made] uppon the feast daie of St. Michell tharchangell which shoulde be in the yeare of our Lorde God one thousande fyve-hundred and eightie, att the dwellinge howse of the said Edmund Lamberte, in Barton-on-the-Heath in the said countie of Warwicke, that then the said graunte, bargaine, and *sale*, and all the covenauntes, grauntes and agreementes therin conteyned, shulde cease and be voyde, as by the said indenture, whereunto this defendante for his better certentie doth

> referre himself, maye appeare; and afterwards, the saide complainante John Shakespeere, by his Deede Pole and Liverie. . .

Deede Pole refers to posting for public notice; and Livery, to the writ known at the common law that the heir on arrival at his majority, had the right to sue out to obtain the possession of the seisin of his lands at the hands of the king.

> . . . theruppon made, did infeoffe the said Edmunde Lamberte of the saide premisses to have and to holde unto him the said Edmunde Lamberte and his heires for ever; after all which, in the terme of Ester, in the one and twenteth yeare of the Queenes Majesties raigne that nowe ys, the said complainantes in due forme of lawe did levye a fyne of the said messuage and yearde lande, and other the premisses, before the Queenes Majesties justices of the common plees att Westminster, . . .

John Lambert turns to the hard evidence in the court record for the conveyance evidenced by the Note of a Fine levied when an estate "in Awston Cawntlett" (i.e. Aston Cantlowe, "Asbies Estate") was mortgaged by "Johannem Shakespere at Mariam uxorem" to "Edmundum Lambert" for "quadraginta libras sterlingorum," Easter Term, 21 Elizabeth, 1579.[31] Such a fine for alienation could indicate a sale or a mortgage, the distinction William Lambarde in his office (1591) had through his treatise, private papers, rulings and regulations of rates, attempted to clarify. In his current Mastership (1597) he still presided specifically over the division having special interest in Alienations.

> . . . unto the saide Edmunde Lamberte, and his heires, sur conuzance de droyt [Norman legal phrase for transferance of right], as that which the said Edmunde had of the gifte of the said John Shakspeere, as by the said pole deede, [cf. *Twelfth Night* I. v. 156–157] and the chirograph [i.e. engrossing, or handwriting] of the said fine, whereunto this defendante for his better certentie referreth himselfe, . . .

Lambert is standing upon the written evidence of the indenture.

> . . . yt doth and maye appeare; and this defendante further sayeth that *the said complainante did not tender or paye the said summe of fortie powndes unto the said Edmund Lamberte, . . .*

At common law, without written proof on the Shakespeares' part to the contrary, Lambert would have an open and shut case, as it undoubtedly appeared he did before the Court of Queen's Bench in 1590 at which time the Shakespeares probably were convinced to withdraw. Furthermore the Shakespeares in their Chancery Bill in 1597 admit that they did *not* "*paye* the said summe;" however their point, for which they have no written evidence was that they "*did tender* the said summe." Whereas the two words in the phrase "tender or paye" are conventionally but not legally meant to be virtually redundant, in this case the Shakespeares are contesting that they met their half of the obligation as well as half of the legal terms, at least in intent, but the instruments of conveyance do not record this.

> . . . [they did not pay to] this defendantes father, uppon the saide feaste daye, which was in the yeare of our Lorde God one thowsande fyve hundred and eightie, accordinge to the said provisoe in the said indenture expressed.

This date is reiterated because common law strictly followed the letter of the law on the payment. The sum had to be returned at the place and on the day specified, neither before, nor later. Before "equity of redemption," or a grace period on loans and mortgages became firmly established as such in Chancery, a crude form of the later practice could be had in a writ out of Chancery similar to an injunction which would prevent the entering of the land, or wasting of the property until complete title was settled.

> By reason whereof *this defendantes said father* [Edmund Lambert] *was lawfully and absolutely seized of the said*

> *premisses* [as of 1580 when payment was not made] in his demeasne as of fee, and aboute eleven yeares laste paste [Lambert exaggerates the time-span which the Shakespeares telescope] thereof, dyed [in 1587] seized; by and after whose decease the said messuage and premisses with thappurtenances descended and came, as of rights the same oughte to descende and come, unto this defendante, as sonne and nexte heire of the said Edmund; . . .

As in the case of Henry IV passing the English throne on to Prince Hal, and thus Henry V being a rightful ruler by due inheritance (despite Bolingbroke's usurpation and shaky claim), so John Lambert claims possession, independent of original dispute, of Asbies by the simple right of the due process of inheritance.

> . . . by vertue whereof this defendante was and yet is of the said messuage, yearde lande and premisses, lawfully seized in his demeasne as of fee, which *this defendante hopeth he oughte both by lawe and equitie to enjoye*, . . .

John Lambert is playing the same game as the Shakespeares in appealing not just to law and justice but in Chancery to its special claim to equity.

> . . . accordinge to his lawfull righte and tytle therein; and this defendante further sayeth that the said messuage, yearde lande and other the said-premisses, or the moste parte thereof, have ever, *sythence the purches* [i.e. since the purchase; Lambert is being careful to continue to refer to it as a sale!] therof by this defendantes father, byne in lease by the demise of the said complainante; . . .

What follows has a remarkable shift in tone from legal formalism to an outright vindictive attack upon the Shakespeares' motives, poisoning the well of clear and conscionable intent.

> . . . and the lease thereof beinge nowe somewhat nere expyred, wherby a greater value is to be yearly raised thereby, they, the said complainantes, doe now trowble and moleste this defendante by unjuste sutes in law, . . .

Particularly for having filed two Bills on the case, and now for purely pecuniary motives after a considerable time of inaction, the Shakespeares may be engaged in chicanery which is actionable in Chancery. Lambert could appeal to equity against the overuse of rights to harass someone unjustly.

> . . . thinkinge thereby, as yt shoulde seme, to wringe from him this defendante some further recompence for the said premisses then they have alreddy received; . . .

Lambert's reply returns to a more controlled language.

> . . . without that, that yt was agreed that the said Edmunde Lamberte shoulde have and enjoye the said premisses in anie other manner and forme [*Costard.* 'In manner and form following, . . . (*cf. Love's Labour's Lost* I. ii. 201–216).], to the knowledge of this defendante, then this defendante hath in his said answeare heretofore expressed; and without that, that anie deedes or evidences concernynge the premisses that of righte belonge to the said complainantes are come to the handes and possession of this defendante, as in the said byll [*i.e. Shakespeares' Complaint*] is untruly supposed; and without that, that anie other matter, cause or thinge, in the said complainantes byll conteined, materiall or effectuall in the lawe, to be answeared unto, confessed and avoyded, traversed or denied, is true, to this defendantes knowledge or remembrance, in suche manner and forme as in the said byll the same is sett downe and declared. All which matters this defendante is reddy to averre and prove, . . .

The documents are on Lambert's side; as far as can be determined equity should be on Shakespeare's, but it is seventeen years after the mortgage due date (1580–1597). Lambert closes:

> . . . as this honorable courte shall awarde, and prayeth to be dismissed therhence with his reasonable costes and charges in this wrongfull sute by him unjustly susteyned.[32]

The Shakespeares' submission of a Replication to Lambert's Replication in response to their Bill of Complaint indicates how hot their pursuit of the case was;

how closely, precisely and quickly the Shakespeare party was onto the situation in Westminster. Someone was providing information in London, not always accurate, and responses were slow from Stratford; in addition since solicitors, barristers, commissioners, and Clerks and Masters of Chancery had to have their fees from this case, at least "reasonable costes and charges," it was William who was sustaining the operation, as his father had neither the means nor the propensity to be doing it at Westminster. Also the endeavor is in keeping with Shakespeare's concerted efforts to push for a grant of arms, and for purchases of lands and house. Thus the persistence of the Shakespeares can be felt in their Replication to John Lambert:

> The said complaynantes [i.e. 'John Shakespere and Mary his wiefe, plentiffes'], for replicacion to the answere of the said defendant [i.e. 'John Lamberte, defendant'], saie that theire bill of complaynt ys certayne and sufficient in the lawe to be answered; which said bill, and matters therein contayned, these complainants will avowe, verifie, and justifie to be true and sufficient in the lawe to be answered unto, . . .

The Shakespeares want to make certain that the case will be adjudged actionable, this can ultimately be decided by one of the Masters or the Clerks.

> . . . in such sorte, manner and forme as the same be sett forthe and declared in the said bill: and further they saie that thanswere of the said defenndant is untrue and insufficient in lawe to be replied unto, . . .

They are meeting accusation with accusation.

> . . . for many apparent causes in the same appearinge, thadvantage whereof these complainantes praie may be to theym nowe and at all tymes saved, then and not ells; for further replicacion to the said answere they saie that, accordinge to the condicion or proviso mencioned in the said indenture of bargaine and sale of the premisses mencioned in the said bill of complaynt, . . .

As did Lambert to them, they are attacking him upon his own admission.

> . . . he this complaynant, *John Shakespere, did come to the dwellinge-house of the said Edmunde Lambert, in Barton-uppon-the-Heathe* [*Sly.* 'I'll answer him by law. I'll not budge an inch, . . . Am not, I Christopher Sly, old Sly's son of Burtonheath, . . . Ask Marian . . . of Wincot. . . ." (*Taming of the Shrew* Induction.)], *uppon the feaste daie of St. Michaell tharchangell*, which was on the yeare of our Lorde God one thousand fyve hundred and eightie, and then and there tendered to paie unto him the said Edmunde Lambert the said fortie poundes, which he was to paie for the redempcion of the said premisses; whiche somme the said Edmunde did refuse to receyve, . . .

Thus John Lambert is pursuing upon an obvious right, but the Shakespeares are claiming that he is proceeding unjustly upon the advantage provided by a technicality.

> . . . sayinge that he [John Shakespeare] owed him [Edmund Lambert] other money, and unles that he the said John, would paie him altogether, as well the said fortie poundes as the other money, which he owed him over and above, he would not receave the said fortie poundes, and imediatlie after he, the said Edmunde, dyed, and by reason thereof, he, the said defendant, entered into the said premisses, and wrongfullie kepeth and detayneth the said premisses from him the said complaynant; . . .

What follows is a legal formula similar to the termination of Lambert's Replication.

> . . . without that, any other matter or thinge, materiall or effectuall, for these complaynantes to replie unto, and not herein sufficientlie confessed and avoyded, denyed and traversed, ys true; all which matters and thinges thes complaynantes are redie to averr and prove, as this honourable court will awarde, and pray as before in theire said bill they have praied.[33]

This case is pursued with considerable vigor from before November, 14, 1597 until after October 23, 1599, during three years in Chancery at the height of William

Lambarde's Mastership there from December 1597 to January 1601. During this time Shakespeare may have borrowed, or received the copy of William Lambarde's *Archaionomia* which contains the dramatist's signature. Meanwhile the case continues as evidenced by Orders of the Court of Chancery:

> *Quinto die July* [July 5, 1598] John Shackspere and Mary, his wief, plaintiffes, John Lamberte, defendant. A commission ys awarded to examyne witnesses on bothe partes, directed to Richard Lane . . .

Richard Lane of Alveston, Esquire, and Thomas Greene and William Shakespeare joined in 1609 in a plea of equity to the then Lord Chancellor, Egerton, Lord Ellesmere in a Chancery suit to protect the income they received from Stratford tithes. One of the personages they sued was George Lord Carew of Clopton. "'Richard Lane and William Shackspeare, and some fewe others of the said parties, are wholly, and *against all equity and good conscience*, usually dryven to pay the same.'"[34] ". . . and for that it is most agreeable to *all reason, equity and good conscience* that every person . . . should be ratably charged. . . . and for that *your orators have no means, by the order or course of the common laws* of this realm, to enforce or compel any of the said parties to yield any certain contribution toward the same, and so are and still shall be *remediless therein unless they may be in that behalf relieved by your Lordship's gracious clemency and relief to other in such like cases extended.*"[35] Richard Lane on several occasions acted in the capacity of Shakespeare's friend. Later a member of the Lane family was to cause William some grief.

In addition to Richard Lane as a witness in Stratford to the commission for the Shakespeares was another of William's friends and business acquaintances:

> . . . John Combes . . .

John Combe's brother Thomas entered Middle Temple in 1608. Their family, as had the Marstons, attended Middle Temple for generations, inheriting rooms there. Shakespeare purchases in 1602 and 1610 some 120 acres of land from John and William Combe. John left Shakespeare £5 in his will, and Shakespeare left Thomas his sword. To balance Lane and Combe two other gentlemen were selected, one was probably not of the family from whom Shakespeare had just purchased New Place:

> . . . Thomas Underhill and Fraunces Woodward, . . .

Underhill and Woodward were selected by John Lambert. Richard Lane and John Combe as William Shakespeare's associates, rather than any of his father's, were selected as witnesses to be examined in Stratford by the commission sent under the Chancery order. This evidences the dramatist's direct involvement in the case as witnesses contemporary to the transaction of 1580, or familiar with John's business are not selected. Friends and partners of William in legal and financial affairs were chosen. Eccles (p. 29) is incorrect to simply presume the witnesses for the commission were selected by John Shakespeare.

> . . . gentlemen, iij or ij. of them, returnable octavis Michaelis, by assente of the attorneyes, Powle and Hubard, and the plaintiefes to give xiiij, daies warnings.[36]

These were indeed significant attorneys for this case! Edward Huberd was one of the Six Clerks of Chancery, an office Edmund Spenser, author of *The Faerie Queene*, held for Ireland in the 1580's. One of the chief duties of the Clerks, often neglected but not in this case, was that of acting as attorneys. Stephen Powle, the other attorney in the Chancery order for the Shakespeares, was another of the Clerks. The year before this case was introduced to Chancery, Stephen Powle, as deputy to the clerk of the Crown was officially summoned to record the ceremony in which Queen Elizabeth made Egerton Lord Keeper in May 1596. Stephen was the son of Thomas Powle who, along with William Lambarde, was one of the four Masters of Chancery and had been clerk for examining letters patent of alienation. In his father's later years, from 1596 on, Stephen was also serving as his deputy. Stephen Powle, Thomas Powle and William Lambarde worked together as Clerk and Masters of Chancery involved with Alienations at the time of Shakespeare's case appearing in that department. *As his father's deputy, one of William Shakespeare's two London attorneys from* 1597 *to* 1599 *would have acted as William Lambarde's clerk during the same time.* The Chancery papers include another order for a commission, either a copy, or a remnant of the earlier duplicate Bill or another commission of which John Lambert complained:

> *Lune, decimo die Julii.* [July 10, 1598] John Shackespere and Marye, his wief, plaintiffes; John Lambert, defendant. —A commission ys awarded to examyne witnesses on both partes, directed to Richard Lanne, John Combes, Thomas Underhill and Frances Woodward, gentlemen, or two of them, returnable octavis Michaelis, by the assent of the attorneys, Powle and Hubard, and the plaintiffes to give xiiij. dayes warnings. (*Ibid.*)

Lambert is not idle as he continues his defense the next year, 1599, with a lawyer from a famous family. Shakespeare's eagerness to pursue this case has created a complication insofar as two Bills have been filed.

> xviij.° die Maij. [*May* 18, 1599] John Shakespeare, plaintiff; John Lambard [i.e. Lambert, perhaps Lambarde pricked up his ears at this point.], defendant.—Forasmuch as this Court . . .

It would be interesting to know who was presiding.

> . . . was this presente day ynformed by Mr. Overbury, beinge of the defendantes councell, . . .

John Lambert's attorney is none other than Nicholas Overbury. Nicholas was the father of Sir Thomas Overbury, who had just become a member of Middle Temple in 1597 and wrote in his character of a *Mere Common Lawyer* that "No way to heaven he thinks so wise as through Westminster-Hall."[37] Sir Thomas was a courtier, and a series of trials after his death in 1613 disclosed that he had been poisoned in the tower by the Earl of Somerset.[38] In *Winter's Tale* (II. iii. 96) Shakespeare cites an old proverb from Sir Thomas Overbury's "Character of a Sergeant": "The devil calls him his white son; he's so like him, that he is the worse for it."[39]

> . . . that the plaintiff did fyrst exhibyte a bill unto this Court against the defendant, as well by his owne name as in the name of his wyef, . . .

This bill in John's name alone would have presented a legal problem since it was Mary's inheritance which he shared by marriage. It must be technically established as falling to her first before John has any claim, and then he does not have sole interest as he shares it with Mary and his eldest son.

> . . . to be relyved towchinge a mortgage of certene landes lyinge in the county of Warr. made to the defendantes father, whose heyre the defendant is, and afterwardes exhibyted a bill in his owne name only concerninge such matter in substaunce as the former bill doth; and althoughe the plaintiff hath taken out two severall commisyones upon the later bill [July 5 and July 10, 1598], yet he hath not examyned any wytnesses thereupon.

Possibly the year's delay on the Shakespeares' part was the result of knowing that their witnesses had no access to the information they needed corroboration on.

> It is therfore ordered that, yf Mr. D. Hunt, one of the Masters of this Cowrt [i.e. Master Dr. John Hunt, Master of Chancery] . . .

John Hunt, along with William Lambarde, Sir George Carew (Carey) and Thomas Powle, was one of the four Masters of Chancery.

A description of the Masters' functions from W. J. Jones (*The Elizabethan Court of Chancery*) illustrated by the names from the case under discussion will be helpful at this point.

> Normally, the lawyers chosen were impersonal [Nicholas Overbury for Lambert and J. Stovell for the Shakespeares] and would act in a fairly reserved and formal fashion. Judges, to whom a point of law had been referred [as in the Chancery case in 1599], or to whom the matter in law had been dismissed [as in the case when it was before the Court of Queen's Bench in 1590], might be required to arbitrate and determine the entire matter. The Lord Chancellor [the Lord Keeper, Sir Thomas Egerton, Lord Ellesmere] and the Master of the Rolls [Thomas Heneage and then William Lambarde who was first Keeper of the Records of the Rolls Chapel appointed by Egerton on May 26, 1597 and then Keeper of the Records of the Tower on January 21, 1601 while still retaining his Mastership of Chancery] were ready, if the parties [*Shakespeare* v. *Lambert*] were agreeable, to attempt such an agreement. Sometimes the Master of the Rolls [Lambarde] would co-operate with some of the Masters [Dr. John Hunt, Master of Chancery]. At other times, only Masters—perhaps as many as four of them together [William Lambarde, George Carew, John Hunt and Thomas Powle (possibly Stephen Powle as his deputy)]—would be appointed to arbitrate [as four did in 1579, 1584, 1593, 1600 and 1602]. It is even possible to find one of the Six Clerks [two of them being at this time Stephen Powle and Edward Huberd] being called upon to play his part in an attempt to determine a case without the necessity of a judicial hearing. If attempts of this nature were unsuccessful, the normal practice of reporting the facts to the court would be employed, and once again the finger of suspicion would point at a litigant who had prevented the achievement of a settlement.

The *Shakespeare* v. *Lambert* suit is settled once again out of court. It appears that Lambert retains the land and the Shakespeares do not have to pay the mortgage debt, fines or Lambert's court fees. Jones continues:

> None the less, the Masters [Hunt, who worked with Lambarde on the jurisdiction of St. James' Court[40]] and often

> other lawyers [Powle and Huberd, Overbury and Stovell] would try again and again to get the parties to agree, even if they felt that the suit was essentially unfit for the court. An arbitration seemed more effective than a dismission in preventing further litigation in some other place.
>
> When the attempt was being made by judges and other lawyers, or when commissioners were sitting near London, . . .

The Shakespeares' three commissions ordered out of Chancery would have sat far from London in Stratford, an expensive operation.

> . . . the Lord Chancellor and Master of the Rolls readily offered their services as umpires should the discussions reach a stalemate. The Masters too would act as umpires [Did Hunt and Lambarde meet with Shakespeare and Lambert in 1599, with Powle and Huberd?] and might meet with the arbitrators as often as four times [as they did in 1559, 1562, 1563, 1564, 1575, and 1601]. Many legal conundrums had to be sorted out which in later times might well have been settled out of court from the beginning through consultations of the respective legal advisers. In Tudor times this could rarely happen, and the only sanction of reliability could be found in at least beginning formal proceedings in some court of law.

Only by chance Jones picks up for illustration on a personal level a remark by one of the figures in the *Shakespeare* v. *Lambert* Chancery suit.

> We can appreciate the glum comments of Master Hunt [the Master referred to in Shakespeare's Court Order of May 18, 1599] who reported [in Morgan *v.* ap Williams (1597)] the successful end of a case with the agreement of the parties, finding them at length weary, one of another, and myself also of them both.

Jones notes that by the 1600's if a case were dismissed to arbitration, any unsatisfactory settlement did not prevent the submission of a new bill on the same matter.

> It has been noted that many references and arbitrations were successfully achieved through the participation of

> judges from other courts and by other lawyers. More will have to be said on this topic, since it clearly bears on the question of the relationship which existed between the Chancery and other courts, noticeably those of common law."[41]

"Mr. D. Hunt" turns out, then, to be Master Hunt. Therefore the case has moved by Huberd's and Powle's consent from the Clerkship level to that of the Masters for consideration. This investigation into the case resulted from the filing of two complaints in what was substantially a single action, and the Shakespeares' delaying a year before acting upon the two commissions consequently granted by Chancery.

> It is therfore ordered that, yf Mr. D. Hunt, one of the Masters of this Cowrt, shall, upon consideracion of the said bills, fynde and report that bothe the said billes doe in substance conteyne one matter, then the defendant [i.e. John Lambert] ys to be dismissed from one of the said billes, . . .

Hunt probably determined that there was, substantially, "one matter," and had one complaint withdrawn, which would explain why it is no longer extant. So Lambert was correct in his earlier furious claim that ". . . they, the said complainantes, doe now trowble and moleste this defendante by unjuste sutes [note the plural] in lawe, thinkinge therby, as yt shoulde seme, to wringe from him this defendante some further recompence for the said premisses then they have alreddy received, . . ." This is what John Lambert had charged in his Replication of November 24, 1597, and now on May 18, 1599 Master Hunt was being ordered to look into the matter. John Lambert is to be dismissed from one of the bills

> . . . with such costes as the said Mr. D. Hunt [i.e. Master Hunt, Dr., or Dr. John Hunt, Master of Chancery] shall tax and asseasse; and the plaintiff . . .

Note the singular; Mary is not mentioned in this court order as she was not in the duplicate bill being dismissed.

"... the plaintiff did fyrst exhibyte a bill ... as well by his owne name as in the name of his wyef, [which is in the records] ... and afterwardes exhibited a bill in his owne name only. ..." (which is not extant). The court continues to speak in very strong language against the delays on the part of the Shakespeares.

> ... the plaintiff *ys to proceede to the hearinge thereof withe effect*, and the defendant shal be at lyberty to chaunge his commissyones, ...

This is a court favor granted to Lambert, and punitively not to the Shakespeares; and it is exercised by John Lambert a month later.

> ... yf he will and the plaintiffes attorney is to be warned hereof.[42]

It is clear that this order is obtained from Chancery for the defendant, John Lambert, by his lawyer, Nicholas Overbury, to counter the Shakespeares' superfluous and harassing actions in Chancery. The ire of the court is aroused, resulting in the Shakespeares being rebuked for wasting Chancery's time, and granting Lambert the request of his lawyer to change witnesses from those he had listed in the order of the year before. The Shakespeares had weak evidence for their case, which appears across the years as an injustice to them that followed the dramatist for twenty-one years from when he was fourteen until he was thirty-five. The justice they expected could have been recognized through the concept, not yet formulated, of "equity of redemption." *Now* Chancery was not turning a kind ear to their protracted and rather costly suit seeking some action.

The next to the last order on record in the case is a result of Lambert's accusation and resulting favor by the court:

> xxvij.° die Junij. [June 27, 1599] John Shackspeere and Margaret [i.e. Mary, but John Lambert's wife's name was Margery], his wief, plaintiffes; John Lamberte, defendant.

> A commission ys awarded to examine witnesses on bothe partes, directed to Richard Lane, John Combes, [remaining the same for the Shakespeares but changing from Thomas Underhill and Frances Woodward for Lambert to] William Berry and John Warne, gentlemen, iij. or ij. of them returnable octavis Michaelis, by assente of the attorneyes, Powle and Hubard, and the plaintiffes to give xiiij. daies warninge. (*Ibid.*)

There is a listing of a further order under Trinity Term. 41 Elizabeth as *Shackspeere contra Lambert* in 1599, but the end of the volume which contained that leaf is unfortunately missing. Halliwell-Phillipps suggests that the lost note was a duplicate of the June 27th, 1599 Chancery Order (pp, 204-205).

The Shakespeares are still active, and have the last word according to the record.

> *Martis*, xxiij.° *die Octobris*. [October 23, 1599] John Shakespere and Mary, his wief, plaintiffes; John Lamberte, defendant.—If the defendant shewe no cawse for stay of publicacion by this day sevenight, then publication ys graunted. (*p.* 205)

The Shakespeares move for a hearing, which probably indicates the commission (now lost) had obtained depositions from the witnesses. The matter was probably settled outside of court, or by arbitration. However, without a doubt, after having signed Asbies away in 1578 and with litigation at common law from 1588 to 1590 and in Chancery from 1597 to 1599 covering over all a period of some twenty years, what was to be Shakespeare's estate remains with the Lamberts as their possession from Edmund Lambert to his son John. John sold it shortly after the termination of the litigation in 1602 to a Richard Smyth for the familiar sum of £40.[43] Perhaps Chancery had come to the arbitrated settlement that the Shakespeares would not have to pay interest, fines, costs or fees but that Lambert when he sold must sell the land with no unfair advantage, or unreasonable enrichment, that is to not exceed the £40 his father had "purchased" it at.

Beyond a shadow of a doubt, Shakespeare, demonstrably from the legal actions and in his play texts is plagued with a concern for his estate lost, and then his lands and revenue forever lost from the critical adolescent age of fourteen until the height of his career at thirty-five; from the time he had to leave his schooling until just before he lost his father, whose decline had affected Shakespeare's prospects, and whose condition prompted him in his rise to attempt to restore him, as well as himself. Well, he made up for the loss of the Chancery suit, measured in the loss of property, time, worry and money. With Asbies gone, he lost 40 acres outside Stratford in 1599; but he would purchase 107 acres outside Stratford in 1602 for £320, however that would be after his father died. These events would be reflected in *Henry V* (1599) as all his legal activities were, in his art. The play celebrates the moment when England, up to Shakespeare's time, possessed the largest amount of territory. Hal, who had triumphed over his dissolute past, had become Henry V, King of England and France. The play opens with the Archbishop of Canterbury and the Bishop of Ely worrying about a "bill" passing which "If it pass against us,/We lose the better half of our possession." (I. i. 1, 7–8) Canterbury convinces Henry that despite France's claim that Salic law does not allow a woman to inherit land that Henry may not let the French ". . . bar your highness claiming from the female . . ." (I. ii. 33–114) Shakespeare was to have received upon his maturity as eldest son the estate of Asbies inherited by his mother and descending to him from the female side.

5. *William Lambarde and Shakespeare's Case*

AS a Master of Chancery, William Lambarde was preparing a manuscript about the court and the actions brought before it. He was preoccupied by precisely what Shakespeare's case posed as a problem before the law. After Lambarde died in 1601, one of the other Masters and close friend, Sir George Carew (Cary), edited the papers and produced Cary's *Reports* out of the labors of Lambarde, as the original title page indicates. The *Reports* suggests how Chancery might have been lenient toward the Shakespeares had their evidence been sufficient. Jones' discussion of the important passage Carew took from Lambarde indicates the significance this case would have had for the Masters of Chancery and, despite the fact that the case was never tried nor won by Shakespeare, the impact of the litigation's content upon legal history.

> The opening words of Cary's *Reports* provide a classic introduction to a jurisdiction which more than any other called for the issue of injunctions for stay of actions or executions in other courts.

Chancery could reverse common law arbitration, or withstand its decisions at the termination of the Court of Queen's Bench case at which time ordering that the land be returned to the Shakespeares upon simple payment of the mortgage according to equity, if undue advantage were being taken, unjust insistence on a technicality were being maintained, or a promise, a matter of oath or conscience, were not being honored. What follows is Lambarde's opinion on the Shakespeare case as he speaks through his editor, Sir George Carew in the opening paragraph of Cary's *Reports*. The passage is embellished with the specifics of the case.

> 'If a man be bound in a penalty [the forfeiture of the Estate of Asbies] to pay money [the £40] at a day [Michaelmas-Day, 1580] and place [Edmund Lambert's residence at Barton-on-the-Heath in the Cotswolds] by obligation [the Fine filed Easter Term, 1579 in Court of Common Pleas], and intending to pay the same [as was John Shakespeare's avowed contention in his Bill of Complaint before Chancery] is robbed by the way; or *hath entreated by word some other respite at the hands of the obligee* (Italics mine), . . .

This is the Shakespeares' case but with Edmund Lambert as the accidental cause preventing the tendering of the money becoming a successful payment through "entreating by word" that the payment of additional debts on the part of the payee must be made. The requirement was not a part of the original indenture and was initiated by Lambert and John apparently unwittingly accepted. Lambarde continues listing accidents preventing intentions from taking place.

> '. . . or cometh short of the place by any misfortune, and so failing of the payment, doth nevertheless provide and tender the money in short time after [which John was willing to pay from the day it was due on, and had offered again in 1587 and for the whole matter in 1597, hence the intent and ability had remained extant from 1580 to 1599], in these and many such like cases the Chancery will compel the obligee [Lambert] to take his principal [the £40] with some reasonable consideration of his damages (*quantum expediat*) [obviously met by the income received from the land from 1580 to 1599] for if this was not, men would do that by covenant which they now do by bond . . . The like favour is extendable against them that will take advantage upon strict condition for undoing the estate of another in lands, upon a small or trifling default [which is precisely what John Lambert had succeeded in doing, despite Chancery's claim of equity to John Shakespeare, Mary, his wife, and his son William].'
>
> Relief in respect of penalty and forfeiture, quite apart from the conscience of the defendant who might be deemed to be taking undue advantage, depended on an assessment of the elements of accident, mistake, and ignorance. These were vague concepts, depending on the facts and particulars of each case. In other words, the principles of liability rested upon factors which could not easily be defined in the abstract, . . .
>
> (Jones, pp. 436–437).

Of the four Masters, Lambarde and Cary (more than Hunt and Powle) were obviously much disturbed by the inequity inherent in Shakespeare's case and those like his. However at this time in legal history the situation upon which the case rested was particularly difficult to unravel without damaging clear obligations between man and property and faith in the instruments of conveyance. Simply, in the Shakespeares' case they probably could furnish no witnesses to substantiate their claim of Edmund Lambert's promise to return Asbies upon their payment of all the outstanding debts.

On the other hand, as Lambarde and Carew recognized, Chancery had not met in any clear way its obligation to the matter in so far as the Shakespeare land remains with Lambert after being settled out of court, or by arbitration, rather than specific remedy (but, contributing ultimately to a change in legal precedent). That it did not change the law at the time is precisely what Lambarde objects to in the forefront of his work. What might have been Edmund Lambert's kind offer, or "merry bond," as in *The Merchant of Venice*, at John Lambert's hands, allows him to have Shakespeare on his hip. Lambert takes, as Lambarde says, "advantage upon strict condition for [the purpose of] undoing the estate of another in lands, upon a small or trifling default" (of not meeting the payment on a specific day).

The Shakespeare case, and those like it at this time, rankled not only the dramatist, but William Lambarde and Carew as well. In fact just as Lambarde may have been an influence upon Shakespeare's understanding of the higher courts of law through his treatise, so Shakespeare's case in Chancery may have influenced Lambarde enough to seek "equity of redemption" principles for Chancery.

Lambarde, in Cary's *Reports*, initiates the move toward that principle; thus, Shakespeare through his *Merchant of Venice* not only anticipates the arguments, as Mark Edwin Andrews points out, for the supremacy of equity over the common law but Shakespeare's case may have been a major factor in bringing the modern legal concept of "equity of redemption" into existence. Small consolation to Shakespeare but he may have been out to affect the law at this point. His loss may very well have become the world's gain, in so far as there now exists, to be legally enjoyed, a reasonable grace period pertaining to mortgages; protection against unjust rigorous application of documents in case of hardship, unfair advantage being taken of someone's misfortune, or unjust enrichment upon a technicality.

At this time Shakespeare, in his litigations and drama, has reached the point where he is doing things not only for personal gain and sustenance, but also to instruct his audience, convert the learned, and have his ideas on law, justice and equity affect his contemporary judicial institutions. These effects, both from his theatre and his lawsuits, survive his life, his estates, and his theatrical stage, and thus posterity has inherited not only his drama but also his view of justice and equity.

> Then what could death do, if thou shouldst depart,
> Leaving thee living in posterity? . . .
>
> (Sonnet VI)

> Not marble, nor the gilded monuments
> Of princes, shall outlive this powerful rhyme; . . .
>
> (Sonnet LV)

> And yet to times in hope my verse shall stand,
> Praising thy worth, despite his cruel hand.
>
> (Sonnet LX)[44]

Shakespeare and Lambarde were both concerned about equity not only in the particular case but also in preserving the institution of Chancery which administered equitable principles. William Lambarde remained the most active Master of Chancery from this period of 1596/7 until his death in 1601. "One of the major changes between the 1591 and 1600 editions of William Lambarde's *Archeion*, a discourse on the courts of Law, was in the section on the origins, powers and jurisdiction of Chancery. Lambarde, in the second edition, hailed the reforms made by his old friend, the new Lord Keeper [Sir Thomas Egerton, Lord Ellesmere]."[45] Edward Hake of Gray's Inn was writing a dialogue on Equity in 1600 which coincides with the time ". . . after the first open hostilities between Common Pleas and Chancery and shortly before the sharp engagement between Coke [Chief Justice representing common law] and Ellesmere [Lord Keeper advocating the supremacy of Equity]."[46] At the turn of the century, Lambarde, Ellesmere, Hake and Shakespeare were much concerned for equity in Chancery and its reform from within, as it was attacked from without by Coke and the common law jurists. Shakespeare's legal concern in his plays came from this period of crucial controversy.

John Shakespeare and William Lambarde died within a month of each other. The Stratford Burial Register records "1601 Septemb. 8 Mr. Johannes Shakespeare." Shakespeare receives interest in the double house in Henley Street where his mother, maintaining one-third life interest, continues to reside with her daughter Joan (ironically named for her mother's sister who had married Edmund Lambert) now Mrs. Hart, and her family. The final version of *Hamlet* is written at this time and several of its numerous concerns are over inheritance and the interposing of a father's brother "'twixt me and my office" (Edmund Lambert was John Shakespeare's brother-in-law), a relative "A little more than kin, and less than kind;" and of a son attempting to recover "those foresaid lands/ So by his father lost." (Cf. I. i. 36–104). Fortinbras, Laertes and Hamlet are three sons attempting to restore their father's losses and their lost fathers. The play is often read as a memorial tribute to Shakespeare's father and is seen as a study of the complex relationships of passionate love, hate, admiration and remorse between father and son.

> . . . I have that within which passeth show;
> These but the trappings and the suits of woe.
> A little month, or ere those shoes were old
> With which she follow'd my poor father's body,
> Like Niobe, all tears:
> My father!—methinks I see my father.
>
> (I. ii 34–35, 147–150).

And Shakespeare acted Hamlet's father's ghost and

so in a way "became" what he mourned; he became the actor of the living memorial which his fictional art had revered. He replaced his father and continued what his father had attempted. In 1602, following his father's death, Shakespeare makes assurance doubly sure with regard to his title for New Place, clearly learning from John Lambert's example of having to protect property inherited or purchased from someone's inheritance. Court of Common Pleas records for William Shakespeare a Foot of *second* 'fine' levied on New Place confirming sale from Hercules Underhill in Michaelmas, 1602.

Hercules came of age in 1602 and. although not eldest son, was heir, since his older brother, Fulke, had poisoned their father William, shortly after he had sold the house to Shakespeare in 1597. Shakespeare sought firmer assurance for his property from the new heir to avoid any future dispute from the family, or the Crown, since the estate was forfeited upon execution of Fulke in 1598/99. In 1599 Shakespeare may have thought he had lost *both* Asbies and New Place estates! Hercules obtained a grant of his estates upon his majority in 1602.[47] Nevertheless it must have been a frightening moment as captured by Ford in *Merry Wives of Windsor*, "Like a fair house built on another man's ground; so that I have lost my edifice by mistaking the place where I erected it." (II. ii. 224–225).

At the time of Lambarde's death, and with John Shakespeare's death, William was restoring and protecting his losses; but just before Lambarde died he was party to one last important link between himself and the now famous, perhaps for the Crown even notorious, dramatist. Queen Elizabeth appointed Lambarde to be Keeper of the Rolls in the Tower of London on January 21, 1601. Dunkel, Lambarde's biographer, continues:

> [Later] Queen Elizabeth invited him to her privy chamber in Greenwich Palace [where Shakespeare had performed on December 26 and 27, 1594] and he [William Lambarde] of course accepted. She began the interview with the dec-

laration that if 'any subject of mine do me a service [such as compiling an index of the Tower records] I will thankfully accept it from his own hands.' She then opened his book [*Pandecta Rotulorum*] and began to read the Latin, saying, 'You shall see that I can read.' Then she took up a number of Latin words in his text and asked for the legal significance in their use.

Then what follows is the most intriguing and fortuitous of the connections between Shakespeare and Lambarde—that looking into William Lambarde's Latin law book she should make her only recorded reference to William Shakespeare, as by a similar coincidence a copy of a Latin law book by William Lambarde should contain the only signature of William Shakespeare not on a legal document. Her statement is recorded in a diary entry in Lambarde's hand.

When she [Queen Elizabeth] came to the rolls dealing with the reign of King Richard II, she said, 'I am Richard II [she is referring to the historical king and the depiction of him in Shakespeare's *Richard II* where Bolingbroke has him dethroned] know ye not that?'

Lambarde is quick to get the reference to the Earl of Essex rebellion in which the Earl of Southampton and Shakespeare's players had a role some months previously.

Lambarde replied, 'Such a wicked imagination was determined and attempted by a most unkind Gent(leman), the most adorned creature that ever your Majestie made. Whereupon she replied [referring to Essex and then to Shakespeare's play], 'He that will forget God, will also forget his benefactors; this tragedy [i.e. *Richard II*] was played 40tie times in open streets and houses.' . . . she dismissed him, saying, 'Farewell good and honest Lambarde.'[49]

Two weeks later on August 19, 1601 he was dead and placed under an inscription against the south wall of the parish church of East Greenwich:

William Lambarde, of Lincoln's Inn, some time Master in

Chancery, Keeper of the Rolls and Records, of the office of Alienations to Queen Elizabeth . . . *Archaionomia* 1568, etc.

With his friends the Marstons, the Greenes, the Combes, and the Underhills and Humphrey Colles all situated at, or connected with, Middle Temple around 1602, it is not surprising to find Shakespeare overtly entertained and entertaining under the roof of its Great Hall, which he had already immortalized in his verse (*Henry VI Part One* II. iv, the scene in which he had the plucking of the white rose and the red initiating the Wars of the Roses take place against all historical record).

LONDON, THE TEMPLE-GARDEN:
RICHARD PLANTAGENET: Great lords and gentlemen, what means this silence?
Dare no man answer in a case of truth?
SUFFOLK: Within the Temple-hall we were too loud;
The garden here is more convenient.
PLANTAGENET: Then say at once if I maintain'd the truth;
Or else was wrangling Somerset in the error?
SUFFOLK: Faith, I have been a truant in the law,
And never yet could frame my will to it;
And therefore frame the law unto my will.
SOMERSET: Judge you, my Lord of Warwick, then, between us.
(II. 1–10).

Will, this son of Warwick, put on a *Twelfth Night* that kept them not silent in Temple Hall. John Manningham of Middle Temple, the diarist (bless his pen) "records a performance before his society on Candlemas Day, 1602:

February 2, 1602—At our feast wee had a play called 'Twelve Night, or What you Will,' much like the Commedy of Errores, or Menechmi in Plautus, but most like and neere to that in Italian called *Inganni*. A good practice in it to make the Steward beleeve his Lady widdowe was in love with him, by counterfeyting a letter as from his

> Lady in generall termes, telling him what shee liked best in him, and prescribing his gesture in smiling, his apparaile, &c., and then when he came to practise making him beleeve they tooke him to be mad.[50]

Manningham caught Shakespeare's popular gimmick of the twins. As *Comedy of Errors* in 1594 before being performed at Gray's Inn was produced for Elizabeth at Greenwich, so in 1601 she saw *Twelfth Night* at Whitehall before it appeared at Middle Temple.[51] In addition to the sure-fire plot, the jokes and the great songs ("O mistress mine, where are you roaming?" Act II, scene iii; "Come away, come away, death," II. iv; "When that I was and a little tiny boy,/With hey, ho, the wind and the rain, . . ." V. i; and other snatches), Shakespeare did not forget to address himself to his setting. The text is replete with references to exceptions and modest limits of order, proof, argument based upon admission against interest (I. v. 69–78); misprison, Sheriff's post (from which comes Deed Pole where indentures were posted for public announcements), misdemeanor, grand-jury, ". . . you keep o'the windy side of the law. . . ."(III. iv.); action of battery, and being "both the plaintiff and the judge/ Of thine own cause" (V. i.).[52]

Hence, with his lengthy case, his appeals to conscience, his encounter with Masters and Clerks of Chancery, his play at Middle Temple, Shakespeare's relationship to Chancery, equity, the Lord Keeper (Chancellor), William Lambarde and the Inns of Court was a continuing one from 1595 to 1602. William had extended into the period of 1596 to 1602 his commitment to performing plays before a juristic audience, having a legal vocabulary in his plays, pursuing litigations in Westminster, reading the law writers and being involved in influencing the theory and practice of equity which he had initiated in "the lost years" from 1585 to 1595. His "hidden life" was a preparation for the times more familiar to us and these times in turn help corroborate his activities during the, up to now, "silent years."

6. Measure for Measure[53] *and King James.*

AFTER 1603 and the death of Queen Elizabeth, the new English King James, from Scotland, with his principles of Divine Right, became the throned Monarch. Insofar as Scotland had no separate jurisdiction for equity in the manner that England did, Chancery was threatened from a new direction by the King's desire to assert his prerogative. Particularly ominous was his ordering a pickpocket hanged without trial during his Progress from Scotland to London.[54] Because of plague, this Progress ended with the King residing at Hampton Court outside London, where Shakespeare's *Measure for Measure* (1604) was designed for his entertainment. The play served as a complicated mirror for His Majesty. It warned against using the law to interfere arbitrarily with the fabric of society by either strict or loose following of the law and its letter. Angelo, the Duke of Vienna's deputy, in attempting a moral reformation of Viennese society by rigorous interpretation of statutes, exposes a flaw. It can be quite impractical to alter custom by a rigid application of the law. The returning Duke, on the other hand, engaging in rectifying Angelo's administrative difficulties, exposes the disruption caused by personal and arbitrary manipulation of the judicial system, even if it is for the purpose of offering remedy for injustices. The intervention of prerogative action despite commendable motive, just as a strict application might be for a high moral purpose, nevertheless does violence to precedent, form, due process, and procedure designed to protect the law and preserve individual rights. King James was being told to be humane, and just, and to follow English precedent, interpretation and equity in his judicial capacity. The audacity of this program is tempered by the convention of art instructing and being in the tradition of an Inns of Court entertainment, such as *Gorboduc* before the Queen, or *Mirror for Magistrates*.

In *Measure for Measure*, Vincentio, the Duke of Vienna,

gives Angelo the power of equity: ". . . your scope is as mine own,/So to enforce or qualify the laws/As to your soul seems good." (I. i. 65–67).

> Hold therefore, Angelo.—
> In our remove be thou at full ourself;
> Mortality and mercy in Vienna
> Live in thy tongue and heart: old Escalus,
> Though first in question, is thy secondary.
> Take thy commission.
>
> (I. i. 43–48).

Angelo represents strict application of the law and, like Portia, Isabella is the mercy-figure (parodied by the bawd ("Madam Mitigation" [I. ii. 45]):

> ISABELLA: No ceremony that to great ones 'longs,
> Not the king's crown nor the deputed sword,
> The marshal's truncheon nor the judge's robe,
> Become them with one-half so good a grace
> As mercy does.
>
> (II. ii. 77–81.)

Isabella is even more conceptually specific about technical differences between pity and clemency when it pertains to judicial discretion:

> Ignomy in ransom and free pardon
> Are of two houses: lawful mercy
> Is nothing kin to foul redemption.
>
> (II. iv. 111–113).

Shakespeare's mercy-figure has learned from the equity writers, such as Lambarde and Hake, a concern for case law and precedent, which prevents misuse of prerogative powers. Isabella appeals for equity against the double threat of a tyrannically strict constructionism and an equally tyrannical personal intervention in the law. William West of Inner Temple and Thomas Ashe of Gray's Inn say that equity is called "equal" and a "reasonable measure" which helps interpret the legal technicality as well as the Biblical significance of the play's title, underscoring the delicate balancing of the philosophical, theological, legal, political, social, and personal issues the problematical nature of justice represents.

The metaphysical problems are based upon a secular legal case. Isabella pleads for the release of her brother from the death penalty. He has been charged with fornication for getting his betrothed with child, a reflection of Shakespeare's past, welling up as his personal concerns turn again toward residence in Stratford. Angelo, the Deputy for the absent Duke, is willing to release his prisoner if Isabella, who is about to become a nun, will sleep with him; but in lieu of that he hides behind a strict juridical interpretation:

> ANGELO: Your brother is a forfeit of the law,
> And you but waste your words.
> ISABELLA: Why all the souls that were were forfeit once,
> And he that might the vantage best have took
> Found out the remedy. How would you be
> If he which is the top of judgment should
> But judge you as you are? O, think on that!
> And mercy then will breathe within your lips
> Like man new made.
> ANGELO: Be you content fair maid,
> It is the law, not I, condemn your brother.
>
> (II. ii. 70–80)

William West wrote in his *Symboleography* (A_2):

> Other lawyers do term it *Summum Jus*, Law in the highest degree, or most exact, and it is so taken of them when man stands more upon the letter of the Law, then [sic] upon the meaning of the writer, or maker of the Law. In which behalf, it so falleth out oft times, that under a colour of knowledge of the Laws, many grosse and dangerous errors be committed.

Angelo is removed by the return of the Duke and is brought to trial, raising the issue which was bothering Edward Hake at this time, that of the "constitutional right of injunctions against enforcing a right and imprisoning one who has followed form of law."[55] Isabella, representing Chancery's use of equity, changes from one who has just argued against the severity of the law to one who insists upon equity following the law:

> For Angelo,
> His act did not o'ertake his bad intent,
> And must be buried as but an intent
> That perished by the way. Thoughts are no subjects,
> Intents but merely thoughts.
>
> (v. i. 455–460).

This reflects Isabella's forgiveness, clemency, and mercy, but also it is precisely the equity decision handed down by Queen's Council in *Hales* v. *Pettit*. Shakespeare had already used portions of the case found in Plowden's *Reports* for the gravediggers' scene in *Hamlet*. The decision, in part, reads:

> For the imagination of the mind to do wrong without an act done, is not punishable in our law; neither is a resolution to do that wrong, which he does not, punishable, but the doing of the act is the only point which the law regards. . . .

Shakespeare, through *Measure for Measure*, is tutoring King James in English jurisprudence, precedent, and case law. Through Isabella, Shakespeare has also engineered the argument for Chancery to remedy, but not replace, common law on the one hand and, on the other, has illustrated how Chancery must instruct procedure and not become merely an arm of arbitrary-prerogative authority, in so far as it must, like common law, abide by its own precedents.

There is no question but that the King heard Shakespeare on this, and his other points pertaining to equity, and early in his reign. From the account of Edmund Tylney, Master of the Revels, for the year from November 1, 1604 to October 31, 1605 one finds the following seven plays by Shakespeare performed before King James:

November 1, 1604—"The Mour of Venis" (*Othello*) the first recorded performance.
The Sunday following—*The Merry Wives of Windsor*.

December 26, 1604 (St. Stephen's Night)—*Measure for Measure*; the first recorded performance.
December 28, 1604 (Innocents' Night)—"The plaie of Errors" (*The Comedy of Errors*).
Between New Year's Day and Twelfth Night (January 6, 1605)—*Love's Labour's Lost.*
January 7, 1605—"the play of Henry the Fift" (*Henry* V).
Shrove Sunday, 1605—*The Merchant of Venice.*
On Shrove Tuesday a play called the Merchant of Venice, again commanded by the King's Majesty.

So from November, 1604 until Shrove Tuesday, 1605, King James heard Shakespeare on justice and law, equity and mercy by witnessing: 1] the trial of Othello in the Council-Chamber of Venice (I. ii.) where arguments for necessity override Brabantio's claims on his daughter; 2] the references to contempt of court and Star Chamber in *The Merry Wives of Windsor*; 3] Isabella in *Measure for Measure* and her various trials, hearings and prison scenes; 4] *The Comedy of Errors* and Shakespeare's first use of equity in Aegeon's trial and the Duke's clemency; 5] *Love's Labour's Lost's* various penalties at the law, decrees, references to William West's treatise on equity, duties of a Chancery solicitor (II. i.), and "quillets"; 6] the trial and discourse on appeals and the King's mercy in *Henry V* (II. ii.); and to cap it all off, the prototype of the representation of equity and mercy 7] Portia in *The Merchant of Venice.* Evidence exists that this didactic menu pleased the King, because he requested a second performance of *The Merchant of Venice* within three days.

In the same season, in private performances, Shakespeare gave the King seven lessons on equity: 1] recognizing in Council national necessity over family claims (*Othello*); 2] exercising power to handle riots quickly in Star Chamber (*Merry Wives of Windsor*); 3] following precedent of King's Council (*Measure for Measure*); 4] exercised by head of state according to a balance between statute law and natural law (*Comedy of Errors*); 5] allowing human necessity to prevail over arbitrary decree (*Love's Labour's Lost*); 6] in the King's mercy being recognized but not exercised to the detriment of the realm (*Henry V*); and 7] being achieved by a most rigorous adherence to the written letter of the law (*Merchant of Venice*). King James was being taught by a dramatist who had just been through a three-year-case of equity in Chancery. This considerable number of plays with such a thematic unity, all constructed and selected by the one dramatist, came to the ears and eyes of King James as he contemplated alterations in the judicial institutions in his attempt to amalgamate them and bring them under his direct control. Fortunately, Shakespeare would feel, this was ultimately thwarted with his aid. It can be presumed that what struck the King most was equity (or mercy):

> 'Tis mightiest in the mightiest it becomes
> The throned monarch better than *his* crown; . . . .
> (*Merchant of Venice* IV. i. 158–189).

Josephine Waters Bennett in her *Measure for Measure as Royal Entertainment* has suggested that the Duke is designed by Shakespeare to imitate King James, not only to merely flatter but to offer him an objective study of himself. If this play specifically were designed to serve this purpose in its first performance, then the other plays by Shakespeare selected to accompany it may very well have been chosen, among other reasons, for their thematic content and instructional purposes relating to English equity.

Shakespeare had learned the mode of instructing figures in high office from his experiences at the Inns of Court, where at least two of his plays had already been performed.[56] Carey Conley in *First English Translators of the Classics* said that the literary movement at the Inns of Court often had declared political motives. Philip J. Finkelpearl describes this situation in his study of *John Marston of the Middle Temple:*

> They, along with their patrons, the new nobility, aimed to improve and enlighten the nation. Through direct access

> to certain useful classics—especially books on warfare like Caesar's *Commentaries* [*cf. Henry IV Part Two* IV. iii. 46–47] and books to discourage sedition like Lucan's *Pharsalia* [which influenced *Julius Caesar* and *Antony and Cleopatra*]—it was hoped that 'goode governments' could be "throughlie executed and discharged' (as William Bavande of the Middle Temple put it).

North's Plutarch, one of Shakespeare's major sources would be a prime example of this tradition. The collection of *A Mirror for Magistrates* originally supervised by William Baldwin, admitted to the Middle Temple 1557 is directed to "the nobilitye/and all other in office":

> For here as in a loking glas, you shall see (if any vice be in you) howe the like hath bene punished in other heretofore, whereby admonished, I trust it will be a good occasion to move you to the soner amendment. This is the chiefest ende, whye it [this book] is set furth.[57]

"It seems to have been a natural function—it was at any rate their self-appointed task in the sixteenth and seventeenth centuries—for the lawyers of the Inns of Court to 'instruct' their governors on their proper duties and responsibilities."[58] It is unfortunate that art and literature do not serve that purpose today as much as they should and can. Finkelpearl describes the prototypical theatrical production in this convention of the Inns of Court commenting on policy to the head of state in an entertainment.

> The same impulse to advise magistrates lies behind the most famous dramatic production at the Inns during this period [from 1558 to 1572], the Inner Temple's *Gorboduc* of 1562. The desire of the young gentlemen to warn their sovereign in person of the dangers threatening a state which lacks a definite successor may strike us as impertinent, but clearly it did not affect Queen Elizabeth that way. After the first production of the play in the Inner Temple Hall, it was repeated for the Queen a few weeks later at Whitehall Palace; and one of its authors, Sackville, was an especially fortunate recipient of her favor throughout his long career. (*p.* 23).

Sackville was a member of the audience at *Gesta Grayorum* in 1594–1595 where *Comedy of Errors* was given. *Gorboduc* impressed Shakespeare enough to be a source for *King Lear*, and his *Comedy of Errors* was done at Gray's Inn and Greenwich Palace before the Queen in 1594, and *Twelfth Night* at Middle Temple and Whitehall Palace before the Crown 1601/2. Shakespeare definitely had an Inns of Court period from 1594 to 1602 in which he continued a tradition there and in turn was influenced by the setting in the subject matter, plots and purposes of his plays.

William Shakespeare had learned the substance of the law from reading Lambarde, West, Hake, Ashe, Germain, Plowden, Bacon, Coke and others on equity, and had himself been in cases in the high court of Chancery, the Court of Queen's (later King's) Bench, the Court of Common Pleas, and Stratford Court of Records. He had connections at Gray's Inn, Middle Temple, Inner Temple, Lincoln's Inn, Clement's Inn, and Staple's Inn. The dramatist was a man of law from Stratford, Westminster and the Inns who was instructed by the civic leaders of his society and in turn instructed them and their betters. He not only anticipated changes to come correctly, but in no small way Shakespeare affected the course of English jurisprudence in relief from common law in Chancery, through "equity of redemption" of mortgages; he expanded the populace's appreciation for their own complex judicial system, instructed Inns of Court students, lawyers, judges, Clerks, Masters, attorneys, lawyers and officials of the courts in their law, just as his history plays would be credited with instructing subsequent English monarchs. Above all, his plays presented speeches before Chancellors and monarchs about their responsibility to law and justice through their powers of equity and mercy.

V

Shakespeare's Legal Mind

Yet must I not give nature all: thy art,
My gentle Shakespeare, must enjoy a part;
For though the poet's matter nature be,
His art doth give the fashion; and that he,
Who casts to write a living line, must sweat
(Such as thine are), and strike the second heat
Upon the muses' anvil—turn the same
(And himself with it) that he thinks to frame,
Or for the laurel he may gain a scorn:
For a good poet's made as well as born,
And such wert thou. Look, how the father's face
Lives in his issue, even so the race
Of Shakespeare's mind and manners brightly shines
In his well-turned and true-filed lines,
In each of which he seems to shake a lance,
As brandish'd at the eyes of ignorance.

—Ben Jonson[1]

1. *Shakespeare at the Law in the Later Years*

THERE was much of nature in the gentle Shakespeare's art. And the good poet, as Jonson says, labored to render nature into artistic forms, and strove to turn out living lines from life experiences—"and such wert thou." Shakespeare brandished the lance of a keen mind at the eyes of ignorance before the unknowing and the unconscious. He gentled his condition, was honest and sweet to his companions as his art became the vehicle to handle his insights into private violence, the sexual abyss, fears, deviance, and adultery; the public horrors of the blank unrelenting universe; and the dark journeyings of the soul in his later plays (*Macbeth*, *Othello*, *Lear*, *Coriolanus*, *Cymbeline* and *Pericles*) to be redeemed by time and familial, ceremonial, artistic, and religious regeneration in *Winter's Tale* and *Tempest*.

Chapter II looked at the texts of Shakespeare's works for evidence of his knowledge about the technicalities of the law. Chapter IV analyzed Shakespeare's parallel use of his public plays and private litigations to effect changes in the law. This chapter will examine the texts and legal documents to uncover some of the dominant psychological drives and use of the law for protective and preservative purposes in Shakespeare, the man, revealed by his concern about law and his later pursuits at the law. These compulsions, concerns, and accommodations can be disclosed and verified by looking in a coordinated fashion at the later plays, contemporaneous lawsuits and parallel family events. These culminate and authenticate, with an unexpected twist, the paternalistic tendencies and legal concerns revealed in "the silent years."

The story is one of continuity, not only of seeing Shakespeare's father's face behind aspects of Shakespeare's legal and artistic endeavors, but also of making sense of what he wrote and did in his later years, which in turn confirms that the young Shakespeare from 1585 to 1595 was in no discontinuous fashion the "father" of the later man seemingly more familiar from the numerous documents. The critical and analytical arts can, as Shakespeare himself professed to do, create out of the "lost years" (the airy nothing of official documentary evidence) a local habitation in the Inns of Court and the realm of jurisprudence, and a name in his preoccupation with mercy and equity which facilitate social relationships, but are based upon and follow law and justice, which sustain social order. The excuse for reproducing the lengthy passage that follows from *Troilus and Cressida* is not just because it is the backbone of all of Shakespeare's judicial concepts, but because its themes and assumptions run throughout the plays, as the legal phrases and concepts do, and one can note in passing references, even more personal concerns, visions, and emerging trepidations.

ULYSSES: The specialty of rule hath been neglected:
And, look, how many Grecian tents do stand
Hollow upon this plain, so many hollow factions.
When that the general is not like the hive
To whom the foragers shall all repair,
What honey is expected? Degree [*i.e., authority, order*] being vizarded,
The unworthiest shows as fairly in the mask.
The heavens themselves, the planets and this centre
Observe degree, priority and place,
Insisture, course, proportion, season, form,
Office and custom, in all line of order;
And therefore is the glorious planet Sol [*i.e., sun* (and *son*)]
In noble eminence enthroned and sphered
Amidst the other; whose medicinable eye
Corrects the ill aspects of planets evil,
And posts, like the commandment of a king,
Sans check to good and bad: but when the planets
In evil mixture to disorder wander,
What plagues and what portents! what mutiny!
What raging of the sea! shaking of earth!
Commotion in the winds! frights, changes, horrors,
Divert and crack, rend and deracinate
The unity and married calm of states
Quite from their fixture! O, when *degree* is shaked,
Which is the ladder to all high designs,
The enterprise is sick! How could communities,
Degrees in schools and *brotherhoods in cities,*
Peaceful commerce from dividable shores,
The *primogenitive* and *due of birth,*[2]
Prerogative of age, crowns, sceptres, laurels,
But by degree, stand in authentic place?
Take but degree away, untune that string,
And, hark what discord follows! each thing meets
In mere oppugnancy: the bounded waters
Should lift their bosoms higher than the shores
And make a sop of all this solid globe:

Strength should be lord of imbecility,
And the rude son should strike his father dead:
Force should be right; or rather, right and wrong,
Between whose endless jar justice resides,
Should lose their names, and so should justice too.
Then every thing includes itself in power,
Power into will, will into appetite;
And appetite, an universal wolf,
So doubly seconded with will and power,
Must make perforce an universal prey,
And last eat up himself. Great Agamemnon,
This chaos, when degree is suffocate,
Follows the choking.
And this neglection of degree it is
That by a pace goes backward, with a purpose
It hath to climb. The general's disdain'd
By him one step below, he by the next,
That next by him beneath: so every step,
Exampled by the first pace that is sick
Of his superior, grows to an envious fever
Of pale and bloodless emulation:

(I. iii. 78–134)

Shakespeare, in this extremely revealing catalog, indicates not only his awareness of degree and the necessity for its defense but recognizes that all this high design is threatened and is being constantly threatened by ignorance from without and the unconscious from within. Shakespeare usually kept back the blood-dimmed tide with art, ritual, and ceremony (as John Davies had said of Will in 1603—"And though the stage doth stain pure gentle blood,/Yet generous ye are in mind and mood."). He used personal rationality, artistic representation, ritualistic enactment, dramatic catharsis, and ceremonial ordering and reordering, to control what sometimes wells up threateningly from within the dark psyche of the individual, as observed by Iago in *Othello*:

Virtue! a fig! 'tis in ourselves that we are thus or thus. Our bodies are our gardens, to the which our wills are gardeners; so that if we will plant nettles, or sow lettuce, set

> hyssop and weed up thyme, supply it with one gender of herbs, or distract it with many, either to have it sterile with idleness, or manured with industry, why, the power and corrigible authority of this lies in our wills. If the balance of our lives had not one scale of reason to poise another of sensuality, the blood and baseness of our natures would conduct us to most preposterous conclusions: but we have reason to cool our raging motions, our carnal stings, our unbitted lusts, . . .
>
> (I. iii. 322–336)[3]

The external world held its own disruption and loss. The new natural philosophy threw everything into doubt. The Essex Revolt, and other crises goaded England toward the Revolution and the execution of the King. The Virgin Queen died and left no heir. Shakespeare's only son died; then his father, next his mother, and then his three brothers; all died and left him the sole male of his family—alive but the last "Shake-speare" "to be brandish'd at the eyes of ignorance." John Shakespeare had fought to regain his wife's dowry, and Will's inheritance; then the dramatist had taken on that struggle; and meanwhile had obtained his own acquisitions which he was about to leave to the women in his life—his wife Anne (a third of all he possessed and "the second best bed," now felt to be of sentimental significance); and to his two daughters, one of whom was to cause him pleasure (Susanna), the other grief (Judith), both over situations concerning sexual affairs. This is revealed in two trials, legal documents, and anticipated in fears expressed in the later plays.

Shakespeare's later biographical period from 1605 to 1615 is characterized by acquisition and protection of artistic and personal acquirements, reaching once again to Chancery and the Chancellor himself. In 1605, William was at the height of his career. It was back in 1575 that his father was beginning to experience legal difficulties. 1585 was the last time William Shakespeare was mentioned in Stratford before his legal pursuit in Westminster. In 1595 he was involved with legal figures at the Inns of Court and as an actor before the Queen. Now in 1605 the records indicate that he is a member of the King's Servants, and has had seven of his legal plays selected for performance before the Court. The Chancellor recognized Shakespeare May 19, 1603, when he applied the Great Seal to the Letters Patent, enrolled in Chancery, authorizing Shakespeare and his companions to perform plays under royal patronage, and originally issued as warrants under the Signet Seal and Privy Seal May 17 and May 18:

> . . . licence and authorize these o[u]r servantes Lawrence ffletcher [an actor who performed before King James in Scotland and won favor] William Shakespeare Richard Burbage Augustine Phillippes John Henninges Henry Condell William Sly Rob[er]t Armyn Richard Cowlye and the rest of their associates freely to use and exercise the Arte and facultie of playing Comedies Tragedies Histories Enterludes Moralles Pastoralles Stage plaies & such like as they have already studied or hereafter shall use or studie aswell for the recreation of o[u]r loving subjects, as for o[u]r solace and pleasure when we shall thinke good to see them . . . to show and exercise publiquely . . . when the infection of the plague shall decrease as well w[i]thin their now usuall howse called the Globe . . . as also w[i]thin . . . any . . . other convenient places w[i]thin . . . o[u]r said Realmes.[4]

Shakespeare's company acted at least one hundred and seven performances before the Court of King James from the time of this grant in 1603 until the playwright's death in 1616. The Chancellor's office legally recognized Shakespeare's professional and private attainments through royal grants and awards from suits.

Later, Shakespeare, the burgher and gentleman of Stratford, has better-known personal dealings with Chancery, even directly with the Lord Chancellor, the Keeper of the King's Conscience. In 1609, there is a complaint from William Shakespeare and his friends Richard

Lane, one of the witnesses for the commission in the Lambert case, and Thomas Greene, Shakespeare's cousin the Stratford lawyer who boarded in New Place, to the Right Honorable Thomas Lord Ellesmere, now the Lord Chancellor of England under King James. The suit regarded one of Shakespeare's substantial sources of income, the Stratford tithes (as the Duke of Vienna says to Marianna of the moated Grange in *Measure for Measure*, "Our corn's to reap, for yet our tithe's to sow." [IV. i. 76.[5]). The appeal is made "to all reason, equity, and good conscience" to get the Combes, one of whom (John) was the other witness in the commission, and Lord Carew to pay their share, asking for the latter "to appear in the High Court of Chancery;" William Combe responds politely that he will pay. Well Combe might, since Shakespeare is making a purchase of a considerable amount of land from him.

In 1613, there is an enrollment on the Chancery Close Role of a conveyance, dated March 10, of a house in the fashionable Blackfriars' area of London by Henry Walker to Shakespeare, whose plays were being performed in a theatre near this residence. This document bears, after the Lambarde signature in the Folger, the earliest of the seven known Shakespeare signatures and is in the Guildhall Library in London, not far from Shakespeare's Westminster address between St. James' Park and Westminster Hall. The British Museum has the mortgage deed for this conveyance which contains another signature. Shakespeare acquires, by inheritance, or has conveyed to him, four residences; a freehold cottage on Chapel Street, the double house in Henley Street, New Place, and the Blackfriars property. As Hamlet says in the gravediggers' scene, "The very conveyances of his lands will hardly lie in this box; and must the inheritor himself have no more, ..." (V. i. 119–121): Not so, for in 1615, Shakespeare records an action to secure the deed for himself and his heirs in Chancery. The original tract of land had been held by Mathias Bacon, a scrivener and admitted to Gray's Inn, March 1, 1597, and Shakespeare had to enter a friendly suit against his son, who, like John Lambert, had inherited the deeds and documents of conveyance from his parents and Shakespeare had to have access to these to secure title. To do so he exercised, as he did on the Stratford tithes, the right of any citizen in the name of equity to appeal directly to the representative of the King's mercy and grace, Egerton, the Lord Chancellor. As in the case of New Place, so with Blackfriars, Shakespeare sues on each property, in addition to the original purchase, to assure his title and possession, and in the later case to possess the instruments of conveyance to show his ownership if ever challenged, as his father could not on the Asbies properties.

In 1607 it is believed Shakespeare was putting his final touches to the unsuccessful *Timon of Athens*. Timon is a figure to be pitied; a selfish and bitter man of small heart; and of circumstances neither heroic nor sufficiently universal to make a tragic figure or sustain a significant dramatic piece. Shakespeare's artistic judgment failed him; perhaps it was infused with things too close to home, too reminiscent of his father and what the dramatist was still engaged in, and psychologically compensating for. On March 15 and June 7 of 1609 in the Stratford Court of Record where his father had presided, he pursues at law a small debt owed him. This has bothered critics idolizing the Bard, but is in keeping with the man in the plays and court records. Considering his father's financial past, it is not surprising that Shakespeare, although gentle and honest, was an acquirer, and protective about his possessions. Half following Polonius' advice to Laertes (I. iii. 75–77) when a lender, as his father often did not, Shakespeare insisted upon payment or went for recovery. He was "honest" in both directions as Chettle had admitted ("... divers of worship have reported his uprightness of dealing, which argues his honesty, ..."); he had seen the consequence from being slipshod in such matters in his father, and overdramatized the consequences in his *Timon*.

The connections between Shakespeare and Chancery subsequent to the Lambert case resulted from his previous acquisitions, purchases and conveyances. On July 24, 1605, Shakespeare bought from Ralph Huband for £440 an interest in the tithes of Stratford and adjacent villages: ". . . the moiety or one-half of all and singular the said tithes of corn [see *Measure for Measure*, IV. i. 76], grain, blade, and hay . . . wool, lamb, and other small and privy tithes. . . ."[6] The other moiety belonged to the Combe family of Stratford and Middle Temple and would pass to Shakespeare's lawyer-cousin, Thomas Greene, likewise of Stratford and Middle Temple. On May 1, 1602, William buys 107 acres of land from John and William Combe for £320. The deed for this was delivered to Shakespeare's brother Gilbert residing in Stratford to hold for his brother, Will, absent in London. In 1610, Shakespeare, as was his habit by now, confirms and then extends by twenty additional acres the earlier purchase of land from the Combes. Also in 1602, the year of the original land purchase, the dramatist buys copyhold property with a cottage adjacent to New Place:

> MACBETH: O, full of scorpions is my mind, dear wife:
> Thou know'st that Banquo and his Fleance lives.
> LADY MACBETH: But in them nature's copy's not eterne.
> (III. ii. 36–38)

"Copy is not eternal" (lease on life is short) is possibly an early reference to common law, copyhold estate, or tenure, during which the land is held from the lord of the manor, as opposed to freehold, having it forever in one's own right. Copyhold had a terminal or determinate date for the lease. These conditions are frequently played with in the sonnets. In 1613 he obtains the house in the well-to-do section of Blackfriars, London, indicated by the dealings with the Lord Chancellor. So from 1597 to 1613, but mostly, after his father's death from 1602 to 1609,

Shakespeare accumulates an estate of holdings and incomes in Stratford, as his father had failed to do. An irony in one of the incomes was in its being a moiety of certain tithes upon lambs and wool closely allied to his father's trade of glover, and his business dealings in wool.

2. *Shakespeare and His Daughters' Trials*

SHAKESPEARE has employed his knowledge of law to obtain wealth, and his familiarity with equity to preserve and insure it. He has also been using equity, mostly in his comedies. There mercy and equitable procedures (even in their most technical sense) were used as a theatrical device. These permitted him to explore potentially tragic materials, but allowed for a sudden manageable reversal of fate; thus, ultimately maintaining the aesthetic and conventional structure of comedy. Now equity, the failure of it, or its labored attainment, in Shakespeare's Jacobean tragedies and romances evidence some astonishing corroboration of biographical material in Will's own story as the theme of land acquisition and conveyance is pursued through the process of inheritance, this time not from the point of view of the recipient (Mary Arden, Shakespeare, John Lambert, Hercules Underhill) but from that of the testator, William Shakespeare, as he had personified the figure in *King Lear* and with Prospero, in the *Tempest*.

In this later period, when Shakespeare puts a mirror up to the judicial process and mocks a court, as he does in *King Lear* (1605), he assumes it must represent the bifurcated fount of justice he has been advocating in his comedies and pursuing in his court cases.

LEAR: I'll see their [*his daughters', Goneril's and Regan's*] trial first. Bring in the evidence.
[*to Edgar*] Thou robed man of justice, take thy place;
[*to the Fool*] And thou, his yoke-fellow of equity,
Bench by his side: [*to Kent*] you are o' the commission,
Sit you too.
(III. vi. 37–40)

King Lear, among other things, reveals Shakespeare's preoccupation at this time with justice and right due authority; an aging man's concern about his inheritance and his offspring, in the striking absence of a mother; and with laws pertaining to these circumstances. The play can be read as a projection of some of the dramatist's personal involvements evidenced by the biographical events and legal actions Shakespeare is engaged in at the time. His concern over the lack of male lineage is visible in *Macbeth* (1606), where Macbeth has no heirs and goes about killing the sons of others, Duncan's two, Banquo's, Macduff's, and Siward's, and where Duncan settles his inheritance, in like manner as Claudius upon Hamlet (I. ii. 106–122);

> DUNCAN: Sons, kinsmen, thanes,
> And you whose places are the nearest, know
> We will establish our estate upon
> Our eldest, Malcolm, whom we name hereafter
> The Prince of Cumberland;
>
> (I. iv. 35–39).

He also evidences his awareness of legal bonds and obligations between persons in the famous: "He's here in double trust;" (I. vii. 12). Trusting or entrusting someone with an obligation is formalized by the legal act of establishing a trust. A trust is what Shakespeare will have to set up to assume that his estate will devolve upon his daughters, in hopes that it will eventually be received by males of his own flesh.

Lear's main source of action is of a father dividing his estate among his daughters upon their marriages. When he does so, he discovers that his judgment has betrayed himself and that he has brought forth by the laws of the body and by laws of inheritance, to which he is now subject, both good and bad offspring. The play reveals other fears: that of the patrimony being stolen from the son in the subplot of Edmund's stealing the inheritance from his legitimate brother Edgar, recapitulating Shakespeare's experience of Edmund Lambert's holding from his brother-in-law what was to have been Shakespeare's inheritance. The root of evil in both plots is traceable to sexual misconduct. The evil of Goneril and Regan is reflected in their sexual incontinence with Edmund. Edmund blames his evil upon his being Gloucester's natural son. Cordelia, innocent and chaste, remains true but is tragically destroyed by the old man's folly and preoccupation toward his daughters, wherein they become his missing wife, and mother, as well as the daughters of the piece.

> LEAR: Tremble, thou wretch,
> That hast within thee undivulged crimes,
> Unwhipp'd of justice: Hide thee, thou bloody hand;
> Thou perjur'd, and thou simular of virtue,
> That art incestuous.
>
> (III. ii. 51–55)

Lear is portrayed as a father revered by the three daughters, abused by two and mothered by one.

In the first scene of *King Lear*, the audience is witness to familial legal actions relating to inheritance. Lear engages in the legal operations of the divesture of property, the entailment of estate, the reservation in grant, and the construction of a dowry. Documents bearing Shakespeare's third signature on legal papers show that in 1612 he confirmed, in the Belott-Mountjoy suit, that he had participated on November 19, 1604 (the year before writing *Lear*) in the setting up of a dowry by Christopher Mountjoy, his French Huguenot landlord who had property on a corner of Silver Street in London. Later Stephen Belott sued for the fulfillment of the dowry that was to accompany Mary Mountjoy. So, Shakespeare bore witness to an inheritance that another Mary was to gain which had been threatened. That was one dowry; Shakespeare was going to have to arrange for two in his immediate family; and Lear handled three at once. All were threatened by the fathers' capacity and desire to withdraw, or alter, the endowment or inheritance.

Thus, *Lear* abounds in justice, mortality, sexual dilemmas, family, but chiefly celebrates an old man and his idealized good and loyal daughter. Although saying she owes half her love to him and half to her husband, Cordelia returns to console him in life and join him in death. This favoring in Shakespeare's personal life culminated in the marriage of his eldest daughter Susanna on June 5, 1607, to the brilliant Dr. Hall, an accomplished and learned physician who resided in Stratford. Within the proper grace period was born a granddaughter christened Elizabeth Hall, on February 21, 1608, and likely being honored on a secondary level by Shakespeare in the passage on the birth of Queen Elizabeth in *Henry VIII* (1613):

KING: What is her name?
CRANMER: Elizabeth
This royal infant—heaven still move about her:—
Though in her cradle, yet now promises
Upon this land a thousand thousand blessings,
Which time shall bring to ripeness: she shall be—
But few now living can behold that goodness—
A pattern to all princes living with her,
And all that shall succeed: Saba was never
More covetous of wisdom and fair virtue
Than this pure soul shall be: all princely graces,
That mould up such a mighty piece as this is,
With all the virtues that attend the good,
Shall still be doubled on her: truth shall nurse her,
Holy and heavenly thoughts still counsel her:
She shall be loved and fear'd: . . .
. . . . . . good grows with her:
In her days every man shall eat in safety,
Under his own vine, what he plants; and sing
The merry songs of peace to all his neighbours:
God shall be truly known; and those about her
From her shall read the perfect ways of honour,
And by those claim their greatness, not be blood.

And, though Shakespeare then speaks of the living heir to the dead Queen it also sounds as if he is extending a blessing to Elizabeth Hall's hoped-for lineage.

Nor shall this peace sleep with her: but as when
The bird of wonder dies, the maiden phoenix,

Her ashes new create another heir,
As great in admiration as herself;
So shall she leave her blessedness to one,
When heaven shall call her from this cloud of darkness,
Who from the sacred ashes of her honour
Shall star-like rise, as great in fame as she was,
And so stand fix'd: peace, plenty, love, truth, terror,
That were the servants to this chosen infant,
Shall then be his, and like a vine grow to him:
Wherever the bright sun of heaven shall shine,
His honour and the greatness of his name
Shall be, and make new nations: he shall flourish,
And, like a mountain cedar, reach his branches
To all the plains about him: our children's children
Shall see this, and bless heaven.

(V. v. 8–55).

In the same year, following the birth of Elizabeth Hall, on September 9, 1608 Shakespeare's mother Mary is buried. These family events of birth, death and marriage have psychological impact upon the great *Lear* (1605), with his daughters; the strange *Pericles* (1606–1608) and its explicit incest motif between father and daughter; and the problematic tragedy of *Coriolanus* (1608–1609), with Volumnia the dominant mother-figure.

The ambition instilled in the dramatist by the father's rise and prompted to compensation by his father's fearful fall was from 1601 onward redirected to the women in Shakespeare's life being projected in *Coriolanus* upon the mother-figure in Volumnia (emerging first in the wife-mother ambitious drives in Lady Macbeth, balanced by the courtesan seduction from such labors of a Cleopatra) and then upon his daughters as evidenced by *King Lear*. Prospero, in *The Tempest*, like Lear, has a daughter, (Miranda) and no wife; the father projects his fear of the sexual corruption of his offspring upon the character of the natural man, Caliban, as it is in *Lear* upon Edmund the natural son. This fear and concomitant desire to protect his daughters as represented in Lear and Prospero are carried to their explicit culmination in *Pericles*, and in

Leontes of *The Winter's Tale*. The feminine preoccupation is portrayed in *Pericles* by the liaison between Antiochus and his daughter, and the characters of Thaisa, Marina, and their counterparts Dionyza, Lychorida (a nurse) and a Bawd presided over by Diana. Similarly, *The Winter's Tale* presents the wife, Hermione, who is lost and returned upon the maturation of the daughter, along with Perdita, who is ready for marriage; with Paulina, a spokeswoman for this wife-daughter complex of figures against Leontes' jealousy. These plays, written when the males of Shakespeare's generation as well as his parents are dying around him, reveal how Shakespeare's mind was turning from London's Court and the Inns of Court to Stratford, his pastoral fields, and residence, after the earlier loss of his only son, distantly echoed in Mamillius' death in *Winter's Tale*, to concentrate on his new return to his wife, daughters, their marriages, and their offspring, in the way Leontes does in the same play. *Pericles* turns out to be an analysis of the father finding himself in his lost daughter-wife figures. *Coriolanus* is a study of a son's feelings toward his mother, written following Shakespeare's own mother's death.

These personal preoccupations are not devoid of legal representation as sons possess mother's inheritance, as fathers transmit themselves to daughters, and husbands treat wives tyrannically. Along with the characteristic motifs of this period in *Winter's Tale* (1610–1611) Shakespeare presents a last trial scene which depicts a court perverted by the taint with which King James threatened Chancery, his assertion of royal authority. Coinciding with this emerging preoccupation over mothers, daughters, female innocence, mercy and equity, is that of Shakespeare's fear and distaste for the willful and threatening male justice figure of a father, a King, or a Leontes (lion) type, becoming converted in time from malevolence, to folly, to benignity, to benevolence in Claudius, Lear, Leontes and Prospero, respectively, as Shakespeare ultimately controls this figure in his art, and through his art, in his own father and then King James himself.

The court representation is a last bold illustration of "the oppressor's wrong," in this case from the top of the hierarchy as opposed to its welling up from the lack of proper authority in *King Lear.* Leontes' tyrannical court is ultimately redeemed only by the action of natural laws through the agency of time and the patient moderation of the trinity of female mercy-figures, Perdita, Hermione and Paulina. The operative resolution, anticipating *The Tempest*, is more mythic, cosmic, natural, and religious than strictly juristic. However the mechanism begins in familiar form with, in this case, Leontes as judge, jury, and plaintiff against his wife Hermione's alleged adultery, and acts as aggrieved party while in the robes of judicial office. He dismisses evidence even from the higher authority of the oracle, despite his opening declaration:

> Let us be clear'd
> Of being tyrannous, since we so openly
> Proceed in justice, which shall have due course,
> Even to the guilt or the purgation.
>
> (III. ii. 4–7)

He judges on his own behalf, loses his entire family of wife, son, and daughter, who are returned to him in person or substitute when he is regenerated by the operation of remorse through time a generation later. This overlapping of characters through time discloses the psychological substitution the dramatist has been exploring in this play, as noted by Otto Rank, who is credited by Norman Holland in his *Psychoanalysis and Shakespeare* (New York, 1964) for seeing

> ". . . in old Leontes' casting youthful eyes at Perdita an incest motif. In effect, the mother-wife has become young again and is desired in the daughter. The recovery of Hermione and her (in effect) second marriage with Leontes disguises the incestuous wish to marry Perdita." (*p.* 279).

Modern productions have emphasized this alignment

of what Shakespeare pursued with a psychological preoccupation understandable from his biography. The literary theme of incest in this period is developed into a theatrical convention only later in the Stuart tragedies of Beaumont, Webster, and Ford (interestingly, all members of the Inns of Court).

At this time, it is known from Thomas Greene's letters indicating that he is about to move out of New Place in 1610. Shakespeare returns to Stratford. Here in this town with pastoral associations far from London City, he turns to his second daughter, Judith. In writing *The Tempest*, he speaks of a man exercising his magic by which the world is brought to admire his daughter, with the wife-mother absent, protecting Miranda from Caliban and bestowing her upon a Prince, and finally abjuring his fantastic craft, "I'll break my staff, /Bury it certain fathoms in the earth, /And deeper than did ever plummet sound /I'll drown my book." (v. i. 54–57) Holland helps to pursue the theme once again as he observes:

> . . . Prospero combines in himself the father possessing the daughter-mother and also the father-as-ruler avenging himself on those who would steal his power or his love from him. (*p.* 287).

These factors from the plays would be of little value to a biography except that they are borne out by events from Shakespeare's life. His preoccupations with his daughters as handled in his art are met with manifestations of his fears from the real world in sexual slanders upon his favored daughter and sexual corruption foistered upon his less favored daughter both revealed by law suits; one pursued by himself, with Thomas Greene as his legal aide.

As has been noted, Shakespeare's eldest daughter, Susanna, was married on June 5, 1607, to John Hall, a learned man, a distinguished physician, and a noted citizen. Scandal erupted in the Hall household in 1613. As a consequence, on July 13 Susanna sought a writ of slander and brought action for defamation (*cf. Measure for Measure*, II. i. 190) in the Consistory (an Ecclesiastical) Court at Worcester. Susanna's charge was against John Lane, whose uncle, Richard Lane, Shakespeare had asked to be one of the witnesses for the commission out of Chancery on the Lambert controversy and had been of Shakespeare's party in the suit to Chancery on the Stratford tithes. John Lane (Jr.) had accused Shakespeare's daughter by saying Susanna ". . . had the running of the reins and had been naught [i.e. immoral] with Rafe Smith at John Palmer [a small town]." Ralph Smith was a Stratford haberdasher and hatter; his uncle was Hamnet Sadler, the close friend of Shakespeare (for whom he named his son). The males of the second generation of close acquaintances were a threat to the reputation of his daughters; and in the case of Judith, to come, and, at first, Susanna, the Shakespeares struck back at the male contemporaries of the son William no longer had.

With this court case, Susanna has become subject to precisely the slanderous accusation of adultery as in something of a prophetic manner for Shakespeare's biography was Hermione in *Winter's Tale*, anticipated by Desdemona in *Othello*. John Lane, ". . . a ne'er-do-well, was some years later hailed into court for riot and libels against the vicar and aldermen, and was then described as a drunkard."[7] Robert Whatcott was the lawyer who represented Mrs. Susanna Hall and is often not recognized, or is misidentified, by scholars and critics when they encounter his name as one of the witnesses of the dramatist's will. He is another one of the numerous attorneys or representatives working for, or associated with, the Shakespeare family. John Lane did not appear in court to support the rumors he had spread and was excommunicated. Susanna's chastity had been maligned, but like Hermione, she survived the accusation triumphantly, and like Cordelia was ultimately honored by the father, receiving New Place and virtually all his personal property upon his death. Her epitaph upon her tomb after she dies in 1649 reads:

> Witty above her sex, but that's not all,
> Wise to salvation was good Mistress Hall;
> Something of Shakespeare was in that, but this
> Wholly of him with whom she's now in bliss.[8]

So, as he had desired, something of himself against the slings and arrows of outrageous fortune had been preserved.

On February 10, 1616, when she was nearly 31, Judith, the younger daughter of Shakespeare, married Thomas Quiney, the son of Shakespeare's friend Richard Quiney and grandson of John Shakespeare's companion Adrian. Thomas was a vintner, or innkeeper, and was 26, much Judith's junior, which was reminiscent of Will's marriage. Perhaps she had tried to please him, and later even named her son "Shaxper". Unfortunately he died in infancy. Fate was against her. Anthony Burgess narrates the developments of the situation well:

> Marriage to a tavern-keeper was scarcely what Will would have chosen for his younger daughter, especially as it was—like his own—a marriage conducted in suspicious haste. The haste is attested by the fact that February 10 came within the period for special licences. The special license that had been obtained for Will and Anne, all those years before, had been obtained in a regular manner and from the proper authority—the Bishop of Worcester. But Thomas Quiney got his licence from the Stratford vicar, and apparently this was so irregular that he (and not, as would have been just, the vicar) was summoned to the consistory court at Worcester. He [*like John Lane before him*] refused to go, or forgot, and was fined and excommunicated. This was not a very good start to the state of holy matrimony.
>
> The hasty wedding was not the result of what Will, remembering the reason for his own, had most cause to suspect. Judith was not pregnant. But a certain Margaret Wheelar had yielded to the incontinent Quiney some nine months before, and this—a month or so after the wedding—came sordidly into the open.

Quiney must have reminded Shakespeare of his characterization of Angelo in *Measure for Measure* and Bertrand in *All's Well That Ends Well* but, fortunately, in art the objects of their adulterous designs are suddenly switched at the last months for their betrothed. Burgess continues:

> Mistress Wheelar and her new-born child had died and were buried on March 15, 1616. On March 26, with the lawyer, [Thomas] Greene, Will's former lodger, as prosecuting counsel, Quiney confessed in court that he had had 'carnal intercourse with the said Wheelar' and was conventionally sorry about it. He had good reason for being genuinely sorry for, *the day before the trial, his father-in-law had altered his will drastically, much reducing poor Judith's expectation* [italics mine]. She was punished for her unwise match. But the unwise match was to prove punishment enough.
>
> Thomas was ordered to make public penance. He was to appear in the parish church on three successive Sundays [at the end of which time William Shakespeare was to be dead!] . . Thomas was evidently not a good man. He had married into the Shakespeare family under false pretences. *He had failed to produce his share of the marriage settlement—one hundred pounds in land.* Later, he was to be fined for swearing and for allowing drunkenness on his premises. There is a tradition that he deserted his wife, but there is no evidence to it. His date and place of death are not known. His tavern was called, appropriately for Judith, the Cage. The site now houses a hamburger bar. No dignity for either of them, even three hundred years after the death, in 1662, of Judith, a tough woman who has survived much degradation.[9]

The episode of Judith, as well as that of Susanna, shows that the plays of the later period were, strangely enough, prophetic about events to happen in Shakespeare's life. They initially evidenced a fear in the father which, while handled in the art, in turn was to manifest itself in the form of threats from offspring of contemporary friends fortunate to have sons, but not of fortunate character. The Shakespeares took up the law to protect themselves, to punish and reward at a time when the dramatist was personally nearly reenacting the tragedy of the good and evil daughters of *King Lear* and reexperiencing a mood toward daughters captured in the adulterous slander of *Winter's Tale* and the sexual looming of *The Tempest*:

PROSPERO: Then, as my gift and thine own acquisition
Worthily purchased, take my daughter: but
If thou dost break her virgin-knot before
All sanctimonious ceremonies may
With full and holy rite be minister'd
No sweet aspersion shall the heavens let fall
To make this contract grow; but barren hate,
Sour-eyed disdain and discord shall bestrew
The union of your bed with weeds as loathly
That you shall hate it both:

(IV. i. 13–22).

Evil, particularly with sexual overtones, corrupted metaphysically in the art but had erupted in reality after being anticipated in the unconscious. The ordering of the law was invoked for punishment, vindication, reward and the casting away of the unruly sons (Caliban, Edmund, John Lane and Thomas Quiney). The patrimony had been attacked by the ignorant, unknowing and false accusing (Lane and Edmund figures) and the unconscious, willful, and beastly (Quiney and Caliban figures) once again, and close to the end (had it hastened the end?); but this time the legacy had survived, with judicious alterations. Shakespeare's estate, through his use of the law, was to have gone to his son Hamlet; he protected his daughters to receive it by legal means, and kept it intact for some future male heir by the reach of law through time.

3. *Last Will and Testament*

JUDITH'S marriage was in February; Quiney's trial was in March; and Shakespeare was dead in April, of 1616. All his fears had come upon him and the blows had come across the generation from sons of friends. During this later period he had also witnessed his three younger brothers' deaths: Edmund, who had been a player, was buried in Southwark on December 31, 1607; Gilbert was buried in Stratford on February 3, 1612; and Richard, there also, on February 4, 1613. He, as the only surviving, male Shakespeare of any generation, made his will on January 25, 1616; altered it March 25th, the day before the Quiney trial; signed it three times in April; died probably the 23rd; and was buried in Stratford April 25, 1616, following the burial on April 17th of his sister Joan's husband William Hart.

Despite its seeming dryness and formulaic phrasing the preoccupations of Shakespeare's mind concerning particular people, property, and the placement of all he had so painstakingly acquired can be strongly felt. Surprisingly the document also acts as a recapitulation of many of the legal concepts and technical phrasing Shakespeare employed in his plays. It was all familiar to him, and some legal figures, such as the Chancellor, Lord Campbell, thought the will must have been constructed by Shakespeare himself; others, such as E. B. Everitt, have gone so far as to find it was written in Shakespeare's own legal hand. The testament was probated on June 22, 1616 by his son-in-law Dr. John Hall.[10] Thus the Will is brought forth on parchment, a testament that his daughters heard bequeathing a rich legacy unto their issue and even now one can seem to see, through the legal phrases, "him that made the will." The will shall be read, you will hear the will, as Shakespeare had written in *Julius Caesar* (III. ii, 137–163).

Shakespeare's will begins:

> On the 25th day of March in the year of the reign of our lord James, now King of England, etc., the fourteenth, and of Scotland the forty-ninth, and in the year of our Lord, 1616.
>
> Testament of William Shackspeare[11]

Testaments were what noverints were named after for having to produce them in fair and proper copy as part of their trade. Joan of Arc in one of Shakespeare's earliest plays, *Henry VI Part One*, says in a defiant metaphor to Talbot "Help Salisbury to make his testament:" (I. iii. 17).

> In the name of God, Amen. I, William Shackspeare of Stratford-upon-Avon in the county of Warwick, gent, in perfect health and memory, God be praised, do make and ordain this my last will and testament . . .

The Painter had observed to the Poet in *Timon of Athens* that "To promise is most courtly and fashionable: performance is a kind of will or testament which argues a great sickness in his judgment that makes it." (V. i. 29–32, and see *As You Like It*, II. i. 47).

> . . . in manner and form following [*Costard.* "In manner and form following, . . ." (*Love's Labour's Lost* I. i. 204)].
>
> That is to say: First I commend my soul into the hands of God my Creator, hoping and assuredly believing through the only merits of Jesus Christ my Saviour to be made partaker of life everlasting [*Isabella.* "Why, all the souls that were were forfeit once;/ And He that might the vantage best have took/ Found out the remedy." (*Measure for Measure* II. ii. 74–76)]; and my body to the earth whereof it is made.
>
> Item, I give and bequeath . . . (*cf. Pericles*, II. i. 126–140.) . . . unto my daughter Judith one hundred and fifty pounds of lawful English money to be paid unto her in manner and form following, that is to say: one hundred pounds [*in discharge of her marriage portion*] . . .

As in *Winter's Tale*: *Shepherd.* "I give my daughter to him, and will make/ Her portion equal his." (IV. iv. 395–396), which is what Shakespeare was doing to match Thomas Quiney's alleged portion. This is the kind of bargain he had witnessed in the Belott-Mountjoy suit and similar to the dowry arrangements at the opening of *Lear*.

> . . . within one year after my decease with consideration after the rate of two shillings in the pound for so long a

> time as the same shall be unpaid unto her after my decease, and the fifty pounds' residue thereof upon her surrendering [*of*] or giving of such sufficient security as the overseers . . .

The overseers of Shakespeare's will were Thomas Russell and Francis Collins. Thomas Russell lived four miles south of Stratford in Alderminster and probably knew Shakespeare also in London when the dramatist had lodgings in Silver Street. His stepson, Leonard Digges, wrote two poems in praise of Shakespeare. Francis Collins, some believe to be the one whose hand the will is in, was associated with Thomas Greene. Francis went to Clement's Inn, referred to by Shallow and Slender in *Henry IV Part Two*, as did John Greene; it is believed he drew up the indentures for Shakespeare's purchase of Stratford tithes; he was an attorney in the Court of Record, which Shakespeare's father had earlier been the judge of as High Bailiff, and he witnessed deeds and wills of Shakespeare's friends with their other mutual legal friend Thomas Greene.[12] Many of the legal phrases in these passages (decease, rite of usance, residue, security, estate, etc.) Shakespeare had already used in their technical aspects in his plays.

> . . . as the overseers of this my will shall like of to surrender or grant all her estate and right that shall descend or come unto her after my decease or [*that she*] now hath of, in, or to one copyhold[13] tenement with the appurtenances [a word familiar from the Asbies' litigations] lying and being in Stratford-upon-Avon aforesaid in the said county of Warwick, being parcel or holden of the manor of Rowington, unto my daughter Susanna Hall and her heirs forever.

As in *Henry VIII* (1613) where the King makes Cardinal Wolsey ". . . forfeit all your goods, lands, tenements,/ Chattels, and whatsoever, . . ." (III. ii. 342–343) and ". . . several parcels of his plate, . . ." (l. 125) so Shakespeare insists that Judith give up all her rights (compensated for by £50) to the copyhold cottage and land across from New Place to Susanna. Susanna subsequently does receive the property on April 18, 1617. Shakespeare clearly wants no land, lease, or conveyable property of his to fall to Thomas Quiney via Judith (as the Arden lands which fell to his mother had been lost by his father), and furthermore wants Susanna to hold New Place entire and in expanded peace.

> Item, I give and bequeath unto my said daughter Judith one hundred and fifty pounds more, if she or any issue of her body be living at the end of three years next ensuing the day of the date of this my will, during which time my executors to pay her consideration from my decease according to the rate aforesaid. And if she die within the said term without issue of her body, then my will is and I do give and bequeath one hundred pounds thereof to my niece [i.e., granddaughter by Susanna] Elizabeth Hall, and the fifty pounds to be set forth by my executors during the life of my sister, Joan Hart, and the use and profit[14] thereof coming shall be paid to my said sister Joan, and after her decease the said fifty pounds shall remain amongst the children of my said sister, [William, Michael and Thomas (the latter died in 1661)] equally to be divided amongst them. But if my said daughter Judith be living at the end of the said three years, or any issue of her body, then my will is and so I devise and bequeath the said hundred and fifty pounds to be set out [by my executors and overseers] for the best benefit [i.e., interest[15]] of her and her issue, and [*the stock* [i.e., principal]] not [*to be*] paid unto her so long as she shall be married and covert.

The intention is that Thomas Quiney and hence poor Judith are to receive no property and furthermore that the £150 is not to be paid to Judith as long as she is under the legal protection and principle of having to share with her husband Thomas Quiney. The interest of the money is for her benefit only after three years, and the principle only when Quiney is no longer part of the family. Even this sum has the slight entail of hope for an issue which is seemingly met in Judith's son, whom she dutifully named Shaxpere Quiney, but is disappointed in his early death.

> . . . but my will is that she shall have the consideration yearly paid unto her during her life and after her decease the said stock and consideration to be paid to her children [i.e., the deed of gift Shylock was forced to make upon Lorenzo who had stolen his daughter Jessica, and that John Shakespeare had not made on any of his properties such as Asbies for William.] if she have any, and [bypassing Thomas Quiney] if not to her executors or assigns [*cf. Hamlet* v. ii. 157], she living the said term after my decease. Provided that if such husband as she shall at the end of the said three years be married unto or attain after do sufficiently assure unto her and the issue of her body lands answerable to the portion by this my will given unto her and to be adjudged so by my executors and overseers, then my will is that the said 150 pounds shall be paid to such husband as shall make such assurance, to his own use.

Thomas Quiney never produced the 150 pounds value of land that he alleged he would as his half of the dowry settlement.

> Item, I give and bequeath unto my said sister Joan. . . .

Joan Hart, as we have seen, three weeks later would be made a widow, and was living, as she had all her life, with her three young sons in the house on Henley Street where Susanna, Judith, and Hamnet had been reared, which was finally left to Shakespeare as the one inheritance coming to him clear upon his mother's death, from the female side.

> . . . 20 pounds and all my wearing apparel, to be paid and delivered within one year after my decease, and I do will and devise unto her [*the house*] with the appurtenances in Stratford wherein she dwelleth for her natural life under the yearly rent of twelvepence. Item, I give and bequeath unto her *three sons* [Italics mine] . . .

At this point we are reminded of *Macbeth* describing a situation similar to Shakespeare's condition which the will so carefully attempts to remedy.

> They hail'd him father to a line of kings.

> Upon my head they placed a fruitless crown,
> And put a barren sceptre in my gripe,
> Thence to be wrench'd with an unlineal hand,
> No son of mine succeeding. If't be so,
> For Banquo's issue have I filed my mind;
> For them the gracious Duncan have I murder'd;
> (III. i. 60–66)].

> . . . three sons *William* [Joan had named her eldest son for her famous older brother] Hart,—Hart, . . .

Shakespeare had forgotten the name of his nephew: It was Thomas, and he was ten at the time in 1616. Ironically he lived until 1661, surviving his two brothers and his line is still extant.[16] The one male who survived that was closest to the Shakespeare family line, at the time of the writing of the will, William Shakespeare, gent. could not spring from recollection's vaults.

> . . . and Michael Hart, five pounds apiece, to be paid within one year [Judith had to wait three years] after my decease.
> Item, I give and bequeath unto [*the said Elizabeth Hall*] . . .

Elizabeth Hall is Shakespeare's only grandchild to reach maturity.

> . . . all my plate that I now have at the date of this my will.
> Item, I give and bequeath unto the poor of Stratford aforesaid ten pounds; . . .

Shakespeare's father had been relieved of his duty to pay a poor tax because of his own narrow straits.

> . . . to Mr. Thomas Combe my sword;[17] . . .

In 1598, Thomas Combe's brother John had been selected as a witness to the commission out of Chancery on the *Shakespeare* v. *Lambert* matter. Thomas Combe sold land to Shakespeare in 1602; had a brother William (1586–1666/7) who studied at the Middle Temple and answered Shakespeare in Chancery on the Stratford tithes.[18]

> . . . to Thomas Russell, Esq., five pounds; . . .

The year before the writing of this will John Greene of Clement's Inn, and Shakespeare's cousin, held a court for Thomas Russell's manor;[19] Shakespeare probably knew Russell in London and Stratford.

> . . . and to Francis Collins of the borough of Warwick in the county of Warwick, gent., thirteen pounds, six shillings, and eightpence, to be paid within one year after my decease.

It is erroneously thought by some (Tucker Brooke and Mark Eccles[20]) that the will is in the legal hand of Francis Collins. The money to him in the will is his fee, as was that to Thomas Russell. They were the two lawyers Shakespeare appointed as the overseers of his will. The pamphlet from the Public Record Office in London attempts to unscramble the matter, ignoring a major possibility.

> A number of authorities [Campbell, the Lord Chancellor, E. B. Everitt, etc.] have stated flatly that Shakespeare wrote his own will, but a comparison of the writing in the body of the will with that of the firmest signature on the third sheet shows that this was not so.

But, of course, Shakespeare may have engrossed the will in his legal hand (traces of which are evidenced in his Belott-Mountjoy signature he signed four years before in 1612) at the time he made up his will in January and then March of 1616; and then signed his will in his personally erratic autograph style three times on the day of his death. The Public Record report continues:

> Nor, in all probability, is it the hand of Francis Collins, the Warwick lawyer who supervised its preparation, for specimens of Collins's hand in other documents differ considerably from the writing in the will. The likeliest theory is that the body of the will was written by Collins's clerk, though the lawyer himself appears to have added the words 'witnes to the publishing hereof Fra: Collyns' which appear at the bottom left-hand side of the third sheet.

In other words the alternative suggestion still furnishes neither a known person nor a hand appearing elsewhere, hence the possibility that Shakespeare not only constructed but also wrote his own last will and testament cannot be totally dismissed as of yet. A third party added the list of the formal witnesses.

> Beneath this entry [by Collins], possibly all written in a third hand, are the names of the other witnesses 'Juliyus Shawe John Robinson Hamnet Sadler Robert Whattcott'. The only specimens of Shakespeare's own hand are the three signatures.[21]

Francis Collins the following year in which he was to die (1617), became town clerk of Stratford, a position held by Shakespeare's cousin Thomas Greene and an office under which it has been suggested Shakespeare may have earlier worked out a clerkship.

> Item, I give and bequeath to Hamlet Sadler [for whom Shakespeare named his only son] 26s. 8d. to buy him a ring: *to William Reynolds, gent., 26s, 8d, to buy him a ring*; . . .

William Reynolds (1575–1632/3) was a neighbor living in Chapel Street and family friend; his grandfather Hugh Reynolds may have served in civic capacity with Shakespeare's father.

> . . . to my godson, William Walker, 20s. in gold; . . .

Shakespeare's godson and namesake William Walker, the son of the alderman Henry Walker, was christened in Stratford on October 16, 1608.[22]

> . . . to Anthony Nashe, gent., 26s. 8d. and to Mr. John Nashe 26s. 8d., . . .

Anthony and John were brothers. John Nash was sued in Queen's Bench for trespass in Easter Term 1588 in the same year as *Shakespeare* v. *Lambert* began in that court. He held Stratford tithes, as did Shakespeare; and both brothers witnessed the Combes' deed to Shakespeare in 1602. Anthony left considerable holdings ". . . to his son Thomas (1593–1647), who studied at Lincoln's Inn and married Shakespeare's granddaughter [Elizabeth Hall] in 1626."[23] Shakespeare, showing to what extent his thoughts had left London and his craft, as an afterthought, then turns to his company of players and adds to the will the gift for some of the membership of the going price for good memorial rings:

> . . . [*and to my fellows, John Hemings, Richard Burbage, and Henry Condell 26s. 8d. apiece to buy them rings*].

Burbage had been his closest and longest associate in the theatre and Heminge and Condell were to prepare Shakespeare's greatest legacy in the First Folio in 1623 (the year Shakespeare's wife Anne died and probably all rights to manuscripts were then relinquished). It is appropriate that Shakespeare remembered at last the two who would, in memorializing him, insure the memory of his works for all time.

Then Shakespeare turns to his eldest and most favored.

> Item, I give, will, bequeath, and devise unto my daughter Susanna Hall [*for better enabling of her to perform this my will and towards the performance thereof*] all that capital messuage or tenement with the appurtenances [*in Stratford aforesaid*] called the New Place, wherein I now dwell, and two messuages or tenements [his parents' house which he had inherited from his mother] with the appurtenances situate, lying, and being in Henley Street [which his sister Joan will rent for twelvepence a year as long as she lives] within the borough of Stratford aforesaid; and all my barns, stables, orchards, gardens, lands, tenements, and hereditaments whatsoever, situate, lying and being, or to be had, received, perceived or taken, within the towns, hamlets, villages, fields, and grounds of Stratford-upon-Avon, Old Stratford, Bushopton, and Welcombe, . . .

This was a considerable amount of property including several dwellings and hundreds of acres. This is where the Asbies estate in Wilmcote from his mother to his daughter and granddaughter would have been included.

> . . . or in any of them, in the said county of Warwick; and also all that messuage or tenement with the appurtenances wherein one John Robinson dwelleth, . . .

The house in Blackfriars had been rented to John Robinson.

> . . . situate, lying, and being in the Blackfriars in London, near the Wardrobe; and all other my lands, tenements, and hereditaments whatsoever, to have and to hold all and singular the said premises with their appurtenances unto the said Susanna Hall for and during the term of her natural life, . . .

Then Shakespeare turns to the revealing entail which represents his fruitless search for a male heir to continue his line which he had rescued, magnified, and extended.

> . . . and after her decease to the first son of her body lawfully issuing and for default of such issue to the second son of her body lawfully issuing and to the heirs males of the body of the said second son lawfully issuing, and for default of such issue the same so to be and remain to the fourth, fifth, sixth, and seventh sons of her body lawfully issuing, one after another, and to the heirs males of the bodies of the said fourth, fifth, sixth, and seventh sons lawfully issuing in such manner as it is before limited, to be and remain to the first, second, and third sons of her body and to their heirs males. And for default of such issue the said premises to be and remain to my said niece [i.e. granddaughter, Elizabeth Hall] and the heirs males of her body lawfully issuing: and for default of such issue, [only then and finally] to my daughter Judith and the heirs males [Shaxpere Quiney dies in infancy] of her body lawfully issuing; and for default of such issue to the right heirs of me the said William Shackspeare for ever. [*Item, I give unto my wife my second best bed with the furniture.*]

The Public Records' pamphlet offers a reasonable explanation for what has become a most notorious line by Shakespeare, rivaling anything from the plays and perhaps the second-best-known fact of Shakespeare's biography, the paramount one being that he married Anne Hathaway in the first place.

By a famous interlineation towards the end of the third sheet Shakespeare's wife received 'my second best bed with the furniture'. The bequest was not necessarily a slight, for the dramatist's motive in leaving the bulk of his possessions to his daughter was clearly the hope of establishing a line through his daughter's male heirs. Beds and similar items of household furniture were quite commonly the sole bequest from a husband to a wife. Quite commonly too she would receive the second best article whilst the best went to the eldest son.

If Anne were to remarry, the possessions or properties would leave the family line, but she could enjoy them under an unwritten life interest. The pamphlet continues with some puzzlement:

> The insertion of this item as an apparent afterthought is less easily explained, but it is conceivable that the bequest was accidentally omitted when the page was recopied.[24]

Shakespeare continues to dispose of particular moveables:

> Item, I give and bequeath to my said daughter Judith my broad silver gilt bowl.

This was separated earlier from all other possessions which were to go to Susanna. The bowl was undoubtedly of value; and it, ironically befitted the surroundings of an Inn, and a tapster-husband who was a notorious drunkard, reveller and rioter.

> All the rest of my goods, chattel, leases, plate, jewels and household stuff whatsoever after my debts and legacies paid and my funeral expenses discharged I give, devise, and bequeath to my son-in-law, John Hall, gent., and my daughter Susanna his wife, whom I ordain and make executors of this my last will and testament. And I do entreat and appoint [*the said*] Thomas Russell, Esq., and Francis Collins, gent., to be overseers hereof, and do revoke all former wills and publish this to be my last will and testament ["'Poor deer,' quoth he, 'thou makest a testament/ As worldings do, giving thy sum of more/ To that which had too much:'" (*As You Like It* II. i. 47–49)]. In witness where-

of I have hereunto put my hand the day and year first above written.

By me *William Shakespeare*[25]

Shakespeare, in failing health, also signed, the two previous sheets. The document was witnessed by Francis Collins, Julius Shaw, John Robinson, Hamnet Sadler, and Robert Whatcott. Mr. Julius Shaw, who lived in the second house from Shakespeare's in Chapel Street, when witnessing Shakespeare's will was bailiff of Stratford, the post Shakespeare's father John had once held. Mark Eccles says that John Robinson and Robert Whatcott ". . . may have been servants of Shakespeare or of Hall".[26] This is unlikely in so far as they were probably the Robert Whatcott who was Susanna Hall's attorney in the court case and defended her against slander in Worcester, and possibly the John Robinson who was renting Blackfriars from Shakespeare in London at this time. Undoubtedly Hamnet and Judith Sadler had been at the christening of the twins in 1585 and so Shakespeare's son's namesake was there as a witness for the will at the end. Shakespeare, as a father had lost a Hamlet, and now this Hamlet had lost the father of a Hamlet: "'Tis sweet and commendable in your nature, Hamlet,/ To give these mourning duties to [Hamlet's] . . . father." (I. ii. 88–89).

The will was probated on June 22, 1616. Shakespeare died April 23, 1616 and was buried on April 25, 1616 in the Holy Trinity Church in Stratford where he was baptized on April 26 (hence possibly died on the day-date he was born, April 23) fifty-two years previously in 1564.[27] The divesting of the estate Shakespeare had acquired since his father's fall from civic height was witnessed by men associated with what John Shakespeare had attained when all was well. Francis Collins was about to be Town Clerk, Reynolds' grandfather may have served with John, Walker's father was an Alderman, and Julius Shaw was High Bailiff of Stratford. The to be world-renowned dramatist had died in Stratford finally in the civic, social, financial, and gentlemanly situation his father had reached at his height, then lost, but had returned to him and then sustained after his death by his son. This had been achieved through legal knowledge in action and in art.

Shakespeare, after leading a life full of legal connections at Westminster and the Inns of Court, dies in a house purchased from a lawyer family of the Inner Temple, possibly in the room once rented by his lawyer cousin of Middle Temple, whose brother was of Clement's Inn, situated across the street from two Stratford lawyers (Court and Roache), and has his will witnessed by the lawyers Collins and Whatcott, and by Robinson who could have been the one living in Shakespeare's London residence which was formerly owned by a member of Gray's Inn. Furthermore, he left property to his granddaughter who would marry a member of Lincoln's Inn, and property to Thomas Combe who joined Shakespeare in a Chancery suit and whose brother studied at the Middle Temple. Surprisingly, in addition to the many legal themes of the plays touched upon in the will, every one of the major Inns of Court (Lincoln's, Gray's, Middle Temple, Inner Temple, and Clement's Inns) are associated with figures or events connected with Shakespeare's last testament.

When Joseph Greene, the vicar of Holy Trinity in Stratford, discovered a copy of Shakespeare's will in 1747, his comments appear to have entertained, as did those of Lord Campbell, the possibility that Shakespeare composed, if not even wrote, the will himself.

> The Legacies and Bequests therein, are undoubtedly as he intended; but the manner of introducing them, appears to me so dull and irregular, so absolutely void of ye least particle of that Spirit which Animated Our great Poet; that it must lessen his Character as a Writer, to imagine ye least Sentence of it his production[28]

The demonstrable connections between the document, the plays, and Shakespeare's legal preoccupations pertaining to inheritance, conveyances, property laws, indentures, equity, establishing lineage, primogeniture, and order, and transference through the female line make the will far from dry reading. As has been seen, Shakespeare's Last Will and Testament is animated with the spirit of his preoccupations in his foregoing life, plays, and legal action, thus summarizing his various legal, judicial and equitable concerns. The document also provides the focus the legalistic portion of Shakespeare's intellect would have to have to make the variety of seemingly disparate and irrelevant events in his life have a unity which was perceived and understood by the dramatist, but which has evaded biographers and critics.

Another of the witnesses to the dispersal of Shakespeare's attainments was Julius Shaw. As High Bailiff of Stratford he symbolizes in this narrative a return through conscious accomplishment of a son across the years of paternal decline, failure, dismissal, ostracism, and deprivation to attain a position analogous to his father's height when he was first citizen of Stratford, presiding as a judge, having estates, houses, lands, and family, and wanting to be styled Gentleman. The High Bailiff of Stratford, that his father was, was present at the distribution of his estates.

4. *Tributes to Shakespeare's Dramatic, Poetic and Juristic Mind.*

AFTER his death, John Heminge and Henry Condell whom Shakespeare had remembered in his will, edited the First Folio of his plays in 1623. In their Dedication and brief Epistle to the Readers they frame their directive in legal terms, most perhaps because they knew their audience, but possibly because they knew something about their man:

> . . . since your Lordships [i.e., the Earl of Pembroke, a member of Gray's Inn, and the Earl of Montgomery] have been pleased to think these trifles something heretofore, and have *prosecuted* [Italics will be mine] both them

> and their author, living, with so much favor, we hope that (they outliving him, and he not having the fate common with some [i.e., Ben Jonson, who came out with his own *Works*], to be *executor* to his own writings) you will use the like indulgence toward them you have done unto *their parent* ["Look, how the father's face/ Lives in his issue, . . ." Ben Jonson on Shakespeare]. There is a great difference whether any book choose his patrons or find them. This hath done both. For so much were your Lordships' likings of the several parts, when they were acted, as before they were published the volume asked to be yours. We have but collected them, and *done an office to the dead, to procure his orphans guardians*: . . .
> . . . therefore, we most humbly consecrate to your Highnesses these remains of your servant Shakespeare: . . .

The editors then address the readers.

> Well, it is now public, and you will *stand for your privileges*, we know: to read and *censure*. Do so, but buy it first: that doth best commend a book, the stationer says. Then, how odd soever your brains be or your *wisdoms* make your *license* the same and spare not. *Judge* your six-penn'orth, your shilling's worth, your five shilling's worth at a time, or higher, so you rise to the *just rates*, and welcome. But, whatever you do, buy! *Censure* will not drive a trade or make the jack go. *And though you be a magistrate of wit, and sit on the stage at Blackfriars or the Cockpit to arraign plays daily, know, these plays have had their trial already and stood out all appeals, and do now come forth quitted rather by decree of court than any purchased letters of commendation.*[29]

Heminge and Condell are undoubtedly making their appeal to the Inns of Court readers and the like who enjoyed the plays and can afford the volume but they might also be remembering a trade that gave their *Johannes fac totem* the knowledge of the law he had and the skill in calligraphy they had just praised so.

> It has been a thing, we confess, worthy to have been wished that the author himself had lived to have set forth and overseen his own writings; . . . His mind and hand

went together, and what he thought he uttered with that easiness that we have scarce received from him a blot in his papers.[30]

This is very remarkable, since theatre managers were perpetually complaining about unintelligable manuscripts, which had to go to copyists; disturbing, corrected copy; and late and incomplete submissions. A dramatist's papers, reports Henslowe, come in slowly, and some of them are "not so fayr written all as I could wish", and in another instance one of the dramatists replied "I send you the foule sheet & ye fayr I was wrighting as y^r^ man can testify"; and another that he "will not fayle to write this fayr and perfit the book."[31] Not only was it astounding to the editors that he wrote his manuscripts so fast, with seemingly no revision but that he produced them in his own hand in fair copy condition. As we have seen, this is something Ben Jonson found equally remarkable, despite the critical use he puts it to:

> I remember, the players have often mentioned it as an honor to Shakespeare that in his writing, whatsoever he penned, he never blotted out line. My answer hath been: Would he had blotted a thousand; which they thought a malevolent speech. I has not told posterity this but for their ignorance, who choose that circumstance to commend their friend by wherein he most faulted, and to justify mine own candor, for I loved the man and do honor his memory (on this side idolatry) as much as any. He was, indeed, honest, and of an open and free nature; had an excellent fancy, brave notions, and gentle expressions, wherein he flowed with that facility that sometime it was necessary he should be stopped: *Sufflaminandus erat* ['He had to be checked'], as Augustus said of Haterius. His wit was in his own power; would the rule of it been so too. But he redeemed his vices with his virtures: there was ever more in him to be praised than to be pardoned.[32]

Although Jonson was critical of Shakespeare's facility, he, nevertheless, in his Eulogy to the Folio, granted that Shakespeare's poetic lines were well turned. In his sonnet prefacing the Second Folio in 1632, John Milton refers to Shakespeare warbling his native woodnotes wild and proclaims that "Thy easy numbers flow." This does not do sufficient justice to Shakespeare's education, reading, contacts, influences, poetry, and plays, which show him to be as learned as Jonson was forced to acknowledge in his Eulogy:

For if I thought my judgment were of years [*mature*],
I should commit thee surely with thy peers,
And tell how far thou didst our Lyly outshine,
Or sporting Kyd, or Marlowe's mighty line.
And though thou hadst small Latin and less Greek,
From thence to honor thee I would not seek
For names, but call forth thund'ring Aeschylus,
Euripides, and Sophocles to us,
Pacuvius, Accius, him of Cordova [*Seneca*], dead
To life again, to hear thy buskin tread [*high tragedy*]
And shake a stage: or, when thy socks [*Comedies*] were on,
Leave thee alone for the comparison
Of all that insolent Greece or haughty Rome
Sent forth, or since did from their ashes come.[33]

Shakespeare's contemporaries as a whole were at a loss about whether to ascribe to Shakespeare a natural or a learned wit, and the dilemma resided in a single mind, that of Jonson's. Shakespeare he said could, or could not, rule his natural wit, he flowed with such ease that "Nature herself was proud of his designs" (the untutored genius); but he found he must not give nature all and in gentle Shakespeare his art must enjoy a portion of the endeavor.

There is, however, a harmony in this misleading dichotomy of a natural poet and a learned intellect. This has been obscured by not relating the life of Shakespeare closer to his artistic products, and vice versa. One of the aspects of Shakespeare that separated him from the other Elizabethan playwrights and increased his universality was his maintenance of both his natural qualities and his artistic talent. To these can be added his technically astute intellect. These attributes are reflected symbolically in his two loci, London and Stratford to which now a third place can be added. Perhaps Westminster can be viewed as a link between his city and craft life and town and family life through the legalistic side of his personal experiences and writing material.

His legal knowledge and associations formed a bridge from the everyday to the civilized levels of learning obtainable at the Inns of Court. The data show a man who could write pastoral comedies and courtly tragedies, combining the inner world of man's thought with nature in *Lear*, *Macbeth*, *Hamlet* and *Richard II* while doing so with the intellectual and political in the green world of *As You Like It*, *Love's Labour's Lost*, *A Midsummer Night's Dream*, and the *Tempest*. His litigations show that the plays had not only intellectual and political, but also legal points to make; and they also indicate a firm connection to his family; his parents, John and Mary; his siblings, Joan, Edmund, Gilbert, and Richard; his wife, Anne; his children, Susanna, Judith and Hamnet, and their posterity, Elizabeth Hall and his three nephews, William, Thomas and Michael Hart. These connections are amplified by the plays, and underscore the plays' concerns about family and inheritance, whether it is that of a Lear, a Macbeth, or a Hamlet in the tragedies; or of an Antipholus or an Orlando in the comedies; or a Henry IV or a Richard II in the histories; or a Prospero or Leontes in the romances. The result of these insights into the man behind the dramas and the mind behind the man reveals not a split personality, nor a figure who on the one hand would only '. . . hear poor rogues/Talk of court news; . . ." (*Lear* V. iii. 13–14) nor, on the other, one only concerned with country matters. Shakespeare saw these as a continuum of human relationships, best exemplified by the spectrum in *A Midsummer Night's Dream* from Theseus, Duke of Athens, to Bottom, guided by personal psyches not irretrievably institutionalized.

This was not an attitude simply handled by such labels as "conservativism," whether medieval, feudal or archaic in its origins, because (as has been seen) it stems from his thorough study of certain areas of his contemporary thought, particularly in law and specifically represented by his researches into the current legal concept of, and controversy over, equity. It is with this legal and philosophical idea that, by being the focus of this book, brings into critical cognition, beyond any equivocation, Shakespeare's ability as a person, a poet, a thinker, a dramatist, a family man, a businessman, an actor at the Globe, at the Inns of Court, or before the Crown to be undifferentiated in at least one area of his vital concern.

He was a champion for equity as a general concept, and in the technical form associated with Chancery. This analysis produces less difficulty in reconciling the works to the man and the life to his thought. There have been those who found it difficult and this led them to the Bacon heresy. The solution was to postulate a brilliant mind and a legally trained author of his plays, but not William Shakespeare. Those holding that belief are ". . . unable to reconcile the plays, those most wondrous achievements of human intellect, with the Shakespeare who bought and sold land and theatrical shares and drew up a last will and testament 'as plain and prosaic as if it had been the production of a pig-headed prerogative lawyer.' "[34]

Samuel Taylor Coleridge had the same problem as Ben Jonson about Shakespeare's being a master craftsman and also a poet of natural gift. At one point Coleridge saw that the dramatist, ". . . no mere child of nature, no *automaton* of genius, no passive vehicle of inspiration, possessed by the spirit, not possessing it, first studied patiently, meditated deeply, understood minutely, till knowledge, become habitual and intuitive, wedding itself to his habitual feelings, and at length gave birth to that stupendous power, by which he stands alone, . . ." and yet at another point Coleridge declares ". . . he was that child of Nature, and not the creature of his own efforts."[35] These distinctions are for the most part not significant to the modern consciousness but that is because it has inherited the resolution of them from John Keats' penetrating observation, which in turn has done its own type of damage.

> Shakespeare pos[s]essed so enormously—I mean *Negative Capability*, that is when man is capable of being in uncertainties, Mysteries, doubts, without any irritable reaching after fact & reason.[36]

This is a perception of Shakespeare which continues the popular notion that we know very little about the man. The damage from this can be considerable, particularly in terms of its effect upon contrasting the philosophic mind Coleridge attributed to him, and Shakespeare's intellect and thought as these related to his ordinary day-by-day life. These phrases, when misapplied, give the false security, license of interpretation, relative freedom from knowledge, and pleasure in pure subjective response and self-projection inherent in the assumption that there is no possibility of discerning Shakespeare's personal attitude, position, opinion, philosophic stance, or particular cause he championed from his works: Above all, that there is little possible gain in attempting to harmonize the works with the seemingly uninteresting and irrelevant information pertaining to the person of the poet-dramatist-philosopher; and so the works and the life are unnecessarily kept apart or one unfortunately totally ignored for the other.

This study has looked at the documents of a man who experienced progressive layers of legal experience, insight and responsibility. Out of necessity at first he picked up this background since he had to acquire a trade, perhaps that of a lawyer's clerk, to meet the family obligations. These responsibilities were economic and were extended later, as evidenced by the legal transactions, in his acquisition of property, capital and equity of a financial kind which his father had failed to hold on to. It is easy to recognize this as an aspect of Shakespeare's shrewdness in being able to provide for himself, so that he could pursue the dictates of his craft somewhat independently from the system of patronage and the immediate fluctuations of the theatrical market. But on a more complex level this should be seen as part of a single thread of consciousness concerned about the justice and equity of the law in his art, business, family, personal life and in the depths of his soul. Formerly, scholars and biographers willingly accepted his accomplishments as paradoxically those of an untutored genius, the widely read but unschooled poet, warbling his native woodnotes wild, and a good businessman to boot.

But researches into the Stratford School; Frank Kermode's "On Shakespeare's Learning";[37] Howard B. White's views of the dramatist as a philosopher (*Copp'd Hills Towards Heaven: Shakespeare and the Classical Polity*. The Hague, 1970); and J.A.K. Thompson's *Shakespeare and the Classics* demonstrate that as Kermode has so aptly put it, we finally have ". . . a plausible representation of a great poet: a man of great intellectual force, who employs it in his poetry." (p. 22). To this may now be added an intense interest in learning, a desire to act upon it, to use it, to teach it, to anatomize it and ultimately to present it in dramatic and dialectical situations. Furthermore, he used this learning in his daily life to effect legal and social change.

I disagree completely with Tucker Brooke who says, ". . . Shakespeare's wisdom was not of the kind which colleges supply. We need no biographical evidence to assure us that the author of the plays was not indebted to the universities; and the academic attitude on the part of his critics has often proved the least profitable of all."[38] On the contrary, in addition to all the other personal ties and artistic responsibilities, I believe there was another discrete area of schooling for him of reading, study, learning and talk, that of England's "Third University," the Inns of Court, where he acquired interests possibly originating in a trade but culminating in a crucial avocation.

It has been thought that the legal terminology in Shakespeare indicates only the personal knowledge needed, and superficially obtained, to protect and acquire property, or that arose from a commercial need to have his plays popular for a specialized audience. This is to an extent true, but it is certainly not the complete motivation. There is substantial evidence of Shakespeare having developed a program of explicating, renovating, and defending, to meet the needs of all levels of society, the system of English law with its common law courts and competing courts of equity, offering provision for appeals to higher courts which allowed for and maximized evenhanded justice. He explained this in his plays, argued for its preservation before his audience, and exercised its rights in his personal life. This program did not come overnight, nor was it won or maintained easily, as can be witnessed by his own unsuccessful case, the ignorance concerning the specialized and complex system by the uninitiated, the abuse by person and of procedures from within, and the threats of manipulation from without. In the area of equity, Shakespeare does not abide our question. Shakespeare's artistic, social, political, economic and legal activity had to have an impact upon the Crown. The King, the prerogative courts and jurists were increasingly persuaded at this time, and Shakespeare played a part in that persuasion, that common law fulfilled its responsibility (in general, and particularly in the overcoming of the lack of any grace period for loans, or equity of redemption on mortgages) to achieve absolute justice and fairness through the presence of the King's Conscience in Chancery, a court of equity acting as the "Gate of Mercy" as Shakespeare had said in Act IV of *The Merchant of Venice*:

> That, in the course of justice, none of us
> Should see salvation . . .
> But mercy is above this sceptred sway;
> It is enthroned in the hearts of kings,
> It is an attribute to God himself;
> And earthly power doth then show likest God's
> When mercy seasons justice.

This very involvement in equity Shakespeare inherited from his father. One of John's civic duties, as Affeeror in 1559 was to assess "amercements." Amercements were payments invoked and controlled by the mercy of the court. These were local court penalties which were nonstatute fines, thus discretionary and calling for the direct application of judicial equity on the part of John Shakespeare. His son in one of his late plays has the Fool prophesy the impossible as ". . . When every case in law is right; . . ." (*Lear* III. ii. 86). Shakespeare had attempted to obtain justice for years in lower courts and sought equity, and an opportunity to expand equitable rulings, on mortgages in Chancery. From early to late, Shakespeare had been surrounded by operations striving to bring the abstractions of true justice, right and fairness into reality through the judicial principles of equity.

A major legal event in the year of Shakespeare's death (1616) proved in legal history to make the dramatist a juristic prophet. It indicated he was a man quite ahead of his time, a visionary about political realities in his understanding of English jurisprudence. The Chief Justice of the United States Supreme Court Harlan F. Stone said, "Often, in listening to *The Merchant of Venice*, it has occurred to me that Shakespeare knew the essentials of the contemporary conflict between law and equity."[39] Very likely *Merchant of Venice* at the Swan and *Shakespeare* v. *Lambert* in Chancery had their effects upon William Lambarde; and *Merchant of Venice* at Court and *Comedy of Errors* at Gray's Inn affected Ellesmere, to be Lord Chancellor of the Court of Chancery. In addition, *Merchant of Venice*, if not influencing or encouraging, at least correctly anticipated what was to happen in a case just before Shakespeare died. The analogous elements from the play will be aligned with the case so that the similarities will become more readily apparent. The Houston lawyer, Mark Edwin Andrews, presents the pertinent description:

> In 1615 [*actually March to July of* 1616], a somewhat similar case (*Glanvill* v. *Courtney*) [*Shylock* v. *Antonio*

> *like Shakespeare* v. *Lambert in the same year as the play in* 1597] arose on a bond. Lord Chief Justice Coke [*the Duke of Venice of the play*] entered a judgment for the plaintiff. Lord Ellesmere, the Lord Chancellor [*Portia of the piece*] issued an injunction [*not for any error in judgment but for the 'hard conscience of the party' as was so in the character of Shylock*] by a decree, thus preventing the enforcement of the judgment on the bond. King James I [*who had seen the play twice in the same week at Court*] appointed Sir Francis Bacon to head a commission to advise the King, once and for all time to come, as to whether or not the Chancellor had the power to enjoin the enforcement of a common law judgment. Bacon [*who had participated in the revels of which Comedy of Errors had been a part in Gray's Inn*] advised the King that the Chancellor had this power.[40]

In the year of his death, Shakespeare was vindicated in his accurate prediction of the victory of equity over common law in his *Merchant of Venice*. The decision appeared too late for him to know of it. Thus, the legal event exists as a memorial to Shakespeare's juristic imagination.

All three cases, *Shakespeare* v. *Lambert*, *Shylock* v. *Antonio* and *Glanvill* v. *Courtney* move from the procedures of the Court of King's (Queen's) Bench to those of the Court of Chancery. What did not happen in Shakespeare's own case; what was confirmed by *Glanvill* v. *Courtney* in the year of Shakespeare's death in 1616, and given considerable significance in Cary's *Reports* was: ". . . if there was an irreconcilable difference of opinion between the Lord Chancellor [i.e. Chancery and prerogative principles of evolving equitable interpretation and jurisdiction] and the Lord Chief Justice[i.e., judge of the common law tending to a rigid adherence to established precedent] the decree of the Court of Equity should prevail over a judgment at law."[41] Andrews says later as the result of his researches into the analogies between Shakespeare's play and Chancery cases that, "If I were asked to name the three men in all England who were most profoundly affected by Shakespeare's *The Merchant of*

Venice, I should unhesitatingly name the following [which is done without direct evidence]: Sir Edward Coke, Sir Thomas Egerton, later to become Lord Ellesmere, and Sir Francis Bacon" (p. 21). To which this study can now add the four Masters of Chancery and two of the six Clerks of Chancery: William Lambarde, George Carew, John Hunt, Thomas Powle, Stephen Powle and Edward Huberd, and also Lambert's attorney Nicholas Overbury, the father of Sir Thomas, and, of course, King James, himself.

This list of those in law influenced by Shakespeare in his lifetime would thus include those in the top nine judicial offices of the realm from the Crown to the Clerks. This struggle between common-law judges and Chancery had gone on from 1300 to 1616 (*cf.* Andrews, pp. 34–41). Shakespeare had appropriately used medieval and religious dramatic devices such as the mercy-figures and Biblical allusions which gave his presentation something of an archaic or conservative fashion but these were part of the heritage of the controversy.[42] He was not ignorant of *Realpolitik* and had the ability to influence the bringing about of the humane use of law against the bureaucratic fixity of the common law courts and tyrannical use of law by the king in the prerogative courts.

Andrews expertly explains how the Chancellor had argued in a similar situation relating to authority:

> Ellesmere, having in mind the flexibility of equity and the elasticity of its writs, is reported to have said in behalf of the King's prerogative, before the council where all the judges had been summoned to decide the matter: '. . . that every precedent must have a first commencement, and that he would advise the Judges to maintain the power and prerogative of the King; and in cases in which there is no authority and precedent, to leave it to the King to order it according to his wisdom and the good of his subjects, for otherwise the King *would be no more than the Duke of Venice.*'[43]
>
> . . . the King would have no power to enforce his proclamation; and, in the opinion of Lord Ellesmere, the King

> would have no more power to enforce his own proclamations than the Duke of Venice, in the trial scene, would have to uphold his own judgment in favor of Shylocke. *(p. 41)*

Furthermore, like the Duke without the benefit of Portia, King James, if he does not have the prerogative of proclamation cannot have Chancery exercising judiciously the equity of interpretation of statute, justifying it with the common law, and having it affect his people equitably. This would allow for just changes in the law through studied application of the statute through the prerogative courts presided over by the Chancellor as in Chancery, Star Chamber, Exchequer and others.

No more fitting an epitaph for Shakespeare can be found with regard to the preoccupation of his mind and work that this study has traced than Sir Francis Bacon's and Henry Yelverton's summation of the Commission's findings in the case of *Glanvill* v. *Courtney* in which the Crown sided with Chancery over common law (King's Bench), on July 18, 1616 three months after Shakespeare signed his last will.

> *Now, forasmuch as mercy and justice be the true supports of our Royal Throne, and that it properly belongeth to us, in our princely office, to take care and provide, that our subjects have equal and indifferent justice ministered to them: and that where their case deserveth to be relieved in course of equity, by suit in our Court of Chancery, they should not be abandoned, and exposed to perish under the rigour and extremity of our laws:*—We . . . do will and command, that our Chancellor, or Keeper of the Great Seal, for the time being, shall not hereafter desist unto our subjects upon their several complains (now or hereafter to be made) such relief in equity (not withstanding any former proceedings at common law against them) as shall stand with true merits and justice of their cases, *and with the former ancient and continued practice and proceeding of our Chancery*; and for that *it appertaineth to our princely care and office only to judge over all our Judges*, and to discern and determine such differences as at any time may or

> shall arise before our several Courts, touching the jurisdiction and the same to settle and decide as we in our princely wisdom shall find to stand most with our honour, and the example of our Royal Progenitors, in the best times, and the general weal and good of our people, for which we are to answer unto God, who hath placed us over them: . . . (*p.* 40)

This was signed for King James by Bacon (*Per Ipsum Regum* [sic] Francis Bacon). Bacon knew that what had from Shakespeare reached his and the Chancellor's ears in at least *Comedy of Errors* would be welcomed for concept and turn of phrase by the ear of the King who had asked to have repeated from Shakespeare "And earthly power doth then show likest God's/ When mercy seasons justice."

Furthermore, what has not been noted is that the delicate blend of *Measure for Measure* is represented in the fact that the commission insists that on the one hand all the judges are subject to the top of judgment (in this case the King's), and on the other that all justice in any case will be meted out according to former practice and precedents of Chancery. This reflects the legal instruction Shakespeare had incorporated in the entertainment where the Duke oversees and overrides Angelo, thereby judging his judges, but with the advice of Isabella, the mercy-figure signifying the advice and opinion of the Chancellor according to the equitable procedures of Chancery.

Therefore, Shakespeare was not merely a passive recipient or reflector of his times. He actively, in at least the one area of equity, and vigorously pursued a program for effecting change in, and reform and the preservation of, English jurisprudence with its strange but equitable bifurcation as represented in the existence of Chancery alongside King's (or Queen's) Bench. Shakespeare participated in effecting English Equity in five crucial ways. 1] His performances of *Comedy of Errors*, *Love's Labour's Lost* and *A Midsummer-Night's Dream* before members of the Inns of Court served to emphasize the humane and equitable applications of the law often overriding the letter of the law. 2] His own case in Chancery, of *Shakespeare* v. *Lambert*, certainly contributed to the kind of cases reaching the Mastership level of Chancery that brought about equity of redemption evidenced by the writings concerning these matters by the Masters of Chancery, William Lambarde and George Carew. 3] His *Merchant of Venice* was a part of the struggle between Ellesmere (Chancery) and Coke (common law) and helped keep the equity of a statute viable as a right for Chancery, as the King's Conscience to interpret his prerogative. This also permitted the King to retain that prerogative source of law over common law, and Chancery its role of reconciling the King to the common law, or otherwise, as Ellesmere said, not having benefit of interpretation, thereby lacking supporting enforcement from the lower courts. 4] His two performances of *The Merchant of Venice* before the King anticipated Bacon's Commission for the King which declared in *Glanvill* v. *Courtney* that Equity (Chancery) must maintain its supremacy over the common law to protect the citizen against the rigorous, and sometimes unjust strict application, or misapplication, of the law, hence offering mercy as well as justice. 5] His productions of *Measure for Measure* and *Winter's Tale* designed for the instruction of the new King warned James of the consequences of his tyrannical use of English law.

Unquestionably, Shakespeare had a permanent impact upon English legal history, at a point where its influence carried over into the American system of appellate courts, which was shortly to come, constructed by lawyers who had been members of the Inns. It may appear to as diverse critics as Tucker Brooke, Herndl, Schoenbaum, and Norman Holland that Shakespeare was conservative;[44] one who never pursued an idea in a scholarly manner;[45] longed for the good old Elizabethan, or early Tudor, if not medieval times; or that he was a mere businessman, entrepreneur and acquirer of possessions.[46] But the new evidence suggests that, in this area of equity involving for Shakespeare a long, deliberate and energetic personal pursuit, he was not a political or historical conservative,[47] and as borne out by his endeavors' accomplishments, with the performance of the plays before jurists, and his effect upon legal history, that Shakespeare was on the contrary a liberal by anticipating and influencing changes in English laws pertaining to Equity by an understanding of its traditions.

As has been seen, much is known about Shakespeare, and if ordered thematically from the legal documents, the plays and his life, much more significant information can be discerned. These considerations must affect the predominant attitude among critics and biographers about the nature of his mind, the scope of his intellect, the depth of his interests, and the relevance of his active concern. His social and political involvement had impact. Shakespeare's profound legal background provides insight into how he came about doing his plays, how he probably wrote them and with what previously unnoted purposes and designs. In addition to the living monument of his plays, Shakespeare also influenced what was bequeathed in legal history to following generations. He played his part to help major contributions of equity to the Anglo-American legal heritage: equity of redemption, which is enjoyed as grace periods for mortgages and loans (*Shakespeare* v. *Lambert*); equity of a statute, which is one of the chief interpretive functions of the Supreme Court (Lord Ellesmere); and the supremacy of equity over common law, which is enjoyed in the notion of an appellate court system and rights of appeal (Bacon). Through his plays, Shakespeare not only made the intricacy of law available to one level of his audience, but, by his productions and legal actions, infused the law itself with the humaneness which has long been associated with gentle Will, Sweet William, in his thought, life and his works.

* * * *

As a result of the foregoing study, perhaps scholar-detectives will uncover more about Shakespeare through researching his associations with the City of Westminster.

Tax records, or other data in the Public Records Office, may be surveyed to find further substantiation for Shakespeare's presence in the Westminster area sometime be-between 1588 and 1594. Further study of Shakespeare's new signature, in all probability being his earliest, of his calligraphy, and of extant documents in legal hand, or copyist's script, might identify more manuscripts in Shakespeare's hand. A study of law books available to Shakespeare as sources for the plays, and of particular copies containing supposed forged signatures may reveal the dramatist's even greater reading in the law. Tracing down and examining volumes from William Lambarde's personal library could uncover marginalia in Shakespeare's hand, or at least provide books now likely to have been available for Shakespeare to read. Legists may come to discern more references to law in, and therefore seek more sources or influences for, Shakespeare's works. Furthermore, they might find a higher level of legal theory, more advanced political knowledge and a greater complexity of juristic thought in these dramatic endeavors than has been hitherto anticipated, except by Baconists. Critics may find that the "problem comedies" (i.e. *Merchant of Venice* and *Measure for Measure*) are less problematic and more coherent when their various designs are conceived upon specific and ornate legal issues. Biographers will, hopefully, find that many partial, or thematic, analyses, and more complete biographical studies in Shakespeare can still be undertaken. This as a result of not only realizing there is much known about him, but that new materials can still be uncovered and put together. New approaches and methodologies can be applied to render his life more completely in itself, and more fully available to the specialist and non-specialist reader.

It now can be decisively concluded that Shakespeare's seventh known signature found in Lambarde's *Archaionomia* of the Folger Shakespeare Library must be a part of any future study of Shakespeare's life, and any consideration of the extent of his legal background. Furthermore, in experiencing the process by which the signature's presence becomes a significant artifact from Shakespeare's life, we can also discover how a new cross-disciplinary, thematic approach to Shakespeare's works and biography unfolds a greater harmony between the two. Looking at law and equity in his daily life and his plays, uncovers a man more believable as a person and more vitally involved, through his works, in the issues of his day. We can explode the two insidious myths of his being, on the one hand, a poet in an ivory tower turning out fine works as caviar to the general, or, on the other, simply being a good dramatist only in order to earn a living; notions contaminating those approaches to Shakespeare showing him both a calculated artist and a socially conscious thinker. The elements were so mixed in him he could perceive intellectual problems with fullness and clarity, rendering them of interest, pleasure and purpose to a wide audience. This is discerned by following one of many threads through his rich life and art. Shakespeare learned much about, and at the law. It is instructive to observe him moving in his everyday experiences and his philosophical thought from the male, justice figures who preserve order (but can also threaten the law's end of achieving justice) to include the female, mercy figures who represent overriding equity and absolute justice as theoretically found in Elizabethan Chancery. This blend of law and equity, justice and mercy was just one of the crucial elements in the human experience that William Shakespeare found in his life, cherished, and wrote down as his particular legacy to us and our heirs forever.

Acknowledgments

THIS BIOGRAPHICAL STUDY was chiefly sustained by Wesleyan University's generous support through research grants and a sabbatical (1969–1970) to the Warburg Institute, University of London, with the pleasant presence of Dr. Joseph Trapp, where my interest in the interconnections between legal and literary history developed. As a Ford Foundation Fellow (1971) and a Fellow of the Center for the Humanities (1972) at Wesleyan, I was able to continue this interest in courses, research and writing. I am most grateful to Victor Gourevitch, the Director of the Center, for providing the scholarly auspices under which the following study was brought into a first draft and the material was first offered in a Center talk.

I want to express my particular gratitude to the staff at the Folger Shakespeare Library, Washington, D.C., for their assistance in my research on the Shakespeare signature in the Library's possession; O. B. Hardison, James G. McManaway, Giles E. Dawson, Richard J. Schoeck, Laetitia Skipton-Kennedy Yeandle, Lydia Bronte, and Kirsten Mishkin. Louis Marder has been an invaluable source of information in connection with Shakespeare, his signatures and Elizabethan law, as has Roderick L. Eagle on the provenance of the Lambarde book in which the signature in the Folger appears. Students at Wesleyan who were helpful in my research were Michael Busman, particularly on maps and court cases, and Jeffrey Aker on Stratford. For reading the manuscript and making valuable additions I am deeply indebted to Joseph G. Harrison, Seth Davis and Katy Butler; also to William B. Coley and Richard M. Ohmann for making helpful editorial suggestions, and to Tania Senff for typing the manuscript and Alain Munkittrick for helping with the photographic sections.

I wish to recognize teachers, scholars and writers of Shakespeare and his period who have continued to inspire my interest in the dramatist and his social setting: C. L. Barber, Roy W. Battenhouse, William Wiatt, Charles Forker, Stephen Orgel, Theodore Baird, Gilbert Hunt, Norman Rabkin, Jonas A. Barish, Norman N. Holland, David Bevington, Philip J. Finkelpearl, Richard Leighton Greene, Catherine Drinker Bowen, Wilbur Dunkel, Marchette Chute, A. L. Rowse, Leslie Hotson, and Anthony Burgess. Those in the field of history who have provided aid concerning English law and encouragement from their discipline have been: Eugene Golob, Willard M. Wallace, Jeffrey Butler, Philip Pomper, Richard Buel, Gerald Strauss, Arthur Hogue, Leo Solt and Walter Sedelow. I have learned much about psychoanalytic approaches to literary text from enjoyable work and teaching with David G. Winter.

Above all I take pleasure in extending my affectionate thanks to Thomas Lipscomb for initiating the project; to J. Hillis Miller, Richard Slotkin, Tony Connor, Franklin Reeve and William Manchester for sustaining the endeavor with their enthusiasm and colleagueship; and to my wife and children for enduring with good humor my preoccupation with the delightful enterprise.

I wish to acknowledge the following for permission to reproduce published material: The Clarendon Press, Oxford, England for passages from E. K. Chambers' *William Shakespeare: A Study of Facts and Problems;* from Clarendon Press and Samuel Schoenbaum, the author of *Shapespeare's Lives*, and W. J. Jones, the author of *The Elizabethan Court of Chancery*; to Gerald Duckworth & Co. Ltd., London, and F. E. Halliday, the author of *The Life of Shakespeare;* Alfred A. Knopf, Publishers, New York, and Anthony Burgess, the author of *Shakespeare;* Columbia University Press, New York and Giles E. Dawson, the author of "Authenticity and Attribution of Written Matter" in *English Institute Annual,* 1942; John Rylands Memorial Library, Manchester, England; Folger Shakespeare Library, Washington, D.C.; Rutgers University Press, New Brunswick, New Jersey, and Wilbur Dunkel, the author of *William Lambarde;* Scott, Foresman and Company, Chicago, Illinois; Controller of Her Majesty's Stationery Office; and the University of Colorado Press, Boulder, and Mark Edwin Andrews, author of *Law versus Equity in "The Merchant of Venice."*

Also I want to thank the following for their kind and gracious permission to reproduce photographic material: The National Portrait Gallery, London; the Trustees, Shakespeare Birthplace Trust, Stratford-upon-Avon; the British Tourist Authority; the Trustees, British Museum, London; the Folger Shakespeare Library, Washington, D.C.; the Trustees, Sterling Library, Yale University; the Trustees of the London Museum; the Controller of Her Majesty's Stationery Office; the Trustees of the Guildhall Library, City of London; the Trustees of the Henry E. Huntington Library and Art Gallery, San Marino, California; the Trustees of the Royal Shakespeare Theatre; the Syndics of the Fitzwilliam Museum, Cambridge, England; the Trustees, Victoria and Albert Museum, London; the Marquess of Lothian; the National Monuments Record, London; the Vicar and Churchwardens, Holy Trinity Church, Stratford-upon-Avon; and the Lord of Verulam.

W. Nicholas Knight
MIDDLETOWN, CONNECTICUT

March 15, 1973

Notes

Chapter I

1. Charles Severn, *Diary of John Ward* (1839), p. 183.
2. As in E. K. Chambers. *William Shakespeare.* Oxford; 1930. II, p. 245.
3. *Ibid.*, pp. 252–253. See Chambers (I, 17) for possible explanation of the passage.
4. A colleague at Wesleyan University, Prof. Richard L. Greene, suggested in a departmental presentation that this ballad may be like those accompanying rituals mocking prominent townsfolk who remarry early, by placing deer's horns on the doorway, mumming, holding a mock trial, and affixing a ballad to the door. Shakespeare may have been involved with some such prank, which caused him embarrassment, possibly ostracism, and which gave rise to the deer-poaching tale.
5. Chambers, *op. cit.*, pp. 253–254.
6. *Ibid.*, pp. 264–265.
7. For the most detailed explosion of the highly favored story of Shakespeare's being whipped by the local justice as a deer poacher, see S. Schoenbaum. *Shakespeare's Lives.* Oxford; 1970, pp. 108–114.
8. William Hazlitt. *Lectures on the English Poets.* London; 1818, pp. 92–93.
9. *The Complete Works of Shakespeare*, ed. Hardin Craig. Chicago; 1951, p. 74. This is the text for the citations from Shakespeare's works.
10. F. E. Halliday. *The Life of Shakespeare.* London; 1961, p. 49.
11. Anthony Burgess. *Shakespeare.* New York; 1970, p. 69.
12. George and Bernard Winchcombe. *Shakespeare's Ghost Writers.* Esher, Surrey; 1968, p. 19.
13. *Cassell's Illustrated Shakespeare*, eds. Dr. F. J. Furnivall and Mr. John Munro. London, 1913, p. xiii.
14. Sir Edward Maunde Thompson. "Handwriting," *Shakespeare's England.* Oxford; 1916, I, 303.

Chapter II

1. A. L. Rowse. *William Shakespeare.* New York; 1964, p. 35.
2. Marchette Chute. *Shakespeare of London.* New York; 1949, p. 46.
3. Cf. F. E. Halliday. *The Life of Shakespeare.* London; 1961, p. 35.
4. S. Schoenbaum. *Shakespeare's Lives.* Oxford; 1970, p. 16.
5. Halliday, *op. cit.*, p. 45.
6. *Ibid.*, p. 46.
7. Roland Mushat Frye. *Shakespeare's Life and Times.* Princeton; 1967, Section 9.
8. James G. McManaway. *The Authorship of Shakespeare.* Folger Booklet on Tudor and Stuart Civilization, 1962, p. 12.
9. Cf. James Orchard Halliwell Phillipps. *The Life of William Shakespeare.* London; 1848, p. 18, where he concludes from the Stratford records that ". . . John Shakespeare could not write his own name!"
10. "Handwriting," *Shakespeare's England.* London; 1916, I, 303.
11. One scholar detects evidence of Shakespeare's law hand in documents coming from Stratford during this period: 1579 Snitterfield conveyance of Shakespeares to Webb, an engrossed indenture in current Secretary. (E. B. Everitt, *The Young Shakespeare: Studies in Documentary Evidence.* Copenhagen; 1954, p. 187.)
12. Jonson's *Every Man in his Humour* IV. iv. [one line] and *Merchant of Venice* V. i. 157–182.
13. *Shakespeare in the Public Records.* ed. N. E. Evans. London, 1964, p. 5.
14. James Orchard Halliwell-Phillipps. *Outlines of the Life of Shakespeare.* London; 1887, II, 235.
15. Rowse, *op. cit.*, pp. 58–59.
16. Anthony Burgess. *Shakespeare.* New York; 1970, p. 22.
17. Information taken from a Bill of Complaint in Latin brought by John and Mary Shakespeare against John Lambert in the Court of Queen's Bench, 1588–1589, respecting an estate at Wilmecote near Stratford-upon-Avon. From the Coram Rege Rolls, Term. Mich. 31–32 Eliz. [Q.B. 27/1311, rot. 516.] Reprinted by Halliwell-Phillipps. *op. cit.* Outlines, II, 11–13. The extremely complex matter of the Arden properties and Mary's inheritance is handled by E. K. Chambers. *William Shakespeare.* Oxford; 1930, II, 35–41 where he also reprints the Bill of Complaint.
18. Halliwell-Phillipps, *op. cit.*, p. 11. This is not, as the conclusion is also not, given in E. K. Chambers, *op. cit.*, p. 35 and hence Chambers here and elsewhere deletes the various attorneys hired by the Shakespeares and the Lamberts.
19. Partial text and translation of Bill by Tucker Brooke. *Shakespeare of Stratford.* New Haven; 1926, p. 9. Neither Tucker Brooke nor

E. K. Chambers reproduce all the testimony in the court cases. For the entire transcripts one must return to Halliwell-Phillipps.

20. Halliwell-Phillipps, *op. cit.*, p. 243.
21. E. K. Chambers, *op. cit.*, p. 117 and Halliwell-Phillipps, *op. cit.*, p. 238.
22. Everitt, *op. cit.*, pp. 47–187.
23. Schoenbaum, *op. cit.*, p. 55.
24. Arthur Freeman. *Thomas Kyd: Facts and Problems.* Oxford; 1967, p. 19.
25. Wilbur Dunkel. *William Lambarde: Elizabethan Jurist* 1536–1601. Rutgers; 1965, pp. 119–123.
26. G.P.V. Akrigg. *Shakespeare and the Earl of Southampton.* London; 1968, p. 193.
27. Hardin Craig (editor of *The Complete Works of Shakespeare,* Chicago; 1951, p. 476n) says the metaphor is that of a court of law (cf. *Othello,* III. iii. 138–141), but that "Unlike many of the sonnets this one does not sustain the figure." On the contrary, the entire sonnet can be taken as depicting a debtor accounting a tale of woe as excuse for his losses to the judges and repaying as he did once in the past through his fears, but at the last moment his double losses and renewed sorrows are obliterated for him by the memory of his friend.
28. G. B. Harrison. *Shakespeare under Elizabeth.* (New York; 1933), p. 310; *Elizabethan Journal* 1591–1594 New York; 1929, p. 361; Leslie Hotson. *Mr. W. H.* New York; 1964, p. 244.
29. Akrigg, *op. cit.*, p. 31.
30. Edward J. White. *Commentaries on the Law in Shakespeare.* St. Louis; 1913, pp. 87–110.
31. Everitt, *op. cit.*, pp. 47–48, 102–103.
32. Chambers, *op. cit.* I, 319.
33. Cf. W. Nicholas Knight. "Julius Caesar and Shakespearean Revenge," *The Erasmus Review.* September 1971, pp. 19–34.
34. Chambers, *op. cit.*, p. 312.
35. Everitt inexplicably, as many earlier scholars, such as Malone, places *Pericles* at this time. The only sense in doing so is that it explicitly has the incestuous content of *Hamlet.*
36. Mark Eccles. *Shakespeare in Warwickshire.* Madison; 1961, p. 102.
37. The complex legal background of Shakespeare's *King John* and *Henry VI* plays is discussed by George W. Keeton. *Shakespeare's Legal and Political Background.* New York; 1967, pp. 118–131, 165–184.
38. Chambers, *op. cit.*, II, 319.
39. *A New Variorum Edition of Shakespeare*: *Hamlet,* ed. Horace Howard Furness. New York, 1963, II, 8–9.
40. As quoted in Everitt, *op. cit.*, pp. 30–32.

41. *Ibid.*, p. 27.
42. Possibly a reference to Don Andrea's famous prologue in *The Spanish Tragedy*, I. i; G. R. Hibbard believes the entire passage could apply to Kyd as well as to Shakespeare (*Thomas Nashe.* Cambridge, (Mass.): 1962, p. 35). This could be so, but Thomas Kyd more than likely resided with the scriveners as his father did in the City of London, and the passage goes on to describe the noverints as coming from outside the City.
43. *Cf.* Everitt, *op. cit.*, p. 29 where he says, ". . . take their way from their residence in the suburbs (since they have been noverint-writers, perhaps Westminster area?). . . ." The Westminster address for Shakespeare in the Folger copy of Lambarde's *Archaionomia* is now a crucial supporting factor for Shakespeare as one of these noverint-writers who wrote the early *Hamlet.*
44. London, 1589, sig. $3^{r\text{-}v}$ as quoted in Arthur Freeman. *Thomas Kyd.* Oxford; 1967, pp. 39–40.
45. Shakespeare's reply may be read in *Henry VI, Part Two*, I. i. 53–259 and most particularly II. 220–229.
46. As quoted in Brooke, *op. cit.*, p. 10.
47. H[enry] C[hettle], *Kind-Harts Dreame* (London, n.d.), sigs. $A_3{}^v$–4;

Chapter III

1. James G. McManaway. *The Authorship of Shakespeare.* Charlottesville: 1962, pp. 30–38. The signature and his neutral attitude toward it may be dimly adumbrated in "There are several books in which Shakespeare's name is written. Some of the signatures may be genuine, but others are obvious forgeries." p. 30.
2. Cited by Louis Marder in a review of Keeton's book in *Renaissance Quarterly*, Vol. XXII, No. 2, Summer, 1969, p. 191.
3. *William Shakespeare, Plays and Poems*, ed. E. Malone (London; 1790), I, i, 104.
4. *Cf.* Horace Howard Furness's *Hamlet.* New York; 1877, II, 5–11; C. A. Brown, *Shakespeare's Autobiographical Poems.* London; 1838, p. 254; and Edward J. White. *Commentaries on the Law in Shakespeare.* St. Louis, 1913, pp. XXXIX-XL.
5. Arthur Freeman. *Thomas Kyd.* Oxford; 1967, pp. 39–48; R. B. McKerrow in his edition of the works of Thomas Nashe; and G. T. Hibbard. *Thomas Nashe.* Cambridge (Mass.): 1962, p. 35.
6. The references to the individual authors are found in Schoenbaum as follows: Lloyd, p. 435; Landor, p. 370; Williams, p. 377; Severn, p. 374; Knight, p. 386; and Holmes, p. 559.
7. Furthermore, E. B. Everitt says, "It is worthy of note that the Folger Shakespeare Library has a copy of a 'Presentment' of boundary for Stratford of 1591 which is in the same penmanship as

Ironside and the Stratford Tithes indenture." *The Young Shakespeare.* Copenhagen; 1954, p. 188.
8. H. T. *Was Shakespeare a Lawyer?* London; 1871, p. 1.
9. Schoenbaum, p. 694. The solicitor's clerk in Jonson's *Every Man In His Humour* in which Shakespeare acted was named Roger Formal.
10. E. K. Chambers. *William Shakespeare.* Oxford; 1930, I, 23.
11. F. E. Halliday. *The Life of Shakespeare.* London; 1961, pp. 39–40.
12. Giles E. Dawson. "Authenticity and Attribution of Written Matter," *English Institute Annual.* New York; 1943, pp. 77–100.
13. J. Q. Adams refers to King James' *Triplici Nodo*, 1609, as the particular volume in the lot he was sending in the modest bid on (Joseph Quincy Adams. *A Report on Progress,* 1931–1941. Published for the Trustees of Amherst College, 1942, p. 30). He corrects himself in his subsequent article to say that the seventh edition of *Microcosmos* was what he was bidding on.
14. The mortgage deed signature is either abbreviated in this form (Shakspe) or the sign of abbreviation over the "e" is a misinterpretation of Shakespeare's attempt to provide some of the letters he did not have room for over the end of his name (*i.e.* "re" above "pe").
15. *A Report on Progress,* 1931–1941 on the Folger to the Amherst Trustees by J. Q. Adams does devote a little more than three pages (pp. 30–32) to an exposition on the find. It is not readily available, not known nor is it listed in bibliographies as containing any such information. It is based upon Dawson's early report, and contains errors corrected and superseded by Dawson's five pages of his longer article written for the English Institute in 1942 and by Adams later four-page article in the *Bulletin of The John Rylands Library Manchester* [England], June, 1943.
16. The only time the photograph of the front has been published before my reporting of the additional features was accompanying Dawson's article in the *English Institute Annual* 1942, Plate II between pages 88 and 89.
17. James G. McManaway. "The Folger Shakespeare Library," *Shakespeare Survey*, ed. Allardyce Nicoll. Cambridge; 1948, p. 61.
18. The exception would be Adams's article appearing in a library journal in England (Joseph Quincy Adams. "A New Signature of Shakespeare?" *Bulletin of the John Rylands Library Manchester.* Vol. 27, No. 2, June, 1943, pp. 256–259 with a photograph from the back opposite p. 257.
19. *The Reader's Encyclopedia of Shakespeare*, ed. O. J. Campbell. New York; 1966, pp. 302, 445, citing no sources for its information, and reproduces the photo from the back.
20. Hereward T. Price. "Shakespeare's Classical Scholarship," *Review of English Studies.* New Series, IX (1958), pp. 54–55.

21. Oddly enough, the passage appears in Dunkel's biography of Lambarde, but without any indication that the subject matter is, or is thought to be, about Shakespeare's *Richard II*. See also, however, Wilbur Dunkel. *William Lambarde*. (Rutgers; 1965), p. 175.
22. She is supposed to have called for the writing of *The Merry Wives of Windsor* by her request to see Falstaff in love, but the source for this is Charles Gildon in his *Remarks on the Plays of Shakespeare* written in 1710. Gildon goes on to say it took Shakespeare only a fortnight to do it.
23. *Cf. The Complete Works of Shakespeare*, ed. Hardin Craig. Chicago; 1951, p. 644.
24. The address in eighteenth-century hand would have to have been entered sometime around 1764 to 1800. Because "Shakespeare" is spelled "Shakspeare", without an *e* between the *k* and *s* and an *a* between the *e* and *r*, more precise data for its entry can be suggested. From 1776 until he was corrected by Malone in 1796, Stevens, the current editor and biographer, insisted that Shakespeare spelled his name with an *a* between the *e* and *r*. This is how Ireland spelled his forgeries and Malone caught him on it, because in 1796 Malone mistakenly concluded the clearest signature on the Will did not contain an *a* in that position. The Lambarde signature is spelled -ere, which rules out Ireland; the eighteenth-century hand has -eare, which suggests a placement between 1776 and 1796 of the address information. Since the eighteenth-century hand does not have an *e* between the *k* and *s* it appears to follow Stevens before he was corrected by Malone; and since it has an *underlined m* in the abbreviation of W*m*, it indicates that it is eighteenth-century, possibly mirroring in its century what it sees as abbreviated in the sixteenth. Furthermore, these differences help rule out the address and the signature hand as having been made by the same person.
25. This is definitely not the case for the two signatures at the Huntington Library in San Marino, California. The one on page one (not the title page) of a copy of *Plutarch's Lives*, London, 1595 is slightly more sophisticated a copy of actual signatures than is Ireland's, particularly the capital *S*. Its *W* is like Ireland's but it is a sketched signature, too carefully executed and placed dead center of a page in one of Shakespeare's most famous sources of which many copies are available (*cf. Huntington Library Bulletin*, IV (1933), 87). The second signature in their possession is clearly not an Ireland forgery or by the person who did the one in Plutarch. It is in *A Collection in English, of the Statutes now in Force*, London, 1598 and is on signature page A, recto. It is sketched, too large, a very knowledgeable imitation, obviously placed to be seen aside references to "Clerks of the peace"'s duties (*i.e.*, to

indicate a source for Justice Shallow and Silence in *Henry IV Part Two*). The signature contains the ornamental dot in the W but there are loops in the legs of the W not seen in any other signature. An unsuccessful S is attempted and added onto and the forger has several goes at the h. It is intriguing since it is in a law book and looks as if it were copying what modern scholars have come to conclude was the ideal form of the signature. I suspect it was constructed since the discovery of the Lambarde signature, possibly imitating the photograph accompanying Dawson's or Adams's articles in 1943 It contains what even might be an oddly shaped superior m as if it were trying to help Adams out in his claim. Paul Needham of The Pierpont Morgan Library in New York and Frederick O. Waage, Jr., of the Huntington brought the volume to my attention; it was owned by Marsden E. Perry before the Huntington acquired it. A signature resembling it, along with two by Raleigh and one by Queen Elizabeth I, cut from a letter and pasted to the back of an eighteenth-century map is in the private possession of Robert H. Trebble in Vancouver, B.C. Brian Bullen, a New Jersey attorney, says he has "A briefe treatise of testaments and last wills" by H. Swinburn published 1590 that may contain along with one or two unreadable signatures one that looks as if it has the letters to nearly constitute Shakespeare's last name. The dates of these volumes seem so sensible in relationship to Shakespeare's years of life (1564–1616) 1590, 1595, 1598. Lambarde's book being printed in 1568, when Shakespeare was only four years old would give a forger pause.

26. Any library or person possessing one of the books from the Lambarde library might want to examine the volume for marginalia which could be Lambarde's and as a remote possibility could be something in Shakespeare's hand, possibly an early hand, conceivably even a law hand. Unfortunately, the Fitzherbert book owned by Lambarde in the Huntington has had its marginalia erased.
27. This indicates how much more desirable it is to have historically significant personal libraries sold or given intact to institutions.
28. *Cf.* also *As You Like It*. V. ii. 34; *Cymbeline* III. i. 23; and *Henry IV Part Two*. II. ii. 134.

Chapter IV

1. This may account for the strange burial entry in the Stratford Register for March 6, 1590 of a "Thomas Green *alias* Shakspere" as a link between the families (*cf.* Mark Eccles. *Shakespeare in*

Warwickshire. Madison, 1963, p. 11). This book is the valuable source for information on Shakespeare's acquaintances in Stratford and the surrounding county. *Cf.* also E. K. Chambers. *William Shakespeare*. Oxford, 1930, II, 17).

2. *The Plays of Christopher Marlowe*, ed. Leo Kirschbaum. Cleveland; 1962, p. 465.
3. Francis Meres. *Palladis Tamia*. 1598. This report lists authors and works of the period and is the major source for dating Shakespeare's plays as pre- or post-1598, and is dedicated to Thomas Elliot of the Middle Temple (*cf.* Philip J. Finkelpearl. *John Marston of the Middle Temple*. Cambridge, (Mass.): 1969, p. 26. Finkelpearl's book is the chief source for information on the social setting for the literary revival at the Inns of Court).
4. I had the pleasure of having my play on the Kennedy assassination (*The Death of J. K.*) performed by the Bar Theatrical society in Middle Temple for three nights in November 1969 and the following Easter, in Hall at Gray's Inn. *Cf. The London Review*. 6, Winter, 1969/70, pp. 55–78.
5. Jasper Heywood. *The Seconde Tragedie of Seneca entitled Thyestes*. London; 1560, sigs. vii r-viii r.
6. Selected from a table of names furnished by Finkelpearl, *op. cit.*, pp. 261–264.
7. S. Schoenbaum. *Shakespeare's Lives*. Oxford; 1970, p. 55. My conjecture is offered in the brackets.
8. Tucker Brooke. *Shakespeare of Stratford*. New Haven; 1926, p. 37.
9. Henry Helmes (who served as the Prince of Purpoole for that year) in his *Gesta Grayorum* not published until 1688.
10. The information is taken from Finkelpearl, *op. cit.*, pp. 42–43.
11. Unfortunately this Sir George Carew (Carey) is neither the figure of the same name whose father, Lord Hunsdon, was the Lord Chamberlain and hence the patron of Shakespeare's acting company (the Lord Chamberlain's Men); nor the third figure of precisely the same name and station from Stratford (Lord Carew of Clopton, Earl of Totness), but undoubtedly all three of these namesakes knew each other at Court in London.
12. Leslie Hotson. *Shakespeare's Sonnets Dated*. London; 1949, pp. 54–55.
13. Leslie Hotson. *Mr. W. H.* New York; 1964, p. 231.
14. Shakespeare's personal earlier encounter with King's Bench has not tainted his respect for its titular office. A whole book can be written upon Shakespeare's study of justice on the governmental level in the *Henry IV* plays.
15. *Cf.* W. J. Jones. *The Elizabethan Court of Chancery*. Oxford; 1967, pp. 44, 62, 68, 111–113, 116–119, 267, 293, 366, 413, 474, 477, and 489; and Wilbur Dunkel. *William Lambarde, Elizabethan*

Jurist. Rutgers; 1965, pp. 110–180. Despite these labors Jones is correct in saying a full-scale study of the life and judicial records could still be attempted to measure the significance of Lambarde as Egerton's major colleague in Chancery. There is a manuscript in preparation by Retha Warniche entitled *William Lambarde: Elizabethan Antiquary.* for Phillimore of Shopwyke Hall, Chichester, England.

16. K. B. 29/234 (Court of King's Bench, Controlment Roll) reads:

> Anglia ss Willelmus Wayte petit securitates pacis versus Willelmum Shakspere, Franciscum Langley, Dorotheam Soer uxorem Johannis Soer, & Annam Lee, ob metum mortis & c.
>
> Attachiamentum vicecomiti Surreie retornabile xviii Martini. [*i.e.*, November 29, 1596, the last day of Michaelmas term].

Discovered by Leslie Hotson's brilliant researches (*cf.* Leslie Hotson. *Shakespeare versus Shallow.* Boston; 1931, p. 9).

17. Jones, *op. cit.*, p. 107.
18. Hotson. *Shakespeare versus Shallow. op. cit.*, pp. 76–77.
19. Jones, *op. cit.*, pp. 477–478.
20. William Lambarde. *A Perambulation of Kent.* London, 1596, p. 233; *cf.* E. K. Chambers. *The Elizabethan Stage.* Oxford, 1930, II, 359.
21. Mark Edwin Andrews. "Law *versus* Equity in *The Merchant of Venice.*" Boulder; 1965. For one of many points that indicate the precision of Shakespeare's reconstruction of the law of his day, compare *Merchant of Venice* III. iii. 26 ff. with the "Case of Market-Overt" given in Coke's *Reports*, Part V, p. 83 and tried at Hilary term 1596 of which Sir Thomas Egerton, Lord Ellesmere, was one of the judges (*cf.* Andrews, pp. 28–29).
22. William West. *Symboleography.* London, 1594, Section 28.
23. Christopher St. Germain. *Doctor and Student.* London, 1715, p. 57.
24. Edmund Spenser. *The Faerie Queene*, eds. J. C. Smith and E. de Selincourt. London; 1970, Book V. Proem, stanza x; Canto X, stanza i; and Book VI, Canto 1, stanza xlii. The second installment of *The Faerie Queene* (Books III–VI) was entered at the Stationers' Hall on January 20, 1596. For an analysis of the Chancery side of the law in the work see W. Nicholas Knight. "The Narrative Unity of Book V of *The Faerie Queene*: 'That Part of Justice Which Is Equity.'" *The Review of English Studies* New Series, Volume XXI, Number 83, August 1970, pp. 267–294.
25. Germain, *op. cit.*, p. 52.
26. Thomas Ashe. *Epieikeia.* Gray's Inn, 1608. Ashe is quoting William West's *Symboleography.*
27. *Cf.* Andrews, *op. cit.*, pp. 74–75 for how the creation of a use after

a use and a trust works in *The Merchant of Venice*. Will Shakespeare's will will be discussed in detail in Chapter V.

28. C. P. 24 (1)/15, C. P. 25 (2)/237, Easter 39 Eliz. I, *Shakespeare in the Public Records*. London; 1964, pp. 12–13.
29. "Lambarde" is a variant on rare occasion for "Lambert" as is "Lamberte," "Lombard," etc. The Lambert and Lambarde names are coincidental and, although in no probability relatives, John Lambert and William Lambarde would have regarded their last names as at least closer than modern spelling would indicate, if not actually taken them as identical. At one point in the Chancery documents John Lambert (Shakespeare's nephew-in-law) is spelled "John Lambarde."
30. The Bill of Complaint is taken from the Estate Records section of James Orchard Halliwell-Phillipps's *Outlines of the Life of Shakespeare*. London, 1887, II, 14–15.
31. *Ibid.*, p. 11.
32. *Ibid.*, pp. 15–16.
33. *Ibid.*, pp. 16–17.
34. Eccles, *op. cit.*, pp. 105–106.
35. As quoted in Brooke, *op. cit.*, p. 61.
36. Halliwell-Phillipps, *op. cit.*, p. 204.
37. As cited in Catherine Drinker Bowen. *The Lion and the Throne*. Boston; 1956, p. 337.
38. *Ibid.*, pp. 364–369.
39. *Cf. The Complete Works of Shakespeare*, ed. Hardin Craig. Chicago; 1951, p. 1227, l. 96n.
40. Jones, *op. cit.*, pp. 365–367.
41. *Ibid.*, pp. 276–278.
42. Halliwell-Phillipps, *op. cit.*, p. 204.
43. Eccles, *op. cit.*, p. 29.
44. Shakespeare is preoccupied in his sonnets with lineage and Time's fell hand declaring that his poetry will survive himself and Mr. W. H., *cf.* LXIV and LXV as examples.
45. Louis A. Knafla. "The Law Studies of an Elizabethan Student," *The Huntington Library Quarterly*, May 1969, p. 238.
46. Samuel E. Thorne, "Preface," Hake's *Epieikeia*. Yale, 1953, p. v.
47. Brooke, *op. cit.*, pp. 43–43 where he goes on to cite Halliwell-Phillipps: "'. . . of so much importance was this considered that, upon the deforciant [i.e. Hercules Underhill] representing in June, 1602, that the state of his health prevented his undertaking a journey to London, a special commission was arranged for obtaining his acknowledgment. This important ratification was procured in Northamptonshire in the following October, Shakespeare no doubt being responsible for the considerable expenditure that must

have been incurred by these transactions.'" These pursuits parallel the unsuccessful litigation over Asbies. For a different interpretation see P. R. Watts 'Shakespeare's "Double" Purchase of New Place,' (1947) 20 *Australian Law Journal*, p. 330 where it is thought Shakespeare purchased the additional two orchards for the same price as the original tract and house.

48. Wilbur Dunkel. *William Lambarde, Elizabethan Jurist* 1536–1601. New Brunswick, 1965, p. 1.
49. *Ibid.*, pp. 177–178.
50. Craig, *op. cit.*, p. 615.
51. Leslie Hotson. *The First Night of Twelfth Night.* New York; 1955.
52. Edward J. White. *Commentaries on the Law in Shakespeare.* St. Louis. 1911, pp. 34–41.
53. Edward J. White (*ibid.*, pp. 42–63) discusses in detail numerous legal passages in *Measure for Measure* under the headings of: Termes of the Law, Deed Laws, Custom shaping Laws, Frailty of all laws—Especially jury system, Action of Slander, Prostitution before the Law, Sentence, Plea for Pardon, Punishment for Seduction, by Venetian Law, the severe Judge, Common Law marriage contract, Plea for Justice, The Equality of Justice, The Law a gazing-stock, when not enforced, Confession of guilt, Loyalty of Attorney, Intent (distinguished from Wrongful Act), Breach of Promise, and Punishment by marriage to Prostitute.
54. George Garrett. *Death of the Fox.* New York; 1971, p. 25.
55. Thorne, *op. cit.*
56. Leslie Hotson suggests *Troilus and Cressida* is "Love's Labour's Won" and was performed at the Inns; Akrigg suggests *Love's Labour's Lost* was designed for such an audience; *Hamlet*, it has been suggested has such a connection (M. D. Legge. "*Hamlet* and the Inns of Court," *Studies in Language and Literature in Honour of Margaret Schlauch.* Warszawa: Polish Scientific Publishers 1966, s. 213–217) and the subject matter and legal vocabulary of *Romeo and Juliet* (and possibly *Two Gentlemen of Verona*) might recommend such a setting, in addition to *Comedy of Errors* and *Twelfth Night.* Shakespeare may have had up to seven plays done at the Inns. There were ample opportunities for these at various holidays and celebrations. The records indicate plays but often not titles or author. Perhaps *Timon of Athens* was designed to instruct such an audience.
57. *The Mirror of Magistrates*, ed. Lily B. Campbell. Cambridge; 1938, pp. 64, 65–66.
58. Philip J. Finkelpearl. *John Marston of the Middle Temple: An Elizabethan Dramatist in His Social Setting.* Cambridge (Mass.); 1969, p. 22.

Chapter V

1. Ben Jonson's Eulogy, part of the introductory matter to the First Folio (1623), as reproduced in Tucker Brooke. *Shakespeare of Stratford.* New Haven, 1926, p. 93.
2. After the death of Shakespeare's son, the rulers in his plays are disturbed by the lack of lineage.

   MACBETH: . . . then prophet-like
   They hail'd him father to a line of kings.
   Upon my head they placed a fruitless crown,
   And put a barren sceptre in my gripe,
   Thence to be wrench'd with an unlineal hand,
   No son of mine succeeding.
   (III. i. 59–64)

   Caesar's first words are:

   CAESAR: Calpurnia!
   CASCA: Peace, ho! Caesar speaks.
   CAESAR: Calpurnia!
   CALPURNIA: Here, my lord.
   CAESAR: Stand you directly in Antonius' way,
   When he doth run his course. Antonius:
   ANTONY: Caesar, my lord?
   CAESAR: Forget not, in your speed, Antonius,
   To touch Calpurnia; for our elders say,
   The barren, touched in this holy chase,
   Shake off their sterile curse.
   ANTONY: I shall remember:
   When Caesar says 'do this,' it is perform'd.
   CAESAR: Sit on; and leave no ceremony out.
   (*Julius Caesar* I. ii. 1–11).

3. See also Edmund's similar declaration in *Lear* (I. ii. 1–22).
4. *Shakespeare in the Public Records*, ed. N. E. Evans. London, 1964, p. 19.
5. *Cf. Hamlet* II. iv. 97; *Henry IV Part One* III. iii. 66; and *Troilus and Cressida* II. ii. 17–25.
6. Brooke, *op. cit.*, p. 53.
7. S. Schoenbaum. *Shakespeare's Lives.* Oxford, 1970, p. 27.
8. *Ibid.*, p. 7.
9. Anthony Burgess. *Shakespeare.* New York; 1970, pp. 254 and 257. E. K. Chambers (*William Shakespeare op. cit.*, II, 117) says erroneously that "there is nothing to show that he [Thomas Greene] ever acted for Shakespeare in a legal capacity." Zelda Teplitz in "King Lear and Macbeth in Relation to Shakespeare" (*The Bulletin of The Philadelphia Association for Psychoanalysis*, Vol. 20, No. 3, September, 1970, provides an interesting discussion of the fictional characters' relations to their female offspring in parallel

with Shakespeare's life. These themes are picked up and anatomized in Norman Holland's excellent book *Psychoanalysis and Shakespeare* (New York; 1964), pp. 258–259, 279, 287, and 329.

10. The bracketed and underlined words were written in after the first draft of the text of the will had been completed.
11. Translated from the Latin by Brooke, *op. cit.*, p. 82.
12. More detailed information is given by Mark Eccles. *Shakespeare in Warwickshire.* Madison; 1961, pp. 116–117.
13. See CXXXIV (Sonnet) for distinction between freehold and copyhold as in *Macbeth* ". . . nature's copy's not eterne" (III. ii.).
14. See *Love's Labour's Lost* IV. ii. 77, *Lear* II. i. 77, and *Tempest* I. ii. 172.
15. The familiar use of the word is found in *Measure for Measure* III. i. 157 and the more technical financial and legal use in *Coriolanus* V. vi. 67.
16. Brooke, *op. cit.*, p. 84 n. 1.
17. "Hold, take my sword." (*Macbeth* II. i. 4); see also *Richard II* III. iii. 132, and *King John* IV. iii. 79.
18. Eccles, *op. cit.*, p. 120.
19. *Ibid.*, p. 117.
20. "Francis Collins was the lawyer in whose handwriting the will is written." Tucker Brooke, *op. cit.*, p. 84. "Shakespeare's will, which is in his [Francis Collins's] handwriting, left [Collins] twenty marks." Mark Eccles, *op. cit.*, p. 118.
21. *Shakespeare in the Public Records, op. cit.*, p. 34.
22. Eccles, *op. cit.*, p. 143. The Stratford Henry Walker is not to be confused with the London Henry Walker from whom Shakespeare purchased the house on March 10, 1613 in Blackfriars.
23. *Ibid.*, p. 122.
24. *Shakespeare in the Public Records, op. cit.*
25. Brooke, *op. cit.*, pp. 82–86 where the orthography of the will is modernized. For a transcription of the will in original spelling, crossings out, and interlineation consult E. K. Chambers. *William Shakespeare.* Oxford; 1930, II, 169–180.
26. Eccles, *op. cit.*, p. 142.
27. Charles Knight is quite assuring in his clever insistence that Anne Hathaway was not neglected at all, although meagerly referred to, by the will. English law guaranteed her one-third life interest in the estate (cf. Schoenbaum, *op. cit.*, p. 386).
28. Joseph Greene in a letter dated September 17, 1747 to James West, Secretary to the Treasury printed in *William Shakespeare, Plays.* ed. G. Steevens (London, 1785), I, 194 n; cited by Smith, *Eighteenth Century Essays*, p. xxxviii; and quoted in Schoenbaum, *op. cit.*, p. 138. Col. J. C. Jeaffreson *Athenaeum* (April 29, 1882. No. 2844) asserts "that Shakespeare's will was in the decedent's

own hand, and supported the thesis with plausible evidence legal and paleographic that the will was the author's original draft." E. B. Everitt. *The Young Shakespeare*. Copenhagen; 1954, p. 184.

29. Brooke, *op. cit.*, pp. 88–90.
30. "Epistle of Heminge and Condell to the readers of the Folio," *ibid.*, p. 90.
31. From Henslowe's Diary cited in E. K. Chambers. *William Shakespeare*. Oxford; 1930, I, 95–96.
32. Ben Jonson. "*De Shakespeare nostrat*[*e*]." *Timber, or Discoveries* (1641) as cited in Brooke, *op. cit.*, pp. 96–97.
33. *Ibid.*, p. 92.
34. Schoenbaum, *op. cit.*, p. 550; the internal quotation is from Robert Jamieson. "Who Wrote Shakespeare?" *Chamber's Edinburgh Journal* (7 August 1852), 88.
35. Samuel Taylor Coleridge. *Biographia Literaria*. Chapter XV in *Coleridge's Writings on Shakespeare*. ed. Terence Hawkes. New York; 1959, p. 65. The last fragment is from *Coleridge's Shakespearean Criticism*, ed. Thomas Middleton Raysor. London: 1930, II. 333.
36. John Keats to his brothers George and Thomas Keats in a letter dated on Sunday December 21, 1817 on a disquisition he had with Charles Wentworth Dilke; *The Letters of John Keats*. ed. Maurice Buxton Forman. London; 1952, p. 71.
37. Paper presented for the Fellows of the Center for Advanced Studies Wesleyan University April 6, 1964 and reprinted in Monday Evening Papers: Number 2.
38. Brooke, *op. cit.*, p. 137 in his essay on "The Personality of Shakespeare."
39. Justice Harlan F. Stone in a letter in 1937 to Mark Edwin Andrews quoted by J. K. Emery, editor, in his Preface to Mark Edwin Andrews. *Law versus Equity in "The Merchant of Venice."* Boulder; 1965, p. ix.
40. *Ibid.*, p. xii.
41. *Ibid.*, p. 4.
42. *Cf.* W. Nicholas Knight. "Equity and Mercy in English Drama 1400–1641," *Comparative Drama* Spring 1972, VI, 51–67.
43. The reference could be to the actual Duke of Venice or it could be to Shakespeare's figure whose familiarity to the King could be presumed. At any rate both the Doge and Shakespeare's Duke lacked not only enforcement of, but could not interpret, nor create, statute. The phrase became a byword for the Stuart kings preoccupied with Divine Right. Charles I repeated the statement (". . . he had no more power than the Duke of Venice") when his authority was challenged by religious questions in Scotland (*cf.* Godfrey Davies. *The Early Stuarts* 1603–1660. Oxford; 1959, p. 88.

44. "The author of the Shakespearean plays, we can say with perfect confidence, was not the advanced political thinker that Bacon was, or Ralegh, or Spenser, or even Marlowe. He was distinctly a traditionalist in politics and social theory. His attitude toward the state and sovereign was not Tudor, but Plantagenet; not Renaissance, but feudal. It represents the feeling of Stratford much better than that of London." Tucker Brooke, *op. cit.*, p. 144. This is revived in Herndl's *The High Design*, in which he shows that even in his Jacobean period Shakespeare held fast to medieval views and notions about natural law as opposed to his contemporaries' sense of political power and personal will. Schoenbaum (*Shakespeare's Lives*) strikes one, in his assumptions, as finding Shakespeare a good reflector of reality but that his knowledge was pedestrian and his concerns passive. Norman Holland ("Shakespeare The Man: Some Conclusions," *op. cit.*, p. 140) says, "He would seem not to be a thinking person; politically and religiously he is conservative to the point of naivete."

45. As evidenced from the plays this study discloses that Shakespeare in his study of equity read some, if not all of the following: William Lambarde's *Archaionomia, Archeion,* & *A Perambulation of Kent, Eirenarcha,* and *Pandecta Rotulorum*: and William West's *Symboleography,* Plowden's *Reports,* Bacon's *Jurisdiction of the Marches,* Christopher St. Germain's *Doctor and Student,* and Thomas Ashe and Edward Hake on *Epieikeia.*

46. *Cf.* Schoenbaum, *op. cit.*, pp. 411, 415, 420, 427 (". . . Shakespeare achieved fame and considerable fortune by writing plays 'under the domination of a commercial spirit.' Halliwell-Phillipps"), 434, and 514.

47. *Cf.* David Bevington. *Tudor Drama and Politics.* Harvard, 1968, pp. 233, 241 and 260 where Shakespeare is described as orthodox and a traditionalist. "The legal and political ideas which he [Shakespeare] incidentally expresses were part of the intellectual equipment [". . . differed little from that of other writers of his time, . . .'] of all educated men of his time, . . ." G. W. Keeton. *Shakespeare's Legal and Political Background.* New York; 1967, p. v. See also Hugh Richmond *Shakespeare's Political and Historical Plays.* For the most part Bevington, Keeton, and Richmond provide abundant data for Shakespeare's sense of current religious, political, historical, social, and legal issues on a highly sophisticated level.

Bibliography of Works Cited

ACHESON, ARTHUR. *Shakespeare's Lost Years in London: 1586–1592.* London: Quaritch, 1920.

ADAMS, JOSEPH QUINCY. "A New Signature of Shakespeare?" *Bulletin of the John Rylands Library, Manchester,* XXVII (1943), pp. 256–259.

———. *Life of William Shakespeare.* Boston: Houghton Mifflin, 1923.

———. *The Folger Shakespeare Memorial Library: A Report on Progress,* 1931–1941. Published for the Trustees of Amherst College, 1942.

AKRIGG, G. P. V. *Shakespeare and the Earl of Southampton.* London: Hamish Hamilton, 1968.

ANDREWS, MARK EDWIN. *Law versus Equity in "The Merchant of Venice".* Boulder, Colorado: University of Colorado Press, 1965.

ASHE, THOMAS. *Epiekeia.* London; 1608.

BARTON, SIR DUNBAR PLUNKET. *Shakespeare's Use of Legal Language.* London: Faber & Gwyer, 1929.

BENNETT, JOSEPHINE WATERS. *Measure for Measure As Royal Entertainment.* New York: Columbia University Press, 1966.

BEVINGTON, DAVID. *Tudor Drama and Politics.* Cambridge, Mass.: Harvard University Press, 1968.

BOWEN, CATHERINE DRINKER. *The Lion and the Throne.* Boston: Little Brown, 1956.

BROOKE, TUCKER. *Shakespeare of Stratford.* New Haven: Yale University Press, 1926.

BROWN, CHARLES ARMITAGE. *Shakespeare's Autobiographical Poems.* London: 1838.

BURGESS, ANTHONY. *Shakespeare.* New York: Alfred A. Knopf, 1970.

CALDIERO, FRANK. "Shakespeare's Signature in Lambarde's *Apxiaonomia,*" *Notes and Queries,* April 21, 1945, pp. 162–163.

CAMPBELL, JOHN. *Shakespeare's Legal Acquirements.* New York: Appleton, 1859.

CARY (CAREW), SIR GEORGE, *Reports or Causes in Chancery* [Out of the labours of Master William Lambert], London, 1650.

CHAMBERS, SIR EDMUND KERCHEVER. *The Elizabethan Stage.* Oxford; Clarendon Press, 1930, 4 volumes.

———. *William Shakespeare.* Oxford: Clarendon Press, 1930, 2 volumes.

CHUTE, MARCHETTE. *Shakespeare of London.* New York: Dutton and Company, 1949.

COKE, SIR EDWARD. *The Reports of Sir Edward Coke, Knt. In English In Thirteen Parts Compleat*, Parts I–XIII, London: E & R Nutt & R. Gosling, 1738.

COLERIDGE, SAMUEL TAYLOR. *Coleridge's Shakespearean Criticism.* ed. Thomas Middleton Raysor, London: Constable & Co Ltd., 1930, 2 vols.

———. *Coleridge's Writings on Shakespeare.* ed. Terence Hawkes, New York: G. P. Putnam, 1959.

COLLIER, JOHN PAYNE. *The Life of William Shakespeare.* London: Whittaker & Co., 1844.

DAVIES, JOHN. *Microcosmos.* London; 1603.

DAWSON, GILES E., "Authenticity and Attribution of Written Matter," *English Institute Annual* 1942, New York: Columbia University Press, 1943, pp. 77–100.

——— and LAETITIA KENNEDY-SKIPTON. *Elizabethan Handwriting* 1500–1650. New York: W. W. Norton, 1966.

DICKENS, CHARLES. *Bleak House.* ed. Edgar Johnson, New York: Dell, 1965.

DONNE, JOHN. *The Poems of John Donne.* ed. Herbert J. C. Grierson, Oxford: Oxford University Press, 1912, 2 vols.

DUNKEL, WILBUR. *William Lambarde: Elizabethan Jurist* 1536–1601, New Brunswick: Rutgers University Press, 1965.

ECCLES, MARK. *Shakespeare in Warwickshire.* Wisconson: University of Wisconsin Press, 1963.

EVERITT, E.B. *The Young Shakespeare: Studies in Documentary Evidence.* Copenhagen: Rosenkilde & Bagger, 1954.

FINKELPEARL, PHILIP J. *John Marston of the Middle Temple.* Cambridge, Mass.: Harvard University Press, 1969.

FLEAY, FREDERICK GARD. *The Life and Work of Shakespeare.* London: Nimmo, 1886.

FREEMAN, ARTHUR. *Thomas Kyd: Facts and Problems.* Oxford: Clarendon Press, 1967.

FRIPP, EDGAR INNES. *Shakespeare: Man and Artist.* London: Oxford University Press, 1938, 2 vols.

———. *Master Richard Quiney.* London: Oxford University Press, 1924.

FRYE, ROLAND MUSHAT. *Shakespeare's Life and Times.* Princeton: Princeton University Press, 1967.

GARRETT, GEORGE. *Death of the Fox.* New York: Doubleday, 1971.

GRAY, JOSEPH WILLIAM. *Shakespeare's Marriage and Departure from Stratford.* London: Chapman & Hall, 1905.

HAKE, EDWARD. *Epieikeia.* ed. Samuel E. Thorne, New Haven: Yale University Press, 1953.

HALLIDAY, FRANK ERNEST. *The Life of Shakespeare.* London: Gerald Duckworth, 1961.

HALLIWELL-PHILLIPS, JAMES ORCHARD. *Outlines of the Life of Shakespeare.* London: Longmans, Green & Co., 1887, 2 vols.

———. *The Life of William Shakespeare.* London: J. R. Smith, 1848.

HARRISON, GEORGE BAGSHAWE. *Elizabethan Journal* 1591–1594. New York: Cosmopolitan Book Corp., 1929.

———. *Shakespeare Under Elizabeth.* New York: Holt Rinehart and Winston, 1933.

HAZLITT, WILLIAM. *Lectures on the English Poets.* London: Stodart, Steuart, 1818.

HEAL, AMBROSE. "Note on Little Crown Street," *Notes and Queries,* 23 October 1943, p. 263.

HELMES, HENRY. *Gesta Grayorum.* London; 1688.

HERNDL, GEORGE C. *The High Design.* Lexington, Kentucky: University Kentucky Press, 1970.

HEYWOOD, JASPER. *The Seconde Tragedie of Seneca entitled Thyestes.* London; 1560.

HIBBARD, GEORGE RICHARD. *Thomas Nashe.* Cambridge, Mass.: Harvard University Press, 1962.

HOLLAND, NORMAN NORWOOD. *Psychoanalysis and Shakespeare.* New York: McGraw-Hill, 1964.

HOLMES, NATHANIEL. *The Authorship of Shakespeare.* New York: Hurd & Houghton, 1866.

HOTSON, LESLIE. *Mr. W. H.* London: Rupert Hart-Davis, 1964.

———. *Shakespeare's Sonnets Dated, and Other Essays.* London: Oxford University Press, 1949.

———. *Shakespeare versus Shallow.* Boston: Little Brown, 1931.

———. *The First Night of Twelfth Night,* New York: Macmillan Co., 1955.

HUGO, VICTOR. *William Shakespeare.* trans. M. B. Anderson, Chicago: McClurg, 1887.

JAMIESON, ROBERT. "Who Wrote Shakespeare?" *Chambers's Edinburgh Journal,* 7 August, 1852, p. 88.

JONES, W. J. *The Elizabethan Court of Chancery.* Oxford: Clarendon Press, 1967.

JONSON, BEN. *The Complete Plays.* London: J. M. Dent & Sons, 1960, 2 vols.

KEATS, JOHN. *The Letters of John Keats.* ed. Maurice Buxton Forman, London: Oxford University Press, 1952.

KEETON, GEORGE W. *Shakespeare's Legal and Political Background.* New York: Barnes & Noble, 1967.

KERMODE, FRANK, "On Shakespeare's Learning," Center for Advanced Studies at Wesleyan University Monday Evening Papers: Number 2, Middletown, Conn.: Wesleyan University Press, 1964.

KNAFLA, LOUIS A. "The Law Studies of an Elizabethan Student," *The Huntington Library Quarterly*, May, 1969, pp. 221–240.

KNIGHT, CHARLES. *The Pictorial Edition of the Works of Shakespeare*. London: G. Routledge, 1838–1841, 3 vols.

KNIGHT, W. NICHOLAS. "Equity and Mercy in English Drama 1400–1641," VI *Comparative Drama* 51–67 (1972).

———. "*Julius Caesar* and Shakespearean Revenge," I *The Erasmus Review* 20–34 (1971).

———. "The Death of J. K.," *The London Review* VI (1969/70). 55–78

———. "The Narrative Unity of Book V of *The Faerie Queene*: 'That Part of Justice Which is Equity.'", *The Review of English Studies*, New Series, XXI, (1970) pp. 267–294.

LAMBARDE, WILLIAM. *Archaionomia*. London; 1568.

———. *A Perambulation of Kent*. London; 1596.

———. *Archeion*. London; 1591.

LANDOR, WALTER SAVAGE. *Citation and Examination of William Shakespeare . . . etc.* London: Saunders & Otley, 1834.

LEGGE, M. D. "*Hamlet* and the Inns of Court," *Studies in Language and Literature in Honor of Margaret Schlauch*, Warsaw: Polish Scientific Publishers, 1966.

LLOYD, WILLIAM WATKISS. "Life of William Shakespeare," *Dramatic Works*. ed. Samuel Weller Singer, London, 1831.

MCMANAWAY, JAMES G. *The Authorship of Shakespeare*. Folger Booklet on Tudor and Stuart Civilization, Charlottesville, University of Virginia Press, 1962.

———. "The Folger Shakespeare Library," *Shakespeare Survey*, ed. Allardyce Nicoll, 1948, I: 57–78.

MARDER, LOUIS. "Review: G. W. Keeton's *Shakespeare's Legal and Political Background*, "*Renaissance Quarterly*, XXII (1969), p. 191.

MARLOWE, CHRISTOPHER. *The Plays of Christopher Marlowe*. ed. Irving Ribner, Cleveland: Odyssey Press, 1962.

MERES, FRANCIS. *Palladis Tamia*. 1598.

Minutes and Accounts of the Corporation of Stratford-upon-Avon and Other Records 1553–1620. ed. Edgar I. Fripp, London: Oxford University Press, 1921–29, 4 vols.

Mirror of Magistrates. ed. Lily B. Campbell, Cambridge, England: Cambridge University Press, 1938.

NASHE, THOMAS. *The Works of Thomas Nashe*. ed. Ronald B. McKerrow, Oxford: Clarendon Press, 1958.

PHILLIPS, O. HOOD. *Shakespeare and The Lawyers*. London: Methuen & Co, 1972.

POHL, FREDERICK J. *Like to the Lark: The Early Years of Shakespeare*. New York: Clarkson N. Potter, 1972.

PRICE, HEREWARD T. "Shakespeare's Classical Scholarship," *Review of English Studies*, New Series, IX (1958), pp. 54–55.

PRYNNE, WILLIAM. *Histriomastix.* London; 1633.

Reader's Encyclopedia of Shakespeare. ed. Oscar James Campbell, New York: Thomas Y. Crowell, 1966.

RICHMOND, HUGH. *Shakespeare's Political and Historical Plays.* New York: Random House, 1967.

ROWSE, A. L. *William Shakespeare.* New York: Harper & Row, 1964.

RUSHTON, WILLIAM LOWES. *Shakespeare a Lawyer.* London: Longman, Brow, Green et al., 1858.

———. *Shakespeare's Testamentary Language.* London: Longmans Green & Co., 1869.

ST. GERMAIN, CHRISTOPHER. *Doctor and Student.* London; 1715.

SCHOENBAUM, SAMUEL. *Shakespeare's Lives.* Oxford: Clarendon Press, 1970.

SEVERN, CHARLES. *Diary of John Ward.* London; 1839.

SEVERN, EMMA. *Anne Hathaway; or, Shakespeare in Love.* London; 1845, 2 vols.

Shakespeare in the Public Records. ed. N. E. Evans, London: Her Majesty's Stationery Office, 1964.

SHAKESPEARE, WILLIAM. *A New Variorum Edition of Shakespeare: Hamlet.* ed. Horace Howard Furness, New York: Dover Publications, 1963, 2 vols.

———. *Cassell's Illustrated Shakespeare.* eds. Dr. F. J. Furnivall and John Munro, London: Cassell & Co., 1913.

———. *The Complete Works of Shakespeare.* ed. Hardin Craig, Chicago: Scott Foresman & Co., 1951.

———. *William Shakespeare, Plays.* ed. George Steevens, London; 1785.

———. *William Shakespeare, Plays and Poems.* ed. Edmond Malone, London; 1790, 10 vols.

SISSON, CHARLES J. "Studies in the Life and Environment of Shakespeare Since 1900." *Shakespeare Survey* III, 1950, pp. 1–12.

SPENSER, EDMUND. *Spenser's Poetical Works.* eds. J. C. Smith and E. de Selincourt, Oxford: Oxford University Press, 1970.

T., H. *Was Shakespeare a Lawyer?* London; 1871.

TAYLOR, JOHN. *Record of My Life.* London; 1832, 2 vols.

TEPLITZ, ZELDA, M. D. "King Lear and Macbeth in Relation to Shakespeare," *The Bulletin of the Philadelphia Association for Psychoanalysis*, Vol. 20 No. 3, September, 1970, pp. 196–211.

THOMPSON, SIR EDWARD MAUNDE. "Handwriting," *Shakespeare's England.* Oxford: Clarendon Press, 1916, pp. 284–310.

TIECK, LEWIS LUDWIG. *The Life of Poets.* Leipzig; 1830.

WEST, WILLIAM. *Symboleography.* London; 1594.

WHITE, EDWARD J. *Commentaries on the Law in Shakespeare.* St. Louis: The F. H. Thomaston Book Company, 1913.

WILLIAMS, ROBERT FOLKSTONE. *The Youth of Shakespeare.* Paris: Baundry's European Library, 1839.

WILSON, JOHN DOVER. *The Essential Shakespeare.* Cambridge: Cambridge University Press, 1932.

WINCHCOMBE, GEORGE AND BERNARD. *Shakespeare's Ghost Writers.* Esher, Surrey: Wolsey Press, 1968.

A Selected Bibliography of Works by Lawyers or On Law in Shakespeare.

The place of publication is London unless otherwise stated.

A. C. "Shakespeare in his Own Age," 61 *Law Society's Gazette*, 240. Review of *Shakespeare Survey No.* 17, 1964.

ADDY, S. O. "Shakespeare's Will: The Stigma Removed," *Notes and Queries*, 16 January 1926, p. 39.

A. H. R. "An Appreciation of Shakespeare's Knowledge of Law on this Tercentenary of his Death," 82 *Central Law Journal* 133 (1916).

ALLEN, SIR CARLETON KEMP. *The Queen's Peace*. Stevens & Sons, 1953.

ANON. "Shakespeare a Lawyer," 2 *Pump Court* 139 (1885); 21 *Canada Law Journal* 189 (1885).

———. "Shakespeare's Lawyers," 32 *Albany Law Journal* 24 (1885); *Irish Law Times* 422; 79 *Law Times* 287 (1885).

———. "Shakespeare's Will and His Wife's Dower," 21 *Legal Observer* 166 (1841).

———. "Shylock and the Law," Review of Griston's *Shaking the Dust from Shakespeare, Times Literary Supplement*, 29 January 1925, p. 68.

———. "The Law and the Bard," 19 *Record of the Association of the Bar of the City of New York*. 325 (1964).

———. "Was Shakespeare a Lawyer?" 6 *Law Journal* 81 (1871).

———. "Was Shakespeare a Lawyer?" 65 *Irish Law Times* 258, 264 (1931).

ARMOUR, E. D. "Law and Lawyers in Literature—IV," 4 *Canadian Bar Review* 315 (1926).

ASSERSOHN, D. P. "Shakespeare in the Sonnets," 61 *Law Society's Gazette* 208 (1964).

AZZOLINI, G. *Shylock e la leggenda della libbra di carne* (Reggio Emilia, 1893), revised and amplified offprint from *L'Italia Centrale* of article entitled "Il Contratto di Shylock nel Mercante di Venezia dello Shakespeare", *Fanfulla della Domenica*, 31 July and 7 August 1892.

BARTON, SIR DUNBAR PLUNKET. *Links Between Ireland and Shakespeare.* Dublin; Maunsel & Co., 1919.

———. *Links Between Shakespeare and the Law,* reprinted from *Law Journal,* vol. 63, pp. 470, 493, 511, 531, 575, 598; vol. 64, pp. 30, 50, 70, 90. (1929). Reprinted by Benjamin Blom Inc., New York, 1971.

BEALE, J. H. "Contempt of Court, Criminal and Civil," 21 *Harvard Law Review* 181 (1908).

BECK, J. M. Foreword to Barton, *Links Between Shakespeare and the Law.* Faber & Ginzer, 1929.

BENTLEY, RICHARD. "Diversities de la Ley," 17 *Illinois Law Review* 145 (1922–3).

———. "Shakespeare's Law," 155 *Law Times* 34 (1923).

BERMAN, RONALD. "Shakespeare and the Law," 18 *Shakespeare Quarterly* 141 (1967).

BOYD, J. O. "Shylock Versus Antonio: or Justice Blindfolded," 21 *Case and Comment* 994 (1915).

BROWN, BASIL. *Law Sports at Gray's Inn* 1594, *including Shakespeare's connection with the Inns of Court, with a reprint of the Gesta Grayorum.* New York; Anchor, 1921.

BRUNE, C. M. *Shakespeare's Use of Legal Terms.* 1914.

BURRUSS, W. B. "Shakespeare, the Salesman," 37 *Commercial Law Journal* 603 (1932).

CALVIN, W. W. "Shakespeare and the Law," 51 *Case and Comment* 6 (1946).

CHAMBERLAIN, J. D. "Legal Experiences of Great Authors," 21 *Case and Comment* 207 (1914).

CLARKSON, P. S. and WARREN, C. T. "Copyhold Tenure and *Macbeth,* III, ii, 38," in vol. 55 *Modern Language Notes* p. 483, Baltimore, 1940.

———. "Pleading and Practice in Shakespeare's Sonnet XLVI," in vol. 62, *Modern Language Notes,* p. 102, Baltimore, 1947.

———. *The Law of Property in Shakespeare and the Elizabethan Drama.* Baltimore: John Hopkins University Press, 1942; reprinted with corrections, 1968.

COWEN, EZEK. "Shylock v. Antonio," 5 *Albany Law Journal* 193 (1872).

COWPER, FRANCIS. "The Prince and the Poet," *Graya,* No. 60, Michaelmas Term, p. 111, 1964.

DAVIS, CUSHMAN KELLOG. *The Law in Shakespeare.* 2nd. ed., St. Paul, Minnesota; West Publishing Co., 1884.

DAWSON, J. P. Review of Andrews's *Law versus Equity in the Merchant of Venice* in 18 *Shakespeare Quarterly* 89 (1967).

DENNIS, W. A. "Portia as an Exemplar," 21 *Case and Comment* 580 (1914).

DEVECMON, W. C. *In Re Shakespeare's "Legal Acquirements,"* Shakespeare Society of New York, No. 12; New York, 1899.

DOYLE, J. T. "Shakespeare's Law—The Case of Shylock," in *The Overland Monthly*, San Francisco, July 1886.

DRAPER, J. W. "Dogberry's Due Process of Law," 42 *Journal of English and Germanic Philology*, University of Illinois, Urbana, 563 (1943).

———. "Ophelia's Crime of Felo de Se," 42 *West Virginia Law Quarterly* 228 (1936).

DUKE, WINIFRED. "The Law in Drama," 38 *Juridical Review* 55 (1926).

E. F. S. "Portia as a Judge," *Weekly Westminster Gazette*, 3 February 1923, p. 12.

ERICKSON, OTTO. "Shakespeare and the Law: A Tercentenary Obiter," 20 *Law Notes* 4 (1916).

FOARD, J. T. "On the Law Case: *Shylock v. Antonio*," *Manchester Quarterly* 268 (1899).

FULLER, R. F. "Shakespeare as a Lawyer," 9 *Upper Canada Law Journal* 91 (1863); reprinted from 21 *Monthly Law Reporter* (Boston) 1 (1862).

GIBSON, S. M. "Shakespeare in the Sonnets," 61 *Law Society's Gazette* 23 (1964).

GREEN, A. WIGFALL, "Shakespeare's Will," 20 *Georgetown Law Journal* 273 (1932).

———. *The Inns of Court and Early English Drama*. New Haven: Yale University Press, 1931.

GREENWOOD, SIR GEORGE. *Shakespeare's Law*. C. Palmer, 1920.

GUERNSEY, R. S. *Ecclesiastical Law in Hamlet: The Burial of Ophelia*. New York: Brentano Bros., 1885.

HANNIGAN, J. E. "Shakespeare and the Young Lawyer," 6 *Boston University Law Review* 168 (1926).

HEARD, FRANKLIN FISKE. *Shakespeare as a Lawyer*. Boston: Little Brown, 1883.

HERRINGTON, W. S. "The Legal Lore of Shakespeare," 3 *Canadian Bar Review* 537 (1925).

HICKS, F. C. "List of Books on Shakespeare and the Law," IX *Law Library Journal* 20 (1916).

———. "Was Shakespeare a Lawyer?" 22 *Case and Comment*. 1002, reprinted from *New York Sun*, 16 April 1916.

HIRSCHFELD, JULIUS. "Portia's Judgment and German Jurisprudence," 30 *Law Quarterly Review* 167 (1914).

———. "What was Iago's Crime in Law?", 14 *Journal of the Society of Comparative Legislation* (N.S.) 411 (1914).

HUNT, J. H. "Law, Lawyers and Literature," 5 *Journal of the Bar Association of Kansas* 234 (1937).

JAUDON, V. H. "Shakespeare and the Law," 1 West Pub. Co. Docket, 799, October 1912.

KEETON, G. W. *Shakespeare and his Legal Problems*. A. C. Black Ltd., 1930.

KEYS, D. R. "Was Shakespeare bred an Attorney?" 2 *Canadian Bar Review* 83 (1902).

LIGHT, HON. J. H. "Law and Lawyers in Shakespeare," 21 *Case and Comment* 185 (1914).

LOVE, J. M. "A Lawyer's Commentary on *Shylock v. Antonio*," 25 *American Law Review* 899 (1891).

LYBARGER, DONALD FISHER. *Shakespeare and the Law: Was the Bard Admitted to the Bar?* Cleveland, Ohio 1965; reprinted from *Cleveland Bar Journal*, March 1965.

MACKENZIE, J. B. "The Law and Procedure in *The Merchant of Venice*," 16 *Green Bag* 604 (1904).

———. "Was Shakespeare Bound to an Attorney?" 14 *Green Bag* 58 (1902).

MACLEAN, R. U. "La Justicia en las obras de Shakespeare," *Letras* No. 36, p. 48, Universidad Nacional Mayor de San Marcos de Lima, Peru, 1964.

MARDER, LOUIS. "Law in Shakespeare," *Renaissance Papers*, University of South Carolina Press, 1964, p. 40.

MARRIAN, F. J. M. *Shakespeare at Gray's Inn—A Tentative Theory.* 1967.

MERCHANT, W. MOELWYN. "Lawyer and Actor: Process of Law in Elizabethan Drama," *English Studies Today*, 3rd. Ser. Edinburgh University Press, 1964, p. 107.

MINOR, P. S. "Shakespeare on Law and Lawyers," 1901, in *Shakespearian Addresses delivered at the Arts Club, Manchester, 1886–1912*, ed. Fishwick p. 223.

MONTMORENCY, J. E. G. DE. "Shakespeare's Legal Problems," in *The Contemporary Review: Literary Supplement*, 1930, p. 797.

NIEMEYER, THEODOR. *Der Rechtsspruch gegen Shylock im 'Kaufmann von Venedig': ein Beitrag zur Wurdigung Shakespeares*, 1952; revised version translated by Herbruch as "The Judgment against Shylock in the Merchant of Venice," 14 *Michigan Law Review* 20 (1915).

NOEL, F. R. "Legal Influences in Shakespeare," 18 *Journal of District of Columbia Bar Association* 353 (1941). (Address delivered before Shakespeare Society of Washington, May 12, 1951).

NORMAN, C. H. "Shakespeare and the Law," letters in *Times Literary Supplement*, 30 June 1950, p. 142 and 4 August 1950, p. 485.

NORMAND, LORD. "Portia's Judgment," 10 *University of Edinburgh Journal* 43 (1939).

PATHAK, ILA. "Shakespeare and the Law," 8 *Vidya* (Journal of Gujarat University), 1965.

PHELPS, CHARLES E. *Falstaff and Equity: An Interpretation.* Boston: Houghton Mifflin, 1901.

———. "Shylock vs. Antonio: Brief for Plaintiff in Appeal," 57 *Atlantic Monthly* 463 (1886).

PHILLIPS, O. HOOD. "Shakespeare and Gray's Inn," 72 *Graya* 107 Michaelmas 1970. (Abbreviated version of Address read to Gray's Inn Historical Society on 7 July 1970.)

———. "The Law Relating to Shakespeare, 1564–1964," 80 *Law Quarterly Review*, I, 172; II, 399 (1964).

PIETSCHER, A. *Furist und Dichter: Studie uber Iherings 'Kampf um's Recht' und Shakespeares Kaufmann von Venedig*. Dessau, 1881.

POLAK, A. L. *More Legal Fictions: A Series of Cases from Shakespeare*. 1946.

POLLOCK, SIR FREDERICK. "A Note on Shylock v. Antonio," 30 *Law Quarterly Review* 175 (1914).

RANDOLPH, A. M. F. *The Trial of Sir John Falstaff*. New York: G. Putnam, 1893.

SALZMAN, L. F. "Shakespeare and the Quarter Sessions," in *The London Mercury*, vol. 15, 1926–7, p. 46.

SEASONGOOD, MURRAY. "Some Law in Shakespeare," 6 *Ohio Law Reporter* 327 (1908).

SENTER, J. H. "Was Shakespeare a Lawyer?" *Vermont Bar Association*, Montpelier, Vermont, 1903.

SIMON, SIR JOCELYN. "Shakespeare's Legal and Political Background," 84 *Law Quarterly Review* 33 (1968).

SMITH, D. *Trial Scenes in the English Drama up to* 1615 (unpublished thesis, Birmingham University, 1960).

SOMERVELL, D. B. "Shakespeare and the Law," *Stratford-on-Avon Herald*, 15 April 1932.

SPRAGUE, H. B. "Shakespeare's Alleged Blunders in Legal Terminology," 11 *Yale Law Journal* 304 (1902).

TELLER, J. D. "The Law and Lawyers of Shakespeare," *New York State Bar Association Report* 1881, vol. 4, p. 162.

UNDERHILL, SIR ARTHUR. in *Shakespeare's England*, ed. Raleigh, Oxford, vol. I, chap. 13 ("Law"), 1916.

WASHER, B. F. "William Shakespeare, Attorney at Law," 10 *Green Bag* 303, 336 (1898).

WATTS, P. R. "Shakespeare's 'Double' Purchase of New Place," 20 *Australian Law Journal* 330 (1947).

WEARS, T. M. "Shakespeare's Legal Acquirements," 16 *Canadian Bar Review* 28 (1938).

WHITE, R. G. "William Shakespeare, Attorney at Law and Solicitor in Chancery," IV *Atlantic Monthly* July, 1859, p. 84.

WIGMORE, J. H. "Shakespeare's Legal Documents," 28 *American Bar Association Journal* 134 (1942).

WILKES, GEORGE. *Shakespeare from an American Point of View, including An Inquiry as to his Religious Faith and his Knowledge of Law*, New York: D. Appleton & Co., 1877; 3rd. ed., 1882.

WINDOLPH, F. L. *Reflections on the Law in Literature*. Philadelphia University Press, 1956.

YEATMAN, J. PYM. *Is William Shakspere's Will Holographic?* Darley Dale, 2nd. ed., 1901.

———. *The Gentle Shakspere: A Vindication*, 1896, 4th ed., Birmingham, 1906.

YOUNG, G. M. "Shakespeare and the Termers," in 33 *Proceedings of the British Academy*, 81 (1947).

Index